The Long Blue Line Disrupted

USS *Serpens* (AK-97) and the Largest Loss of Life in US Coast Guard History

Douglas E. Campbell

&

Robert G. Breen

The Long Blue Line Disrupted

USS *Serpens* (AK-97) and the Largest Loss of Life in US Coast Guard History

Douglas E. Campbell

&

Robert G. Breen

**SYNECA
RESEARCH
GROUP, INC.**

The Long Blue Line Disrupted: USS *Serpens* (AK-97) and the Largest Loss of Life in US Coast Guard History

ISBN 978-0-359-87305-0

Direct all inquiries to Dr. Douglas Campbell at dcamp@aol.com

Cover design by Michelle Rekstad at Rekstad Graphics, rekstad@aol.com.

"As we headed our personnel boat shoreward, the sound and concussion of the explosion suddenly reached us and, as we turned, we witnessed the awe-inspiring death drama unfold before us. As the report of screeching shells filled the air and the flash of tracers continued, the water splashed throughout the harbor as the shells hit. We headed our boat in the direction of the smoke and, as we came into closer view of what had once been a ship, the water was filled only with floating debris, dead fish, torn life jackets, lumber and other unidentifiable objects. The smell of death, and fire, and gasoline, and oil was evident and nauseating. This was sudden death, and horror, unwanted and unasked for, but complete."

Unidentified enlisted man aboard a nearby Navy personnel boat, 29 January 1945.

Navy Department Communique No. 582, March 1, 1945

"The USS *Serpens,* a cargo ship manned by Coast Guard personnel, has been lost in the South Pacific Area as the result of enemy action."

DEDICATION

This dedication goes out to the long blue line of Coast Guard men and women who defended, and are defending, our U.S. shores since the inception of the U.S. Treasury Department's Revenue Cutter Service and Life-Saving Service (which merged to become the United States Coast Guard in 1915); who have risked their own lives to save others; and especially to those who have given their lives for peace and freedom in the process.

After World War II, Fleet Admiral Chester Nimitz applauded the performance of Coast Guard men and women. It was written in the introduction of Malcolm Willoughby's *The U.S. Coast Guard in World War II* and bears repeating: "I know of no instance wherein they did not acquit themselves in the highest traditions of their Service, or prove themselves worthy of their Service motto, 'Semper Paratus' — 'Always Ready.'"

PREFACE

The Coast Guard has been many things to many men and women. The thousands of us who have worn Coast Guard blue hold memories that will be with us for a lifetime. For those of us whose chosen specialty in the service took us to sea, the authors here have captured the magic combination of excitement and action on one hand and boredom and repetition on the other. They cover the endless days of sailings and arrivals, of exotic ports of call and the focus of personal responsibility for performance that only wartime and the sense of imminent combat can bring. They use the two very real tools of recorded logbook entries and letters to loved ones back home to describe life aboard the USS *Serpens* AK 97 during the end of World War II in the Pacific theatre. The daily toil was demanding and enormously important to the war effort and the moments taken to write personal notes of hope and affection buoyed the spirits of both the sailor writing and those at home reading.

The story of the *Serpens* is an important chapter in Coast Guard history. Not only is it a documentation of the most tragic loss of life in the more than 220 years of Coast Guard service to the United States, it's also a validation of our service's founder, Alexander Hamilton, who famously penned a letter of advice to the officers of the newly created Revenue

Marine in 1790. Mindful of why the American Revolution had been fought in the first place, Hamilton challenged the new officers to mark their demeanor "with prudence, moderation and good temper" citing further that the "success and continuance of the establishment (the service) would depend on the qualities" It is a very short link from the Hamilton charge through the sacrifice of such service members as the crew of *Serpens* to the context that frames every sailor and ship in today's Coast Guard as they execute their daily responsibilities for the citizens of our country. A legacy, WHEN KNOWN and only WHEN KNOWN, inspires the service of today. The *Serpens* story is a significant part of that legacy and deserves to be told wide and far.

I currently serve as a Board member for the National Coast Guard Museum Association. We are not only building a building, we are also gathering stories from the history of the service to be told to visitors through exhibits and designed interactive experiences. The future museum is about the brave Coast Guard men and women who serve our nation every day. We want to honor the heritage of over 220 years of service, respect the sacrifice of those serving today and inspire the next generation to carry on the traditions of selfless service. These authors remind us by the very title of this book, that it's often the Disruptions in routine that cause memories that need preserved. THE LONG BLUE LINE DISRUPTED is the story of one such iconic event. The story is told both factually through the ship's log and emotionally through the letters home of those lost in the explosion.

I have had the great honor of commanding Coast Guard ships at war and in the multi-missioned service of our Coast Guard at home in the United States. The *Serpens* is gone, as are some of the cutters I commanded. But today, there are many Coast Guard cutters flying the colors of our country, manned by Coast Guard crews, accomplishing today's missions with the same sense of responsibility as did the crew of *Serpens*. In part, when they read this story, they will stand a bit taller and renew their commitment to Honor, Respect and Devotion to Duty. Those, after all, are the Coast Guard Core Values. That's who we are.

James M. Loy

ADM, USCG, Retired

21st Commandant

ACKNOWLEDGEMENTS

This book could not have been written without the vast search capabilities of the Internet or, then again, without individuals volunteering their support! You would have thought every book on major events during World War II would have been written by now but nowhere can be found a definitive volume on the U.S. Coast Guard's greatest loss of life in the history of that organization. We have a lot of people to thank for all this accumulated knowledge. We're not going to get them all and for that we apologize in advance. But here are a few that made a difference to what you are about to read:

The Maritime Education and Research Society (MERS, a charitable 501(c)(3) foundation), and the estate of the late Robert Nicholas Woll, for partially funding the research effort.

Fold3, a huge on-line database of documents, images, and other material covering American military history, owned by the genealogical organization at www.Ancestry.com. Here are Muster Logs, transcripts of oral history and the War Diaries of USS *Serpens* (AK-97).

U.S. National Archives and Records Administration at www.nara.gov. Special thanks to David Castillo for his help in tracking down the history of the 231st Port Company, 492nd Port Battalion, in Guadalcanal.

U.S. Naval History and Heritage Command at http://www.history.navy.mil/

The Coast Guard Combat Veterans Association (CGCVA), a Non-Profit Association dedicated to extending the knowledge of the Coast Guard's service and participation in those significant historical events in United States history.

The small but very interesting Solomon Islands National Museum in Honiara, Guadalcanal, gives one a very good historical look at the Solomon Islands including, of course, World War II.

The Vilu Military Museum in Lenggakiki, Solomon Islands. Their display of the remains of American and Japanese WWII aircraft and other relics is an experience not soon forgotten.

The *Solomons Star,* the daily newspaper for the Solomon Islands, for publicly supporting our efforts and for getting the word out to their readership concerning our quest for any oral histories from those who remember the day *Serpens* exploded and the days following.

U.S. Army Center of Military History at Fort McNair, Washington, DC, and at http://www.history.army.mil/

Those great bunch of people at www.navsource.org who collect and display what they call 'The Photographic History of the U.S. Navy'.

Glyn Owen, who sits on the Maritime Education and Research Society (MERS) Board of Directors, for visiting and photographing the Liberty ship *John W. Brown* in Baltimore, MD; and for joining our research team in Pensacola, FL, to dive the Liberty ship *Joseph L. Meek* and to fly out to Guadalcanal to dive the remains of USS *Serpens*.

Peter Dunn who lives in Australia and who spent some time combing through WWII history in Australia and New Zealand and for his detailed website www.ozatwar.com.

The National Archives of Australia in Canberra at http://www.naa.gov.au/, the Australian National Maritime Museum in Darling Harbour, Sydney, at http://www.anmm.gov.au/, the National Library of Australia at http://www.nla.gov.au/ and the Naval Historical Society of Australia at https://www.navyhistory.org.au

Stephen J. Chant, former Navy Journalist, great co-worker in days long past and now retired in Burlington, VT.

All those that helped with our "behind-the-scenes" tour of the WWII Liberty ship and now floating museum, the John W. Brown. One of two surviving fully operational Liberty ships preserved in the United States, the ship's non-profit Foundation to help preserve the vessel is always in need of funds. Special thanks to Charles L. "Chuck" Weaver and Dan Donald for the tour. Go to https://www.ssjohnwbrown.org/

Those participating in digitizing complete editions of some 3,600 newspapers at www.newspapers.com – with millions of pages being added every month.

The Historic Naval Ships Association which turned 50 on 10 December 2016. Their original tenets remain to this day - to honor the men and women who joined the naval service of their nation; to educate the public, both young and old about the great naval heritage of their nation; and to inspire men and women to serve their country. Check them out at http://www.hnsa.org.

A call out here for readers to support the United States Coast Guard Enlisted Memorial Foundation, Cape May, NJ. See them at www.cgemf.org/. Also, the U.S. Coast Guard

Chief Petty Officers Association (CGCPOA) and the U.S. Coast Guard Enlisted Association (CGEA) both at www.uscgcpoa.org.

The Coast Guard Purple Heart Initiative, sponsored by the Hampton Roads Chief Petty Officers' Association (CPOA), seeks to recognize the sacrifices and preserve the history of U.S. Coast Guard heroes who were awarded the Purple Heart. Maybe one day we'll add the remaining names of the crew of the USS *Serpens* who are still awaiting their Purple Heart to the list. They are at http://cgpurpleheart.org/.

Thanks goes out to Ellison Kyere, Senior Marketing Officer at the Solomons Tourism office for going out of his way helping us with planning, having the USS *Serpens* wreath made, coordinating tours, etc. This was more than just a job for Ellison – he was genuinely pleased to be helping us pull things together that we needed. And thanks to Travel Solomons for the tour of the east and west sides of the islands and getting us to the Vilu Museum – a remote place that you probably couldn't find on your own!

A special thanks to the Tulagi Dive Shop at the Point Cruz Yacht Club in Honiara, Solomons, for our underwater tours of the *Serpens'* bow and debris field as well as the other underwater ships and aircraft our group dived on. Thoroughly professional and fast to reply on email questions. It should be everyone's "go to" dive shop for the true "Iron Bottom Sound" experience. Special thanks to Troy Shelley (Dive Operator), Alwin James (Divemaster), Catherine Hanson-Friend (Dive Assistant) and Paul Robertson (Deckhand) for making this a memorable experience. So check them out at http://www.tulagidive.com/.

And even more thanks to another Dive Shop – Gulf Coast Dive Pros in Pensacola, FL, and Captain Andy Ross of Niuhi Boat Charters (and his Divemaster Adam Wise) for helping us prepare for our Guadalcanal Liberty ship dives by trying to get us out to the Liberty ship *Joseph L. Meek*. In 1976, she was sunk as an artificial reef and now rests in 95 feet of water seven miles out of Pensacola Bay. The ship sits upright with her sides rising 20 feet off the bottom. While inclement weather spoiled the day, it was a very professionally run operation and highly recommended to all wanting a pleasant and safe dive on to some local Pensacola shipwrecks.

I am sure that some inaccuracies have crept in when it comes to spelling names. Even official records disagree. But any mistakes are ours and ours alone. Additions, deletions, corrections? Please contact me at dcamp@aol.com.

FOREWORD

The term "long blue line" in U.S. Coast Guard phraseology refers to the color of the Coast Guard uniform and depicts the timeline of Coast Guard men and women who have served from the very inception of the Coast Guard. Their customs, traditions, history and heritage reflect an honorable profession. The official motto of the U.S. Coast Guard is *Semper Paratus*, a Latin phrase meaning "Always Ready". These words were never more true than when the Coast Guard, as a whole, went into harm's way during the "Neutrality Patrols" of 1939-1941 and during World War II. There were losses.

The Coast Guard lost a total of 1,917 persons during WWII with 574 losing their life in action, dying from wounds received in action, or perishing as a Prisoner of War. A sampling of events in which Coast Guardsmen died include:

On 29 January 1942 the gunboat USCGC *Alexander Hamilton* (WPG-34) was torpedoed by German submarine *U-132* off Reykjavik, Iceland, at 64°10'N, 022°56'W. She was the first cutter sunk by enemy action during World War II; 26 of her crew perished in the attack. The capsized wreck was scuttled the next day by gunfire from the destroyer USS *Ericsson* (DD-440). The next day, halfway around the world, USS *Wakefield*, manned by a Coast Guard crew, was in

Singapore when she was bombed by Japanese aircraft while still tied to the pier. Five of her Coast Guard crew were killed and nine were wounded. On 9 September 1942 the Coast Guard-manned weather ship USS *Muskeget* (WAG-48) disappeared without a trace while on weather patrol in the North Atlantic during World War II. Her entire crew of 117 USCG officers and enlisted men, plus five civilians, were lost between Norfolk, Virginia, and Iceland. After the war the U.S. Navy determined that she had been torpedoed and sunk with all hands by the German submarine U-755. On 17 December 1942 USS *Natsek* (WPG-170), part of the Greenland Patrol, disappeared in Belle Isle Strait while on patrol. There were no survivors among her 24-man crew. It is believed that she capsized due to severe icing.

On 3 February 1943 a U-boat torpedoed the transport USS *Dorchester* off the coast of Greenland with the loss of 15 Coast Guardsmen. On 27 March 1943, CG-85006 (ex-motor boat *Catamount*), exploded off Ambrose Light, off Long Island, NY, while on Coastal Picket patrol duty. Nine of her 10 crew died. On 13 June 1943 USCGC *Escanaba* (WPG-77) was sunk by explosion off Ivigtut, Greenland, 60°50'N, 52°00'W, by either torpedo or striking a mine. Like *Serpens*, there were only two survivors. The cause for the loss has never been confirmed but 100 Coast Guardsmen were among those that perished that day. On 25 September 1943, the USS *LST-167*, a US Coast Guard-manned tank landing ship, was damaged by a dive bomber off Vella Lavella, Solomons, 07°45'S, 156°30'E. Eight Coast Guardsmen died.

On 9 March 1944 USS *Leopold* (DE-319), a US Coast Guard-manned destroyer escort, was torpedoed by German submarine *U-255*, 650 miles west of Scotland. There were 171 Coast Guard officers and enlisted men on board that were killed. The survivors were rescued by USS *Joyce* (DE-317), another Coast Guard-manned destroyer escort. On 3 May 1944 the German submarine *U-371* was off Algiers in the Mediterranean when it struck the USCG-manned destroyer escort USS *Menges* (DE-320) with a torpedo, destroying her stern, killing thirty-one of her crew. On 27 August 1944 the USS *LST-327*, tank landing ship, was damaged by mine en route from Cherbourg to Southampton, England, killing 19 US Coast Guardsmen. In terms of death by natural disaster during WWII, the Great Atlantic Hurricane of 14 September, 1944, saw the largest loss of US Coast Guard lives. The Category 3 hurricane made landfall at Cape Hatteras, NC, Long Island, NY, and Point Judith, RI. At Cape Henry, VA, sustained winds were reported at 134 MPH with gusts to 150 MPH. USCG Cutters *Jackson* and *Bedloe*, and Lightship *No. 73* on Vineyard Sound Station, foundered. All 12 of the lightship's crew perished. Forty-eight of the 78 crewmen on board the two cutters were lost. On 12 November 1944 the *LST-66*, during the Leyte landings, was hit by a Japanese suicide plane, killing five US Coast Guardsmen. On 8 January 1945, the attack transport USS *Callaway* (APA-35), was involved in the bombardment of Japanese defenses of Lingayen Gulf. Kamikazes damaged *Callaway* at 17°00'N, 120°00'E, killing 16 Coast Guardsmen. But it was on 29 January 1945 that the US Coast Guard suffered its greatest loss.

> *"I felt and saw two flashes after which only the bow of the ship was visible. The rest had disintegrated and the bow sank soon afterwards."* – Coast Guard LCDR Peery Stinson, USS *Serpens* commanding officer.

The quote above refers to the Coast Guard-manned cargo vessel USS *Serpens* (AK-97). On 29 January 1945, while loading ammunition in Lunga Bay off Guadalcanal near the northern tip of the Solomon Islands, a catastrophic series of explosions destroyed the cargo vessel. In terms of lives lost, the destruction of the *Serpens* ranks as the single most largest disaster ever recorded in Coast Guard history.

Wartime censorship notwithstanding, the story of what happened that day some 75 years ago is still shrouded in some mysteries. This book, the first to be written on this subject matter, attempts to shine a light on this dark event by having requested that classified documents be declassified and by requesting other documents through the Freedom of Information Act (FOIA). When at times that failed, Congressional leaders interceded on our behalf. Yet still not all information was forthcoming. The original transcript of the Court of Inquiry which formally investigated the loss in 1945, at one time held by the Office of the U.S. Navy's Judge Advocate General (JAG), has gone missing and there are apparently no copies found to exist. This and other curious events can be found within these pages, including the possibility that *Serpens* may have been destroyed by a torpedo from an enemy submarine rather than by an "accident intrinsic to the loading process."

Dan Bowen, a retired enlisted man attached to the 492nd Port Battalion at Guadalcanal during World War II, was there that fateful night and asked the question that still cannot be answered: "Why?" He writes in the 8 August 1992 edition of the *Tampa Bay Times* (Tampa, Florida), page 132:

> "We should have suspected that our stay would be a lengthy one as we went ashore in semi-darkness, in water up to our knees. To confirm our location, we asked a bored-looking Seabee on shore what he called this place. He said, "Home," and walked off.

"We did determine that we were on Guadalcanal. The date was [ironically] January 29, 1944. The island was supposed to be secured, but nobody told the snipers in the hills. We were the 492nd Port Battalion, made up of four port companies. We were a back-up service battalion whose function was the loading and unloading of ships. We were classified as "non-combat" but had been trained in carbines—and 50-caliber machine guns.

"We were at the 'Canal' for 16 months, off-loading supplies for the personnel on the island, then loading that ship almost exclusively with rolling stock (Jeeps, trucks, tanks, amphibious craft), and then all forms and sizes of ammo, right up to the hatch covers. We could always tell another U.S. invasion was in the works by the number of ammo-laden ships we sent out.

"Over a period of 50 years, names and places seem to fade or disappear, but there is one event that has always stayed sharp in my mind. Sometimes during an emergency, three of our companies would work the same ship in shifts. We were working the USS *Serpens* about a mile offshore from barges and amphibious ducks and loading 5,000 tons of ammo from bottom to top. Each shift had been aboard four straight days and my shift was scheduled to go out the last day at 8 a.m. to button her up and send her on her way by noon.

"It never happened. In the dark of January 29, 1945, with a tremendous roar, the USS *Serpens*, a 200-man Coast Guard crew and 51 men of our B Company (if you can call 19- and 20-year-olds men) disappeared from the face of the Earth.

"In daylight we scoured the beach for miles. Nothing. Was it an accident? A mechanical breakdown? Enemy action? With no survivors and no physical evidence, no one will ever know. And the big question: Why?"

Strange that no book has ever been published about this singular event. Co-authors Douglas E. Campbell and Robert G. Breen have attempted to answer Dan Bowen's question as we approach the 75th Anniversary of the greatest loss of life in the history of the U.S. Coast Guard—and the greatest loss of life in the history of the Army's 231st Port Company of the 492nd Port Battalion—on 29 January 2020.

TABLE OF CONTENTS

HISTORY OF USS *SERPENS* (AK-97)

"The USS Serpens, a cargo ship manned by a Coast Guard crew, has been lost as the result of enemy action, somewhere in the South Pacific, the Navy Department has announced. The Serpens served as a provision ship for American forces in the New Zealand, New Caledonia and Guadalcanal areas between August 1943 and December 1944. Next of kin of all casualties have been notified." Photo is dated 14 July 1944, Official Navy Photograph No. 4088; photo by PhoM3c Arthur C. Hagendorn, Jr. On 14 July 1944 Serpens was at Berth #13, Purvis Bay. Florida Islands, British Solomon Islands, discharging dry stores to forces afloat, including to other Liberty ships SS Peter Burnett and SS Edgar Allen Poe.

In times of war, the Coast Guard or individual components of it can operate as a service of the Department of the Navy. This arrangement has a broad historical basis, as the Coast Guard, or components of what was to become the U.S. Coast Guard, has been involved in wars as diverse as the War of 1812, the Mexican–American War, and the American Civil War (in which the cutter *Harriet Lane* fired the first naval shots attempting to relieve besieged Fort Sumter). On 3 June 1941 President Franklin D. Roosevelt signed an executive order making 2,100 US Coast Guard officers and men available to man four transports, USS *Leonard Wood* (APA-12), USS *Joseph T. Dickman* (APA-13), USS *Hunter Liggett (*APA-14), and USS *Wakefield* (AP-21, formerly the luxury ocean liner SS *Manhattan*), along with 22 other ships manned by US Navy personnel. The last time the Coast Guard operated as a whole within the Navy was in World War II when, on 1 November 1941, Roosevelt signed another executive order reassigning the Coast Guard's duties from the Treasury Department to the Navy.

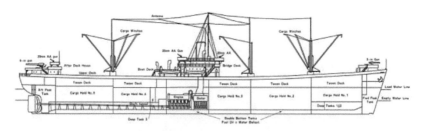

During World War II the U.S. Navy originally assigned the Coast Guard 10 cargo or supply ships (AKs) that were still being built - but after a reorganization among Naval commands the Coast Guard only received one from the Navy's inventory planned to be manned entirely of Coast Guardsmen – USS *Enceladus* (AK-80), commissioned 22 August 1943. The Coast Guard had to wait until 28 March

1943 to receive the first of 14 "Liberty" ships that were dedicated to Coast Guard crews. Those Liberty ships, listed by their commissioning dates and original commanding officers are as follows:

USS *Albireo* (AK-90), 29 March 1943, LCDR Edward M. Benton, USCGR

USS *Cor Caroli* (AK-91), 16 April 1943, LCDR J. A. Lewis, USCGR

USS *Eridanus* (AK-92), 8 May 1943, LCDR F. W. Johnson, USCGR

USS *Mintaka* (AK-94), 10 May 1943, LCDR L. S. Burgess, USCGR

USS *Etamin* (AK-93), 25 May 1943, LCDR G. W. Stedman, USCGR

USS *Murzim* (AK-95), 14 May 1943, LT J. E. King, USCGR

USS *Sterope* (AK-96), 14 May 1943, LCDR Leo P. Toolin, USCG

USS *Serpens* (AK-97), 28 May 1943, LCDR M. J. Johnson, USCGR

USS *Menkar* (AK-123), 2 June 1944, LCDR Edward G. Gummer, USNR (Ferry) then to LCDR Niels P. Thompsen, USCG

USS *Codington* (AK-173), 23 July 1945, LCDR A. F. Pittman, USCG

USS *Sussex* (AK-213), 20 August 1945, LCDR L. N. Ditlefsen, USCG

USS *Craighead* (AK-175), 5 September 1945, LCDR G. M. Walker, USNR

USS *Tarrant* (AK-214), 18 September 1945, LCDR F. A. Simmons, USCGR

USS *Somerset* (AK-212), never commissioned

Liberty ships were slightly over 441 feet long by 57 feet wide. They used a 2,500-horsepower steam engine to push them through the water at 11 knots, equaling approximately 11.5 miles per hour. The ships maintained a range of about

17,000 miles. Crew quarters were located amidships while cargo was fitted into one of the five available holds - three situated forward of the engine room and two in the aft portion of the vessel. Each ship could carry up to 10,800 deadweight tons of cargo and 4,380 net tons - effectively the amount of space available for cargo and/or passengers.

Many technological advances were made during the Liberty shipbuilding program. A steel cold-rolling process was developed to save steel in the making of lightweight cargo booms. Welding techniques were developed to produce the first all-welded craft. Prefabrication was introduced resulting in complete deckhouses, double-bottom sections, stern-frame assemblies and bow units inevitably increasing production output of whole ships. On average it took 592,000 hours to build the ship and the average time of construction for one ship by 1944 became just 42 days.

Serpens required 3,425 tons of steel for the hull along with 2,725 tons of steel plate and 700 tons of metal-shaped walls and bulkheads needing 50,000 castings. A total of 2,751 Liberties were built between 1941 and 1945.

The California Shipbuilding Corporation built 467 of those Liberty and Victory ships during World War II, including one that would eventually be named USS *Serpens* (AK-97). The California Shipbuilding Corporation was often referred to as Calship.

The Calship shipyard was created at Terminal Island in Los Angeles, California, United States as part of America's massive shipbuilding effort of World War II. W. A. Bechtel Co. was given sponsorship and executive direction of Calship. As of 1940, Los Angeles shipyards had not built a large ship in 20 years. By late 1941 though, shipbuilding had become the second largest manufacturing industry in the Los Angeles area.

Calship was created from scratch and began production of Liberty Ships in May 1941. In the early 1940s, contracts from the U.S. Department of Maritime Commission and a number of U.S. Navy contracts led to prosperity shipbuilding business in Los Angeles. The yard was located on 175 acres on the north side of Terminal Island, north of Dock Street, near present-day berths 210-213. It initially had 8 ways, and later increased this to 14. 'Ways' are concrete and wooden blocks, spaced about one-third of a vessel's beam apart, that support each ship under construction. Forty thousand men and women worked under the military contract to construction of 467 vessels over 5 years. The combination of these ships was known as the "Liberty Fleet". These cargo ships were designed for rapid construction with lower costs for them. Thirteen months after commencing production, the yard broke the record by delivering 15 Liberty Ships in June 1942. It delivered 111 ships in 1942, more than any other yard in the United States. In June 1943, it broke the record again by delivering 20 ships for the month, and yet again in December 1943, delivering 23 ships.

Large Navy contracts developed shipbuilding in California. As a result of that, many workers migrated to the work area. Many shipyards sprang up from San Francisco to San Diego. At the peak of shipbuilding in California 282,000 persons were involved. Shipbuilding became a highly efficient wartime industry. The building of vessels and the number of jobs in the shipbuilding peaked in mid-1943.

The Kaiser Steel plant in Fontana, California, was completed in August 1943, which enabled further production increases at Calship. Between 27 September 1941 and 27 September 1945 the yard launched 467 ships.

The Calship yard was known as "the city built on invisible stilts." It was situated on marshy ground, and was built on artificial earth supported by 57,000 piles driven into the mud. Shipbuilding commenced before the fitting-out docks were even completed. The yard's workers came from every region of the United States, reaching a force of 40,000 men and women, only 1% of whom had any shipbuilding experience whatsoever.

Before the keel of *Serpens* was even laid one of her sister ships, USS *Atik* (AK-101), was sunk while deployed as a Q-Ship (warship disguised as a merchantman) in a battle with German submarine U-123 in the North Atlantic on 26 March 1942. In the Pacific, a foreboding of *Serpens'* fate occurred at Lunga Point, Guadalcanal, just yards away from where *Serpens* would eventually explode. On 28 November 1942 the Japanese submarine *I-6* launched its Ko-hyoteki class midget submarine *Ha-10* which proceeded to close in on the cargo ship USS *Alchiba* (AK-95, later AKA-6), anchored off Lunga Point.

During November *Alchiba* had been shuttling supplies and personnel between Guadalcanal and Tulagi. Now, at 0616 on 28 November 1942, in nearly the same position as *Serpens* would be in January 1945, two torpedoes from *Ha-10* exploded on *Alchiba's* port side. At that time, her No. 2 hold was loaded with drums of aviation gasoline and ammunition, and the resulting explosion shot flames 150 feet in the air. The commanding officer, CAPT James Shepherd Freeman, ordered the ship to weigh anchor and run up on the beach. This action undoubtedly saved the ship. Hungry flames raged in the ship for over five days before weary firefighting parties finally brought them under control. CAPT Freeman was awarded the Navy Cross and his executive officer, Commander Howard R. Shaw, was awarded the Silver Star for their leadership in saving this vessel.

A U.S. Marine Corps M2A4 "Stuart" light tank is hoisted from USS Alchiba (AK-23) into an LCM landing craft, K23-1) off the Guadalcanal invasion beaches on the first day of landings there, 7 August 1942. U.S. Navy photo 80-G-10973 courtesy National Archives and Records Administration (NARA).

Salvage operations began soon thereafter. Most of her cargo was saved, and temporary repairs were in progress when *Alchiba* was torpedoed again on 7 December 1942, this time by midget submarine *Ha-38* (launched from *I-24*). This time an enemy submarine's conning tower had been spotted shortly before two torpedoes were fired. One passed close under the cargo ship's stern, but the other struck her No. 4 hold on the port side near the engine room. Although the hold cargo (500-pound bombs) had been unloaded earlier, the blast killed three men, including MM2c Everett M. Stuermer, wounded six others, and caused considerable structural damage. Once the fires and flooding were controlled, salvage operations resumed which enabled the ship to get underway for Tulagi on 27 December 1942.

Some three months later, *Serpens* was laid down under Maritime Commission contract (MCE hull 739) as the Liberty ship SS *Benjamin N. Cardozo*, on 10 March 1943. She was one of three cargo ships launched by Calship on 5 April 1943; the ship being named for the late Supreme Court Justice. It was the 164th Liberty cargo vessel launched by Calship. The ship displaced 14,250 tons, was 441' 6" in length, had a beam of 56' 11" and a draft of 27' 7". Her cruising speed was 11.5 knots and a full complement of officers and men was 206. She was also the 18th Crater-class freighter cargo ship constructed for use by the United States Navy in World War II by the Maritime Commission. She was classified as EC2-S-C1 (EC2 = Emergency Cargo, type 2 and S = steam propulsion) and fitted with one propeller. The launching was sponsored by Mrs. H. P. Needham; wife of Commander H. P. Needham, CEC, USN, who later, as Captain, was the commanding officer of the Naval Construction Battalion Center at Port Hueneme, Los Angeles, CA., as well as Officer-in-Command of Camp Rousseau and the advance base depot. As an aside, the depot at Port Hueneme was the only Seabee receiving barracks on the West coast, the point where all navy construction battalions were sent for final training before shipping out to the Pacific during World War II. In connection with this, the base had a large military training area and technical training grounds where Seabees learned to work and fight with guns, shovels and other tools of their trade. The Seabees also spent time at the depot aboard the land-locked USS *Never Sail*, a simulated Liberty ship on which Seabee stevedores were trained for the unloading of cargo ships at Pacific ports where civilian labor is not available.

The "ship" was fitted out with all the trappings of a real Liberty ship and operated on three watches — 24 hours a day — with 80 men holding down each watch. It was 264 feet long, 57 feet wide and 12 feet high, with decks and cargo hatches like a regular ship.

After receiving primary training in stevedoring at Camp Peary, Williamsburg, VA, which has a similar "ship," special Seabee battalions, mostly, were sent to Port Hueneme and assigned to the *Never Sail*. Here, they received their final training in 10 days. The *Never Sail* put some 600 to 700 men through the mill each week and had been one of the primary actors in breaking one of the worst bottlenecks of the war in the South Pacific — unloading ships where port facilities were primitive and dock workers non-existent.

Out in the field, the port battalion/port company formations were, in essence, longshoremen in uniform. "Stevedore" is an older term similarly used for personnel who loaded and unloaded cargo ships. Up until the 1960's, cargo ships were considered "break bulk" freighters whose cargo holds were loaded/unloaded in single pieces or in cargo nets.

In the days before intermodal transport, the only way to get large quantities of freight overseas was through the use of break bulk freighters. The USS *Serpens* (AK-97) was an example of a Liberty ship, a mass-produced break bulk freighter unique to World War II.

It took a large number of men to load and unload ships like the *Serpens* (more men than the ship's crew) -- to run the booms on the ship; to move the cargo in the holds under the booms or to move the cargo in the hold out from under the booms; to spot the cargo on the shore or onto the lighter (barge); and so on. These were the days before forklifts were readily available on ships--the cargo had to be manhandled into place almost every step of the way. So, to assist the ships' crews, the Port Battalions/Companies were used to make the loading/unloading of the ship's cargo as quick as possible. While shipping companies during peacetime want a quick turnaround in getting their ships in and out of port in order to maximize profit, in wartime, a naval commander wants a quick turnaround to ensure the safety of the cargo ships from enemy attack. The Port Battalions/Companies were key to that concept.

The SS *Benjamin N. Cardozo* was transferred to the Navy on 19 April 1943; renamed USS *Serpens* and given the designation as cargo ship AK-97. She was commissioned at San Diego on 28 May 1943, with the first entry into her U.S. Navy logbook reading: "1130. On this day at this time, this ship was commissioned the U.S.S. *Serpens* by W. J. Morcott, Commander, U.S.N. at Destroyer Base, north side of pier 2 at San Diego, California. The U.S.S. *Serpens*, commissioned and turned over to Magnus J. Johnson, Lt.Comdr., U.S.C.G. for his command." Note: LCDR Johnson was actually USCGR. He was succeeded on 22 July 1944 by LCDR

Peery L. Stimson, USCG. LCDR Johnson went on to command USS *Mintaka* (AK-94), an EC-2 S-C1 Liberty Ship, from 12 December through 18 September 1945. A graduate of the USCG Academy, he retired as a Commander and passed away 24 June 1957.

The commissioning ceremony of USS Serpens (AK-97) on 28 May 1943 at the San Diego, CA, Destroyer Base. View is from forward, looking aft. No photo number; photographer unknown. Photo provided courtesy of CAPT James D. Ellison, USCG (Ret.), who served aboard Serpens as a LTJG.

Serpens remained tied up to the north side of pier 2 as she underwent the conversion process, changing her over from a civilian to a military cargo ship. This included the installation of her 3"/.50, 5"/.38 and 30mm guns. On 1 June 1943 at 1130 she began taking aboard ammunition for those guns. The following day, all preparations were made for getting underway for the first time as a U.S. Naval vessel. At 0600 the engines were turned over and all lines were singled up. At 0645 Tug *#266* came alongside to port as did Tug *#133* at 0647. At 0709 the rest of the lines were cast off and, unmoored and officially underway, *Serpens* stood out from pier #2. By 0715 she was proceeding through the channel under various courses and speeds. At 0808 she departed the channel, passing through the two San Diego anti-torpedo net openings. At 0813 the civilian pilot departed *Serpens* by pilot boat and the rest of the day was spent swinging the ship around to check her magnetic compasses, checking on degaussing, calibrating her radio direction finder and completing calibrations on the magnetic compasses. Returning, *Serpens* anchored in the San Diego anchorage and, anticipating gun firing exercises the following day, a Navy ammunition barge came alongside and provided the ship with additional stores. Within 90 minutes the barge had pulled away, to be replaced by a fuel barge arriving at 0205 on 3 June 1943. Having taken on 69,662 additional gallons of fuel oil, the barge departed at 0540 and at 0612 *Serpens* was again underway. Back out at sea *Serpens'* crew performed various operational drills on the vessel at various engine speeds and at 1547 test-fired the 5"-.38 stern gun. This time they stayed out at sea for 5 days, arriving back to their San Diego anchorage at 0756 on 7 June 1943.

The following day *Serpens* got underway at 1541, loaded with jeep and tank lighters, departing San Diego Bay and passing through two anti-torpedo nets outside the entrance to the Bay. Jeep and tank lighters are barges used for the purpose of ferrying to shore heavy cargo from freighters and transports arriving in theaters of operation. The lighters, once craned off the cargo ship, may either be riding offshore at anchor in the open sea or more likely, anchored in a harbor. Heavy cargo like jeeps and tanks from the ships would be loaded onto these lighters. Then tugs, tow boats, or marine tractors would propel the lighters to the shore for unloading. Now, on 8 June at 1915 and with an ammunition barge in tow, *Serpens* turned north-northwest at slow speed, heading for San Francisco, CA. On 13 June *Serpens* passed under the Golden Gate Bridge and at 1550 moored to starboard at Pier #5, Encinal Docks, Alameda, CA. By 0800 on 14 June all the ship's jeep and tank lighters had been unloaded and with the vessel's hatches rigged to stow cargo, the California longshoremen who had come aboard began taking on cargo, beginning in cargo Hold #3. On the following day, the daily ritual of inspecting magazines and smokeless powder samples as well as checking the small arms lockers and ammunition began. By 17 June, 3,776 tons of general cargo had been loaded aboard *Serpens*.

Ten days later, on 23 June 1943, two sister ships met their fate against the enemy. USS *Aludra* (AK-72) sunk after being torpedoed by Japanese submarine *RO-103* off San Cristobal Island, Solomon Islands, 50 nm south of the eastern tip of the San Cristobal Island. The submarine's Commander, LT Ichimura, sighted a convoy of three transports protected by three destroyers. He torpedoed and sunk the 7,440-ton *Aludra* and damaged the 7,176-ton "Liberty" ship USS *Deimos* (AK-78) in the vicinity of 11-26S, 162-01E. *Deimos*, damaged irreparably, was scuttled by destroyer *O'Bannon* (DD-450) at 11-35S, 162-08E.

The following day, 24 June 1943, *Serpens* sailed west to assume provision ship duties in support of operations in the Solomons. At 1310, with the tug *Sea Queen* assisting in unmooring, *Serpens* stood out into the main channel, proceeding toward San Francisco Bay. At 1715 she passed under the San Francisco and Oakland Bridge and at 1745 passed under the Golden Gate Bridge. The *Serpens* now executed her first operational order that would take the ship and crew to the South Pacific and much closer to the front lines. The orders were from Commander, Western Sea Frontier, and their mission was to move all this loaded cargo to Noumea, New Caledonia.

Serpens crossed the Pacific Ocean at an average speed of 11.5 knots, zig-zagging for the most part. She went to General Quarters whenever another vessel closed but all were found friendly. The main concern during the crossing was the amount of seawater filling the different bilges which required being pumped out when they reached 8 to 12 inches in depth. On 12 July 1943 she was in the Tonga Islands and at 1652 dropped anchor in 13 fathoms (78 feet) of water in Nukualofa anchorage. Shortly thereafter the Captain's gig, lifeboat #2 and motor launch #3 were lowered away and set against the gangway on the starboard side of the ship. Liberty parties were transported back and forth to the island. At 1250 on 19 July all hands were mustered and present and it was "anchors aweigh and underway" for their next port. The following day *Serpens* joined a convoy comprised of SS *Dona Nati*, SS *Wiley Post*, and SS *Calusa* with the minesweeper USS *Constant* (AM-86) as escort. As a side note, *Constant* sailed from Pearl Harbor on 8 March 1943 for Espiritu Santo, arriving 25 March for local escort duty, operating from Espiritu Santo and Noumea in support of the Guadalcanal operation. On 1 June 1944 her name was canceled and she was reclassified as a submarine chaser, *PC-1590*. She continued her service at Espiritu Santo, Noumea, Samoa and Tongatapu until 6 May 1946. She then returned to Pearl Harbor, where she was decommissioned 19 June 1946. She was sunk as a target on 27 January 1955.

At 1819 on 25 July 1943, still in the same convoy, *Serpens* let go her port anchor into 11 fathoms (66 feet) of water – she had arrived at the port of Noumea, New Caledonia, anchored in anchorage #27. The following day she moved over to anchorage #10 in Dumbea Bay. At 1353 a floating crane came alongside to port and began taking the tank lighters off the *Serpens*; at 1620 the last tank lighter was sitting in the water. Coxswain Gregory Sippe, a member of the *Serpens* crew and in charge of the working party, came alongside to starboard in tank lighter *#257* and took nine tank lighters in tow; all headed for the Noumea boat pool. Finished, *Serpens* pulled up anchor at 0627 on 27 July and repositioned to Berth #45.

On 29 July *Serpens* made preparations for getting underway and set her sea watches. At 1330 she pulled her anchors off the seabed and headed out of Dumbea Bay at various courses and speeds, heading for New Zealand. By the next day she was attached to a convoy which included the Navy's ammunition oiler USS *Lackawanna* (AO-40), two merchant ships (MS *Tabinta* and MS *Bloemfontein*), the steamship SS *Oliver Wendell Holmes* and the Navy escort vessel and auxiliary minesweeper USS *Shelldrake* (AM-62). For most of her WWII career, *Shelldrake* crisscrossed the South Pacific, shepherding convoys between bases in the New Hebrides, Solomon Islands, and New Caledonia; also making-occasional runs to New Zealand, Samoa, and Fiji. *Sheldrake* also participated intermittently in patrols off Guadalcanal. On 3 August *Serpens* passed abeam of the Cape Egmont Lighthouse at 0136 and by 1330 was approaching the main entrance of Port Nicholson, New Zealand. They picked up their pilot at 1408 and passed through the anti-torpedo net off Ward Island at 1435. Finally, at 1512 they were moored to King's Wharf, Berth #2, in

Wellington. For the next two weeks they remained in Wellington, unloading general stores and loading commissary stores, including milk. For the crew they also took aboard on several occasions 100 pounds of bread, fresh milk and fish.

On 17 August 1943 all the stevedores were sent ashore and the fresh water hose was secured. The pilot came aboard at 1024 and by 1048 *Serpens* was underway. The pilot boat *Jamie Seddon* came alongside at 1158 and picked up the pilot; LCDR Johnson then took *Serpens* out to sea, passing the Pencarrow Light abeam to port at 1216. At 1818 the following day *Serpens* picked up their next pilot and at 1835 *Serpens* passed abeam of Taiaroa Head light, proceeding into Otago Harbor. At 1932 she laid port side to against Bohn Pier in Port Chalmers, New Zealand. On the following day, 19 August, *Serpens* pulled away from Bohn Pier and, with the tug *Dunedin* to assist, proceeded through Otago Harbor and tied up port side to Victoria Wharf, Dunedin, New Zealand, a distance of 14 miles, at 0819. Within 30 minutes stevedores were loading *Serpens* with supplies, including lumber and nails, for her next anchorage.

On occasion, *Serpens* transported more than supplies between seaports – they also took on passengers. Such was the case at Dunedin when a Captain Duncan of the Royal New Zealand Navy with official orders to Wellington, New Zealand. Also coming aboard was Chief Electrician's Mate (CEM) Arthur Clements Heinen, USNR, who was being transferred off the net tender USS *Butternut* (YAG-60) to *Serpens* for passage to Wellington. On 28 August *Serpens* unmoored her lines and at 0818 stood out from alongside the wharf, with crew and passengers passing abeam of Taiaroa Head Light at 0956. At 1743 the following day *Serpens* was moored starboard side to Berth #2, Aotea Wharf, Wellington, NZ.

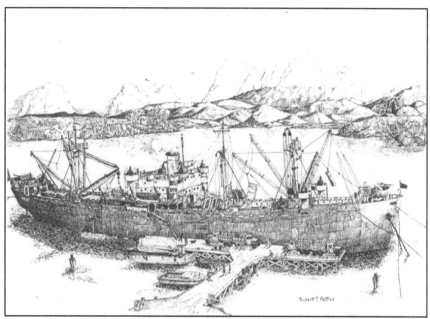

A pen and ink sketch of the USS Serpens. According to former Serpens' crewman Leonard B. Rogers, the artist, Robert C. Pettes, spent a couple of days sketching the Serpens from a nearby hilltop while the ship was tied up in New Caledonia. Pettes dated the drawing 9/23/43. Mr. Rogers son, Charles P. Rogers, graciously donated a copy of the drawing to the USCG Historian's Office. He noted that "the picture took a few days to draw and he [Pettes] started [drawing] at one end [of the ship] and drew it to the other. Note that in the course of that time the wind changed directions and the flags are blowing in different directions." Fortunately, Mr. Rogers' father was transferred before the Serpens was lost.

By 0850 on 3 September 1943 the stevedores were all ashore and *Serpens'* engines were warmed up. With the pilot aboard, they stood out alongside Aotea Wharf and proceeded through Lambton Harbor. Passing through the anti-torpedo net, then Pencarrow Head Light, Baring Head Light and Brother Lighthouse all to her port, *Serpens* was again back at sea. They rendezvoused with their escort ship, USS *Craven* (DD-382) on 7 September. Approximately five hours later the destroyer reported "Man Overboard" and *Serpens* cut speed, slowed and then stopped. They lowered their #3 lifeboat which pushed off in search for the person. With lifeboat away, *Serpens* swung in circles in search of the person as well. Within 20 minutes *Serpens'* lifeboat was recalled and hoisted back aboard. The logbook from USS *Craven* regarding this incident read:

7 September 1943

1410   Sappington, Jewel Birthal, Seaman 1/c, USNR (V-6) fell overboard. Sappington was climbing ladder to superstructure deck on the port side forward. He had a handful of magazines and was climbing ladder with one hand when he was observed to miss the ladder rung – as the ship rolled to port. He fell backwards, hitting his back on the life line, bounced off the life line into the water. A life ring was thrown overboard towards Sappington from the port wing of the bridge. Captain took the conn. Broke out Man Overboard flag, sounded series of five blasts or whistles. Ship was backed immediately to the area about fifty yards from life buoy. Sappington was evidently paralyzed by fall for he sank in four to five minutes after entering water.

1526   Discontinued search, resumed station and commenced patrolling as before.

All resumed course and speed. The following day the escort destroyer departed as *Serpens* slipped between the reefs into Dumbea Bay, Noumea, New Caledonia. At 1411 *Serpens* was anchored in 10 fathoms (60 feet) of water in Berth #45.

On 9 September 1943 *Serpens* weighed anchor, passed through the anti-torpedo net opening and repositioned herself in Fisherman's Bay in 7 fathoms (42 feet) of water. Barges came alongside and the working party unloaded mail sacks and other cargo. That completed, they repositioned again in Fisherman's Bay and remained about 5 miles from Berth #45. On 11 September they hoisted a tank lighter aboard and, with Amedee Island Lighthouse on her starboard beam, proceeded out of Fisherman's Bay. At 0735 the following day she entered Mueo Passage to Port Nepui, New Caledonia. By 0922 she was moored to starboard to the New Zealand Army dock at Port Nepui where the New Zealand Army came aboard to unload cargo from all five holds. By 21 September unloading was complete and *Serpens* took aboard a D-4 bulldozer and a sand and gravel loader, then weighed anchor to reposition herself within the Port Nepui Bay anchorage for preparations in getting underway the following day.

On 22 September *Serpens* pulled up her anchor at 0515 and by 0554 she had passed through the reefs at Mueo Passage and was steaming full speed ahead. Later that morning *Serpens* dropped a target overboard so that the gun crews could practice firing their 3"/.50 and 5"/.38 batteries. Shortly before noon they ceased firing and resumed course and speed for their return to Dumbea Bay, New Caledonia, Berth #43, dropping anchor at 1633. After unloading cargo, they repositioned to Dock #1, Grand Pier, on their port side where U.S. Army stevedores came aboard to continue unloading cargo. On their starboard side USS *Rapaki* came alongside to load four booms as part of *Serpens'* deck cargo. As a side note, the vessel "USS *Rapaki*" was a coal-powered steam crane belonging to New Zealand but during World War II it was requisitioned by the U.S. Navy for use in the Pacific islands.

On 24 December 1925 the Lyttelton New Zealand Harbour Board ordered an 80-ton self-propelled floating crane, called Rapaki. It was named after the settlement close to Lyttelton of the same name. In December 2018 Rapaki was towed to Wynyard Wharf to be broken up. Her sister ship, Hikitia, can still be visited on the Wellington Waterfront and is now the only steam crane still in New Zealand waters. Photo courtesy Alexander Turnbull Library.

Also loaded aboard *Serpens* were paint and engine room supplies from the Naval Supply Depot at Noumea. On 29 September at 0607 *Serpens* stood out from alongside the Grand Pier and repositioned to Berth #24 in Dumbea Bay in preparation for getting underway. At 1315 anchors were aweigh and *Serpens* was "haze gray and underway;" at 1406 she fell in astern of her escort destroyer and at 1533 she passed through the reefs and out to sea. At 2200 the following day her destroyer escort departed to starboard and *Serpens* was on her own.

On 2 October 1943 *Serpens* entered Navula Passage in the Fiji Islands and passed abeam of the Navula Reef Beacon to port at 1240. She anchored in Morri Bay awaiting the pilot and permission to proceed and at 1443 she passed through the anti-torpedo net. At 1650 she was moored forward and aft by anchor buoys in Lautoka Harbor, Vita Levu, in 5.5 fathoms (33 feet) of water. Barges came alongside and stevedores began unloading from holds #1, 3, 4 and 5. At 0810 on 4 October *Serpens* unmoored and proceeded through the anti-torpedo nets and by 1805 had passed through the Suva Harbor nets, still in the Fiji Islands. The War Diary for U.S. Naval Forces, Fiji Islands, on 4 October 1943 stated that at 1806 local time "U.S.S. *Serpens* arrived in Suva from Nandi with U.S.S. *YMS 216* following and providing escort protection." She moored port side to King's Wharf while additional cargo was unloaded and loaded. Departing the following day, the War Diary for U.S. Naval Forces, Fiji Islands, on 5 October 1943 stated that at 1233 local time "U.S.S. *Serpens* and the M.V. *Matua* (British), escorted by U.S.S. *YMS 216*, departed Suva. The U.S.S. *Serpens* was bound for Tutuila." USS *Serpens* crossed the International Date Line and on 7 October, at 1243, was moored to "A" buoy in Pago-Pago Harbor in 10 fathoms (60 feet) of water. Having unloaded additional stores from her various holds, *Serpens* again weighed anchors on 10 October, passing Ofu Island abeam to starboard at 1825. At 0800 on 14 October 1943 she was anchored in 25 fathoms (150 feet) of water off the reef entrance to Taruiai Pass, Penrhyn Island, unloading additional cargo.

On 15 October 1943 a sad event occurred surrounded by a mystery. Robert W. Baronich writes: "My brother Martin P. Baronich, Seaman S2, was killed in an accident aboard USS *Serpens* (AK-97) on October 15, 1943. Any information would be appreciated." The authors could not find the Muster Logs for this time period, nor any Muster Log from any ship with Martin Baronich listed - so having the names of the entire *Serpens* crew for the October 1943 period would be guesswork. Also, the War Diary for USS *Serpens* mentions no such accident although such an event would have been noted, even had Martin Baronich been a shore-based stevedore supporting *Serpens* rather than a crewmember. The authors did find his "Application for Headstone or Marker." On the form it states that his full name was Martin Paul Baronich, Jr., and that he was a Fireman Second Class, USCGR. He was born on 4 June 1922, enlisted on 27 November 1942 and was indeed killed on 15 October 1943. His body was returned home to Biloxi, Mississippi and he was buried in Southern Memorial Park with a Christian emblem on the headstone. Neither the American Battle Monuments Commission nor the Veterans Affairs BIRL Death File lists his name, although his name and other pertinent information (except duty station) appears on the Office of the Quartermaster General (OQMG) Form 623, *Application for Headstone or Marker*.

Departing at 0850 on 16 October, *Serpens* was moored starboard side to the U.S. Naval Dock, Teavanui Harbor, Bora Bora, Society Islands, at 0645 on 19 October, loading all holds. She unmoored from the dock at 0955 on 26 October, passed through the reefs and set a course for Aitutaki Island in the Cook Islands, arriving on 28 October. There they remained for 14 hours and steamed away at 2103 the same day, heading for the Tonga Islands.

November 1943 came and *Serpens* and her plank owner crew were coming up on their 6-month anniversary as Coastguardsmen aboard a military cargo ship in the middle of World War II. At 1348 on 1 November she moored port side to Red Pier, Nukualofa, Tongatabu, Tonga Islands. Here they unloaded Hold #4 and then loaded *Serpens* with other supplies. Their holds fully loaded, they then began loading and securing supplies onto the ship's forward deck. At 1619 on 4 November they weighed anchors and stood out of Lahi Passage, zig-zagging according to plan, heading back to Noumea. They arrived at 1227 on 9 November, dropping anchor in 10 fathoms (60) feet of water at Berth #42, Dumbea Bay, Noumea, New Caledonia. The November 1943 edition of the USCG Magazine published a comment about *Serpens* from an unknown crewmember: "The saltiest cargo-carrying vessel in the fleet is the USS *Serpens* AK-97. Now to eliminate the guff, and to get down to facts, we are still steaming in this mill pond, sometimes called the [CENSORED] and with the C.G. colors flying, leaving a good opinion wherever we go. We are very proud of this ship." At various times *Serpens* shifted berths and sometimes moored to different piers at the Finger Piers for the various unloading sequences, but until early December 1943 she remained in Dumbea Bay.

On 1 December 1943 Commander H. S. Klien, USN, reported aboard as commander of task unit 35.1.7. The task unit that formed up included *Serpens*, USS *Alchiba* (AKA-23), merchant ships SS *Cape Blanco* and SS *Thomas J. Walsh*, and three escort vessels – destroyer escort USS *Agree* (DE-167), minesweeper USS *Constant* (AM-427) and submarine chaser *SC-1046*. CDR Klien announced their destination – Lunga Point, Guadalcanal, Solomon Islands. At 0600 the following day they were all underway and by noon were passing through Havannah Passage, New Caledonia. At 1610 on 4 December merchant ships *Frederick Jackson Turner*, *William Ashley* and *Thunderer*, with three additional escort ships – USS *Dash* (AM-89), USS *Eaton* (DD-510) and USS *Osterhaus* (DE-164) – had joined the convoy. At 0800 on 7 December the convoy and escorts had arrived at Lunga Point. *Serpens* broke off and proceeded with merchant ships SS *Frederick Jackson Turner* and their escort vessel

Osterhaus proceeded to Tulagi Harbor, where *Serpens* dropped anchor in Berth #5 for a brief time. At 1315 they were underway again, this time headed for Gavutu Bay, Florida Island. Two hours later they were anchored and discharging deck cargo and cargo from holds #2 and #5. On 10 December USS *Osterhaus* reported in her War Diary: "proceeded to investigate report of submarine sighted two (2) miles north of Beacon 'L', Guadalcanal, Solomon Islands."

On 11 December 1943 they weighed anchors and proceeded to Lunga Point, where at 1555 they were anchored at Berth #28 and commenced the discharging of cargo. On 14 December CDR Klien departed the vessel and boarded the auxiliary minesweeper *YMS-260*.

On 18 December, while still discharging cargo, *Serpens* received an interesting set of orders. They were to temporarily cease unloading their cargo and proceed to Tillotson Dock, Russell Islands. While there, they were to tie up port side to the dock while their former convoy member, SS *Cape Blanco*, was to tie up against their starboard side. *Serpens* was then needed to use their jumbo boom to unload *Cape Blanco*. This unloading began at 1025 on December 19 through Christmas Eve. At 0606 Christmas Day 1943, *Serpens* got underway and proceeded back to Lunga Point with the escort vessel *SC-521*. At 1234 they were anchored back off Lunga Point when they received another set of orders sending them to Purvis Bay, Florida Island, where at 1616 they were anchored in Berth #14. There they celebrated Christmas with a traditional dinner followed by pumpkin pie, black coffee and cigars.

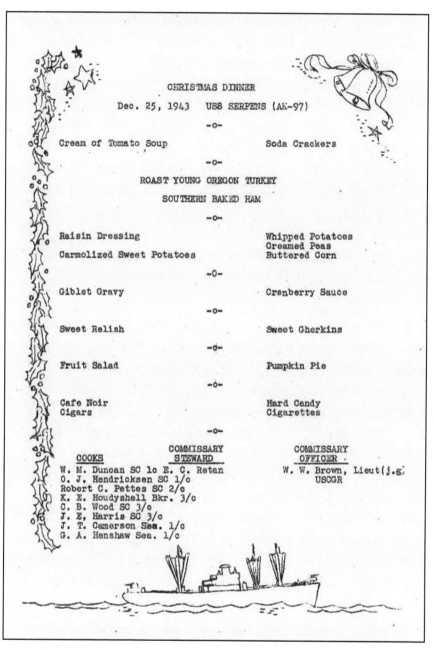

CHRISTMAS DINNER

Dec. 25, 1943   USS SERPENS (AK-97)

—o—

Cream of Tomato Soup   Soda Crackers

—o—

ROAST YOUNG OREGON TURKEY

SOUTHERN BAKED HAM

—o—

Raisin Dressing   Whipped Potatoes
                                        Creamed Peas
Carmolized Sweet Potatoes   Buttered Corn

—o—

Giblet Gravy   Cranberry Sauce

—o—

Sweet Relish   Sweet Gherkins

—o—

Fruit Salad   Pumpkin Pie

—o—

Cafe Noir   Hard Candy
Cigars   Cigarettes

—o—

	COMMISSARY	COMMISSARY
COOKS	STEWARD	OFFICER
W. M. Duncan SC 1c	E. C. Retan	W. W. Brown, Lieut(j.g)
O. J. Hendricksen SC 1/c		USCGR
Robert C. Pettes SC 2/c		
K. E. Houdyshell Bkr. 3/c		
C. B. Wood SC 3/c		
J. E. Harris SC 3/c		
J. T. Camerson Sea. 1/c		
G. A. Henshaw Sea. 1/c		

The following day they repositioned to Berth #12 at Purvis Bay and on December 27 they received a dispatch message from Commander Task Group 35.6 to return to Lunga Point, to be escorted by USS *Kiwi* (apparently another local vessel requisitioned by the Navy during the war.). The orders stated to "arrive before dark December 27th." At 1855 on that day they anchored off Lunga Point. For the next two days they loaded additional cargo and at 0636 on 30 December they fell in line with a convoy *comprised* of Tank Landing Ships (LST's) *166*, *397*, *446*, 447 and *449*. All were escorted by the destroyers USS *Conway* (DD-507), USS *Hudson* (DD-475), USS *Pringle* (DD-477), USS *Renshaw* (DD-499) and USS *Anthony* (DD-515). Their orders were to proceed to Cape Torokina, Empress Augusta Bay, Bougainville Island, Solomon Islands. The following day, New Year's Eve, LST *390*, USS *Saufley* (DD-465) and USS *Menominee* (AT-73) joined the convoy.

On New Year's Day 1944 *Serpens* found herself steaming closer and closer to the enemy. At 0649 they had anchored at Cape Torokina in Anchorage #1 and were discharging cargo into amphibious assault craft built to land tanks onto beaches, called Landing Craft Tanks (LCTs). At 1725 they raised anchor and were underway to Guadalcanal under the same task group when, at 2031, general quarters was sounded as there was a Japanese air attack from where they just departed, Cape Torokina. At 2137 general quarters was again sounded as there was a second Japanese air attack at the same place. The following day, 2 January, at 0456 general quarters was again sounded because of a Japanese air attack on Treasury Island which was broad to port quarter some 15 miles away.

At 0400 on 3 January 1944 *Serpens*, along with escorts USS *Anthony* (DD-515) and USS *Hudson* (DD-475), departed the convoy and proceeded to Russell Islands. At 0720 the two escorts departed company and headed for Guadalcanal, leaving *Serpens* to fend for herself. At 0832 *Serpens* was moored to the #1 buoy in Tillotson Cove, Russell Islands. The following day they repositioned against the dock in Renard Sound and began taking on cargo. With cargo loaded by the morning of 8 January, *Serpens* got underway at 1207 for Guadalcanal, escorted by *YMS-265*. At 1832 they were anchored in Berth #4, Kukum Anchorage. At 0629 the following day they got underway for Doma Cove, Guadalcanal, anchoring there at 0800, and began loading cargo for the next four days.

At 0611 on 13 January *Serpens* unmoored and got underway for a return visit to Cape Torokina, Bougainville Island. She pulled into line with a large convoy that included USS *Adhara* (AK-71), USS *Patapsco* (AOG-1), and LSTs *39, 116, 117, 220, 397, 449* and *485*. The convoy, assigned as Task Group 31.6, was heavily escorted by USS *Waller* (DD-466), USS *Guest* (DD-472), USS *Bennett* (DD-473), USS *Philip* (DD-498), USS *Conway* (DD-507), USS *Eaton* (DD-510), USS *Sigourney* (DD-643) and USS *Sioux* (AT-75). Surrounded by naval destroyers for protection, the crew of *Serpens* may have felt safer from enemy attack, but none could withstand the forces of nature. On 14 January, while underway, they encountered rain and gale force winds. On 15 January they anchored in Berth #2 at Cape Torokina and by 0822 began discharging cargo into the same LCTs as before. During unloading the weather turned worse. At 1555 *Serpens* was ordered by the Commander of the Torokina Naval Base to discontinue operations due to the severity of the weather. Ten fenders, several lines and two steel mooring wires were destroyed before operations ceased. At 1859 the Torokina radio advised *Serpens* that Condition Red had been put into effect – *Serpens* went to general quarters fearing that Japanese aircraft would appear but none did in that weather and they secured from general quarters at 1921.

Between the bad weather which included gale force winds and going to general quarters because of possible enemy air attacks, unloading operations slowed. On 17 and 20 January enemy aircraft did indeed bomb Bougainville Island. At 0425 on 23 January Japanese aircraft bombed the beachhead and dropped one stick of bombs about 3/4ths of a mile from *Serpens* to seaward.

On 24 January 1944, possibly inspired by the closeness of war, SC1c Charles Bernard "Woody" Wood, USCGR, sat down and drew this:

Bill Hitt, LM, USCGR '42-'46, wrote in the Quarterdeck Log (publication of the Coast Guard Combat Veterans Association), Volume 28, Number 2 (Summer 2013), page 13: "I knew that ship [*Serpens* (AK-97)] well and had several friends in the crew, including one close friend, William H. Harlow. My ship, USS *Celtic* (IX-137), crossed paths with *Serpens* on several occasions and we'd have a get-together. *Serpens* made regular runs from Australia to New Hebrides (our base) to the Solomons. She made so many runs to Bougainville, we dubbed her the Bougainville Express."

On 25 January Japanese aircraft again bombed the beachhead; at 0447 an enemy plane was shot down and crashed into the sea about a mile from *Serpens*. Secured from general quarters and unloaded, *Serpens* began loading empty oil drums and at 0815 they got underway for Guadalcanal in a convoy comprised of LSTs *39, 166, 172*, and *472* along with the seaplane tender USS *Chandeleur* (AV-10), USS *Adhara* (AK-71) and USS *Patapsco* (DD-AOG-1) and again heavily escorted by USS *Farenhalt* (DD-332), USS *Fullam* (DD-474), USS *Guest* (DD-472), USS *Bennett* (DD-473), USS *Hudson* (DD-475), USS *Braine* (DD-630), and USS *Sioux* (AT-75). At 1230 on 26 January USS *Chandeleur* and USS *Patapsco*, escorted by three of the destroyers, departed the convoy. At 1500 all the LSTs and one destroyer departed the convoy and headed to Munda. That left *Adhara* and *Serpens*, escorted by *Guest* and *Sioux*, who all proceeded through Blanche Channel and onward back to Guadalcanal.

At 1053 on 27 January *Serpens* was anchored off Lunga Point, Guadalcanal, and at 1455 *Serpens* and USS *Adhara* (AK-71), escorted by *YMS-243*, proceeded to Gavutu Harbor where they re-anchored at 1722 for the next two days. At

1040 on 29 January *Serpens* pulled up anchor and got underway astern of sister ship USS *Sterope* (AK-96), with the ocean-going minesweeper USS *Adroit* (AM-82) as escort, and proceeded to Tenaru Beach, Guadalcanal, where she anchored at 1328 for three hours. At 1640 *Serpens* got underway again in convoy with USS *Antares* (AK-258), USS *Sterope*, and merchant ships SS *John Bartram* and SS *Musa*, escorted by USS *Starling* (AM-64), USS *Adroit* (AM-82), USS *Advent* (AM-83), and USS *Velocity* (AM-128), heading for Espiritu Santo, New Hebrides Islands. Unbeknownst to all, exactly one year later *Serpens* and most of her crew would disappear in a violent explosion back at Lunga Point, Guadalcanal.

Crewmembers aboard U.S.S. Serpens (AK-97) sometime in 1943. Last names, from l to r: Story, Grainey, Creegon and Woods. None of the four were aboard at the time of the explosion. Photo No. 7/12; photographer unknown. Photo provided courtesy of CAPT James D. Ellison, USCG (Ret.), who served aboard Serpens as a LTJG.

On 1 February at 0830 the convoy entered Nawa Channel and at 1030 *Serpens* was anchored at Berth #17, Espiritu

Santo. The following day they repositioned to Pier #5 and began discharging general cargo. On 3 February they unmoored from the pier and anchored out in Segond Channel and on 4 February repositioned to Anchorage #10-1/2 and began taking on cargo. At 0802 on 6 February the weighed anchors and stood out of Segond Channel under orders to "proceed from Espiritu Santo to Noumea, unescorted." By 1130 on 9 February they were again anchored in Fisherman's Bay, Noumea, New Caledonia, and discharging cargo. The following day one of the first officers to rotate off the ship departed at 0907. The *Serpens* logbook reads: "Engineering Officer, W. J. Elliott, Lieutenant, USCGR, departed this vessel to USS *Arthur Middleton* as Engineering Officer of said vessel. Assistant Engineering Officer, Ensign W. C. Kotkas, USCG, this date, assigned as Engineering Officer of the USS *Serpens*."

On 11 February *Serpens* raised her anchors and stood out from Fisherman's Bay under the following orders: "Proceed from Noumea to Auckland via Cape Brett and report to NOB at Auckland for drydocking and availability. After drydocking load dry provisions for fleet issue, requisitioning the stock from Joint Purchasing Board, Wellington. On completion return to Noumea." At 1715 on 16 February the tugboat *William C. Daldy* came along the port side of *Serpens* and assisted *Serpens* to moor starboard side to Queen's Inner Wharf, Auckland, New Zealand. On 18 February, having unloaded cargo, *Serpens* stood out from Queen's Inner Wharf and proceeded to Calliope Dry Dock, assisted by tugs *William C. Daldy* and *Te-Awhina*. By 1409 they were moored both starboard and port inside the drydock and at 1450 the drydock crew began draining out the water. Over the next two days the Engineering Department, led by Ensign Kotkas, overhauled and inspected all sea valves;

cleaned both boilers; inspected and measured clearances, stern tube and rudder; overhauled and adjusted all necessary main engine bearings and overhauled all auxiliary machinery as found necessary.

The Calliope Drydock is a historical stone drydock on the grounds of the Devonport Naval Base, in Devonport, Auckland, New Zealand. It was built in 1888 to service ships of the British Royal Navy, and is still in use today. Pictured is a circa 1908 postcard showcasing the interior of the Calliope Drydock. Photo courtesy www.madoncollections.com.

At 0655 on 20 February they began refilling the drydock with seawater and at 0915 *Serpens* was again afloat. At 1050 she backed out of the drydock, assisted by *William C. Daldy* and *Te-Awhina*, and by 1214 was moored starboard side to the merchant ship SS *Peter White* at King's Wharf. The following day she freed herself from alongside SS *Peter White* and proceeded to Prince's Wharf with the assistance of the same two tugs. On 23 February she shifted over to the starboard side of USS *Cygnus* (F-23) to allow a large transport to moor in her position and then shifted back the following day upon departure of the transport. On 25

February they commenced taking on a cargo of dry provisions for fleet issue.

At 30 minutes past midnight on the morning of 5 March 1944 all loading has been completed. At 0645 *Serpens* unmoored from the Prince's Inner East Wharf and with the assistance of the *William C. Daldy* stood out from the pier and got underway, unescorted, for Noumea. At 1226 on 9 March she anchored in Berth #39, Dumbea Bay, New Caledonia and at 1238 she pulled up anchors and proceeded to Dock #11, Ducos Point, Noumea, New Caledonia, mooring at 1316. The following day they commenced loading dry provisions on board for fleet issue and also craned aboard two "Landing Craft, Vehicles"; or LCVs, received from Boat Repair Unit, Navy #131. These were small wood-hulled vehicle carriers used for initial and subsequent landing waves such as those seen on D-Day along the beaches at Normandy. The LCVs were also used as personnel and cargo carriers. At 0700 on 12 March all loading ceased and preparations were made to get underway. At 0901 *Serpens* unmoored and got underway in a small convoy with merchant ship SS *San Bruno*, escorted by *SC-504*. On 14 March *SC-504* developed engine trouble and the convoy stopped engines in Hillards Channel, Efate Island, in the New Hebrides Islands and waited while *YMS-136* joined the convoy to assist in repairing the engine. The following day they arrived at Segond Channel, Espiritu Santo, New Hebrides Islands, where *Serpens* moored to Buoy #20 at 0942. On 16 March they began unloading provisions and at 1115 they brought on board two LCM-3's from Boat Repair Unit, Navy #140. The "Landing Craft, Mechanized" (LCM) was a landing craft primarily designed for carrying vehicles. They were used to land troops or tanks during Allied amphibious assaults. The LCM-3 variant weighed 2 tons empty and was designed to carry 120,000 lb. (60 tons) of cargo. Loaded up by 18 March, *Serpens* got underway at 1556 in convoy with SS *San Bruno* and escort *PC-1325*, headed back to Havannah Harbor, Efate Island, New Hebrides Islands. They arrived there at 0745 the following day, mooring to Buoy #10. At 1231 they unmoored and got underway for Fila Harbor, Efate Island, anchoring in the harbor at 1552 and by 1730 that afternoon they started unloading operations.

At 0500 on 20 March *Serpens* ceased their unloading operations and at 1033 weighed anchors and got underway back to Havannah Harbor, Efate Island, escorted by *SC-984*. By 1345 they were again moored to Buoy #10 and at 1945 were discharging provisions. At 1445 the following day they had to cease unloading operations and secure all hatches for the rain and high winds heading their way. On 23 March they repositioned to Buoy #14 and continued unloading. On 28 March they repositioned again, this time to Berth #8, mooring port side to USS *Celtic* (IX-137). Celtic was built in 1921 and named *Kerry Patch* by Bethlehem Shipbuilding Corp., Quincy, MA.; acquired by the Navy on 17 January 1944 while it sat at Noumea, New Caledonia. She was commissioned the same day, LT J. S. Loring, USCG, in command. *Celtic* sailed 15 February 1944 for duty as a station tanker, sailing into Noumea, Efate and Espiritu Santo, New Hebrides; Port Purvis, Gavutu, and Empress Augusta Bay in the Solomons. While moored against *Celtic*, *Serpens* took aboard fuel oil from her while sending over diesel oil to *Celtic*. Afterwards, *Serpens* repositioned herself to Berth #12 where she moored at 1525.

At 1623 on 29 March it was "anchors aweigh" again for *Serpens* as she proceeded to Espiritu Santo. At 1925 the steering gear began giving trouble and in the course of the next few hours it went out of operation several times, making it necessary to transfer control of steerage to the after steering station. The following day, at 1333, *Serpens* anchored back in Segond Channel, Espiritu Santo. On the last day of March 1944 *Serpens* again pulled up anchors at 1426 and got underway in convoy with two merchant ships, SS *Thomas Condon* and SS *George Reid* and their escorts, USS *Baron* (DD-166) and USS *Hogan* (DES-6). Their destination was back to Guadalcanal.

The officers of the USS Serpens, date unknown. LCDR Magnus J. Johnson, USCGR, the first commanding officer, is in the back row, third from the right. Photo provided courtesy of CAPT James D. Ellison, USCG (Ret.), who served aboard Serpens as a LTJG.

On 1 April the convoy was still underway toward Guadalcanal when they ran into a storm. The port life net on the *Serpens* was ripped off by the sea and wind conditions. While the seas were being reported as Force Five (Moderate waves taking a more pronounced long form; many white horses are formed; chance of some spray), the winds were measured at Force Seven (near gale, 28-33 knots or 32-38 mph). At 0818 on 3 April the convoy dispersed off Koli Point, Guadalcanal, at which time *Serpens* and escort *Baron* proceeded to Purvis Bay, Florida Island. In the afternoon they had commenced unloading provisions of fleet issue. On 8 April they ceased unloading operations, having unloaded 1,035 tons, weighed anchor and proceeded to Government Dock, Tulagi, where they also unloaded cargo. Early on 11 April, having discharged 1,554 tons of cargo at Government Dock and with 30% of stores remaining, *Serpens* proceeded back to Purvis Bay, Florida Island, where they once again began discharging fleet provisions to forces afloat. By 15 April they had unloaded another 2,590 tons of provisions and had 25% of their cargo still remaining for distribution.

New orders arrived on 16 April for *Serpens*: "with *Serpens* in task unit 35.2.3 in company with USS *Adhara* [AK-71], USS *Kopara* [AK-62], USS *Racoon* [IX-127, originally SS *J. C. W. Becham*], and SS *Platano*, with escorts USS *Daring* (AM-87), USS *PC-1127* and USS *YMS-238*, to leave Guadalcanal 1800, 16 April 1944, for Espiritu Santo; convoy commander to be Captain Blankenship, USN." *Serpens* proceeded to Guadalcanal and *PC-1127* joined *Serpens* at 1040. At 1043 CAPT Blankenship with his staff of signalmen and radiomen reported aboard. At 1700 the convoy sortied off Koli Point in column formation with escorts screening and all set course for Espiritu Santo. Under orders from CAPT Blankenship the afternoon of 18 April was spent undergoing emergency turn drills and at 1032 on 19 April the convoy stood into Bruat Channel. At 1100 the convoy then stood into

Segond Channel where the convoy dispersed and each ship proceeded to their assigned berth. At 1245 CAPT Blankenship departed *Serpens* with his staff. *Serpens* was there at Espiritu Santo to unload provisions. The Naval Supply Depot (NavSupDep) at Espiritu Santo was under orders to load 750,000 packages of cigarettes and 200,000 candy bars onto *Serpens* to round out their next load to Noumea. NavSupDep failed to get this order carried out due to the fact that *Serpens* was there to unload cargo and could not load and unload cargo at the same time. With weather threatening and intermittent showers occurring, this perishable type of cargo could not be delivered via the open float lighters.

Murphy's Law is an adage that is typically stated as: "Anything that can go wrong will go wrong". Its roots can be traced back to Alfred Holt at an 1877 meeting of an engineering society in which he said "It is found that anything that can go wrong at sea generally does go wrong sooner or later." Notwithstanding the 19 April incident with the cigarettes and candy bars, Murphy raised his ugly head again four days later. On the morning of 23 April 1944, *Serpens* unmoored from their buoy in Segond Channel and stood in to Pier #5 at Espiritu Santo where the U.S. Army working party began unloading the remaining cargo. It was later learned that this cargo was placed on another ship and returned to Tulagi, where the cargo was while aboard *Serpens*. The reason *Serpens* could not unload it at Tulagi was because the provisions were intended for direct fleet issue (unloaded directly to other ships) and could not be considered as available for issue to land-based stores. Now they were considered as such and brought back. Two days later Murphy struck again.

On the morning of 25 April, while still unloading at Pier #5, a U.S. Army Tech Sergeant was seriously injured inside *Serpens'* No. 2 hold when the hatch boards and beam were dislodged, resulting in a broken back to the soldier. This led to more stringent safety precautions. From then on, when holds were to be unloaded, all beams and hatch boards were to be removed prior to working the hold and any beams that could not be removed had to be welded in place. Also, a ship's Safety Committee was ordered to be presided over by the Medical Officer to study all possible ways in which a safer handling of cargo and prevention of injury to personnel could be put into effect. This was accomplished and the policy was put into effect.

Unidentified crewmen from USS Serpens (AK-97). Photo provided courtesy of CAPT James D. Ellison, USCG (Ret.), who served aboard Serpens as a LTJG.

This same day, *Serpens* received a request for a loading plan from the Commander, Service Squadron, South Pacific (ComServRonSoPac) as to how *Serpens* was going to load

4,000 tons of dry provisions into four holds while at their next port of call – Noumea. Since the ship's crew had no idea as to details of the dry provisions, the plan was not prepared.

On the morning of 27 April *Serpens* ceased unloading operations, stood out from Pier #5 and proceeded out Segond Channel with orders to proceed to Tulagi unescorted. On the same day the Coast Guard-manned USS *Etamin* (AK-93) was attacked by Japanese planes while anchored in Altape Roads, New Guinea. The resulting fire was brought under control and the vessel was towed to Finschhaven. Three seriously wounded Coast Guard personnel were flown to Port Morresby. The vessel was subsequently reconditioned and saw further service.

While at sea on 28 April the entire ship was sprayed with freon-aerosol insecticide as prescribed by the Malarial Control Board under direction of the ship's Medical Officer. At 1300 on 29 April *Serpens* was moored port side to Dock #2, Grand Quay, Noumea, New Caledonia, and commenced loading cargo for provisioning the fleet.

Having loaded 3,559 tons of stores and dry provisions by 6 May, *Serpens* got underway at 0544 for Guadalcanal in convoy with merchant ships SS *James H. Breasted* and SS *William Ford Nichols*, escorted by *SC-1325*, *SC-1326* and *SC-1328*. Called Task Unit 35.1.3, LCDR M. J. Johnson came aboard *Serpens* as the Task Unit Commander. On 10 May they arrived off Lunga Point, Guadalcanal, at 1039 and received orders to proceed to Tulagi Harbor, where they dropped anchor in Berth #7 at 1237. In Lunga Bay at the same time was a sister ship, USS *Centaurus* (AKA-17). Her War Diary reported: "The convoy arrived at Lunga Point on the 10th of May and the *Centaurus* immediately began loading ammunition and gasoline into all holds. At that time submarine warnings were so frequent that the ship was obliged to shift her anchorage and be ready to slip her anchor cable sometimes twice a day. During this loading period, the ship shifted berths from Lunga Point, Doma Cove, Koli Point and Bunina Point."

Here in Tulagi Harbor, *Serpens'* mission was to provision other ships with the stores they had loaded aboard in Noumea – except there were no ships in the area that needed provisioning. Three days later, having failed to unload any provisions, they got underway at 0650 for the Russell Islands, escorted by *Q-401*. Their new mission was to take the 3,559 tons of stores and provisions and issue them to the LSTs there, then return to Tulagi Harbor. At 1432 on 13 May they anchored in Sunlight Channel, Russell Islands. Over the next five days they unloaded dry provisions into the small LSTs, amounting to only 61 tons of the 3,559 tons aboard. Later in the day on 18 May they departed Russell Islands with escort *ML-402* and returned to Tulagi Harbor. This time they moored port side to Government Dock at 1640 and began discharging their provisions to the Naval Advanced Base at Tulagi rather than to any ships requiring provisioning.

By 20 May 1944 *Serpens* had unloaded 1,025 tons of the remaining 3,498 tons of stored provisions when they were ordered to cease unloading and get underway for Hathorn Sound, New Georgia Islands, to provision ships afloat there. On 21 May they were anchored in Hathorn Sound. On 23 May the *Serpens'* logbook states: "Completed provisioning forces afloat in this area. No dry provisions were needed and the only discharge made was 59 tons of ship's store stock. The trip here was therefore unnecessary and the service rendered was negligible. At 1334 we got underway for Tulagi

Harbor with escort SC-701." They arrived at 1159 on 24 May and anchored in Berth #9.

Unidentified crewmen from USS Serpens (AK-97). Photo provided courtesy of CAPT James D. Ellison, USCG (Ret.), who served aboard Serpens as a LTJG.

One could almost feel the morale of the crew dropping as they were sent from one harbor to another to provision ships that were either not there or didn't need provisioning. Or finding out that cargo unloaded in one port was reloaded onto another ship and sent back to a port where they had just come from and could have easily unloaded it themselves. Or having a U.S. Army soldier break his back aboard their ship. Acronyms first appearing in World War II were becoming the colloquial language of choice – FUBAR, SNAFU... And it continued.

On 25 May *Serpens* got underway at 0550 for Tetere, Guadalcanal, anchoring there in Berth #79 at 1258 where they began provisioning forces afloat. On 26 May Motor

Machinist's Mate Second Class (MoMM2c) Leslie (n) Helsem and MoMM2c Hugo (n) Riccardi reported on board *Serpens*. Previously, on 6 May, MoMM2c Riccardi had written to his wife about getting his new rate, Motor Machinist's Mate: "There were about 15 of the boys in our department that went up for a rate when I did and only four of us made it. It's quite a disappointment for the ones that didn't get it. When I think of it, it has been a long time since the time I was disappointed for not getting the same rate, so I figured I got it the hard way and earned it. So I feel better about it now. Can't show it here, we always wear dungarees and blue shirt. The crow I am supposed to wear has the letters M.O., one on each side of the propeller. The one without the M.O. means he's a Machinist's Mate. M.O. means Motor Machinist's Mate. Machinist Mates cover steam engine and machine shop work."

MoMM2c Riccardi was a prolific writer, sending hundreds of letters home to his wife until his death on 29 January 1945. He mailed 88 letters home to his wife Silvia just while stationed aboard *Serpens*. His letters reflect life aboard *Serpens*, his crewmates, the places he visited, and general life at sea.

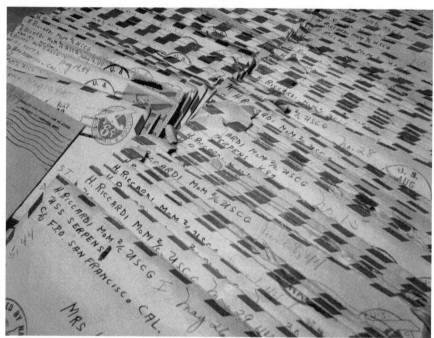

A portion of the more than 200 letters written by MoMM2c and later MoMM1c Hugo (n) Riccardi, USCGR, to his wife Sylvia. They had been married a month before Hugo was shipped out to fight the war; he never returned. Although Sylvia eventually remarried, she kept all of Hugo's letters – which became available after her death – and are now the property of the co-author Douglas E. Campbell.

Riccardi's first letter from *Serpens* was dated the day he reported for duty, 26 May 1944:

"Hello Beautiful, Well here I am aboard ship and so far I am very well satisfied. It took me three days to catch up to it, but I finally caught it. I boarded her today. One of the boys took me through the ship and showed me around her and introduced me to most of the boys, they sure are a very nice group. I met one fellow that was with me at Fairport, so we talked old times. I met Mister Alygood the Lt. that was in charge of our group in California. This ship is considered as one of the best ships around the islands for conditions and having one of the best crews aboard her, so I can be proud of being aboard her. And I sure am going to try and do my share as a member. The chow is very good, we have beer every night and a picture show when ever possible. Pretty good, hey? I guess you were sort of surprised to know of my sudden change, well so was I honey. Well my love, don't worry about me. I am alright and very glad to get back with my own outfit, all Coast Guards, and a swell bunch too. Tell my folks and everyone else that I will write as soon as I get a chance. I'll be dreaming of you always, as ever, so I better hit the sack now and get some rest for my first day of work tomorrow. I'll write to you as soon as possible honey and you keep writing as planned. So good night my sweet, sweet dreams. Your old salt and hubby, Hugo."

MoMM2c Hugo Riccardi from a photo taken while aboard USS Serpens. The negative was mailed home to his wife in Cleveland, OH, to have printed. Photo courtesy Douglas Campbell.

In a later letter Riccardi explains to his wife why it took him three days to catch up to *Serpens*: "So you don't understand why I was chasing the *Serpens* around? Well I just couldn't make connections to get aboard her. They tell me to go to a certain island by inter-island boat, when I get there she has already pulled out. Then I find out she is where I was at first, so I go back. When I get there, she pulled out again so I went there again and finally got on after sleeping in a signal tower all night. I would have been better off if I had stayed and waited for it to come where I was, but that's over and a little experience don't hurt anyone."

The next day, 27 May, they completed all needed provisioning, having discharged 179 tons of provisions and ship's store stock. At 0721 on 28 May they got underway back to Tulagi Harbor and anchored there in Berth #6 at 0959. As there were no ships in the vicinity that needed provisioning, they repositioned from Berth #6 to port side Pier #6 and again began discharging provisions to Naval Advanced Base, Tulagi. The date, 28 May 1944, was the one-year Anniversary of the ship's commissioning and MoMM2c Riccardi writes his wife on 29 May:

"I boarded her just in time, for yesterday was celebrated as one year for this ship being in commission. So we had a swell turkey dinner with all the trimmings including pie and ice cream and beer. And a show in the evening of which I will tell you about in my next letter. I'll say it again, that this is a very fine ship bunch of fellows and well-mannered, and always willing to do something for a mate. We have a recreation room, with piano and a mandolin of which needs strings. Also a tailor shop, barber shop, canteen, and believe it or not, a laundry, for $2.00 a month, swell isn't it? I will write a longer letter as soon as I hear from you. Your hooligan and hubby Hugo."

On 30 May 1944 two friends of Riccardi reported on board: MoMM2c Vernard C. Jacobs and MoMM2c Hubert Taylor. Riccardi writes his wife: "Those two boys I told you about came aboard today so I have a couple of more old friends with me. I like my job pretty well and I hope I can stay on top side." He also remembered to tell his wife about the movies he watched on board: "I have seen the picture of Bette Davis in 'All This and Heaven Too.' It was a very long picture and I think a very good picture. Last night I seen Mickey Rooney in 'Girl Crazy.' It was funny. I never realized he could dance so good, and play the piano so well. He is OK. I wonder how he likes the Army life now?"

By 30 May they had 1,005 tons of provisions and ship's store stock of the 3,559 tons loaded on 6 May still in their holds. Discouraged at what he was seeing, LCDR Magnus J. Johnson submitted comments into the ship's logbook based on three months experience of seeing his Fleet Provision Ship at work:

> The service that a ship of this size and type can render as a Fleet Provision Ship is very valuable. Discharge of provisions from this ship direct to forces afloat minimizes handling of cases and thereby minimizes loss due to breakage. As compared to the usual method of shipping dry provisions to an advanced base where they are stowed in warehouses and then re-issued to forces afloat, there is a great saving in manpower and time. A ship of this size can carry as great a variety of food stuffs as is required or as is carried in any of the advanced bases where provisions would have to be drawn and our handling meets with the approval of the majority of Supply Officers on vessels being provisioned as evidenced by many verbal commendations received. The only disadvantage of this trip has been the lack of

coordination of our movements with those of other ships of the fleet thereby necessitating discharge of the greater part of our cargo to Naval Advanced Base, Tulagi."

With just over 1,000 tons of dry provisions and ship's stores still needing to be unloaded, *Serpens* remained at Tulagi doing just that. Until June 6 *Serpens* continued unloading, first from Pier No. 6, then from the Government Dock. At 0643 on 6 June *Serpens* moved from Government Dock to Anchorage No. 7 in Tulagi Harbor and then at 0916 got underway for Lunga Point, Guadalcanal. There they anchored in Berth No. 36 off Tenaru Beach, discharging the remaining cargo to forces afloat for the next three days. At 1538 on 9 June they got underway from Lunga Point in a convoy with USS *Dephinus* (AF-24), USAT *How Eight* and the merchant ship SS *Horace Greeley*, along with escorts *PC-589* and *PC-606*. Just past Lengo Channel the ships dispersed and *Serpens* steamed independently to Auckland, New Zealand, to reprovision. After five days at sea, MoMM2c Riccardi writes his wife:

"I haven't got my sea legs yet and I'm having difficulty writing this – as yet I have not heaved but I feel like I did. I am hoping I get used to it but it don't look so good. It looks like your old man isn't such a salt at that. Gee but I wish I had that sea bag I sent home. Right now I could use the sweater and will be needing the pea coat. I'll bet it sounds funny for you to read that, first I was telling you warm it was, now I'm telling you of it being cold. Well, I can't tell you where I am going but it sure will be different weather. I will tell you after we are out of there."

A day out from arriving at Auckland, Riccardi writes some more about shipboard life:

"It's a good thing I didn't send my blankets home because I have been using both of them for a while. Tell you more about it later. I like it much better on board ship than I did at Tulagi. Yes, it's much cleaner, no bugs or spiders, lizards and mosquitos to worry about, better chow, good crew, and not so monotonous. I feel much better now than I did at first, I am hoping I get over that sea sickness. It envies me to watch these salty fellows work and feel good the way they do. Well, all I can do is try."

Arriving on 17 June, she tied up port side to Prince's Wharf at 1517 and began loading dry stores aboard until 24 June. The next day after arriving at Auckland Riccardi writes his wife: "Yesterday [17 June] was Sunday, I went ashore to church and prayed for us, came back and had chicken for chow, then took a nap, got up and watched the boys being towed on their surf board, then had chow again, then seen the movies, then hit the sack. Now I am at a place where I can get the mail daily." On 21 June he writes: "Well honey I am feeling fine and getting to feel pretty well acquainted with the ship and its crew."

On 24 June, at 0709, *Serpens* got underway to steam back to Noumea. The next day it seems MoMM2c Riccardi may have found his sea legs. He writes to his wife: "Well honey I am getting so I can take pretty good now and that's a relief, so I am able to do my work. Almost every Sunday we have turkey for dinner, pretty good hey? As yet I can't tell you where I have been but when I can I will tell you everything I did and other things to make a more interesting letter."

At 1205 on 28 June they moored port side to Grand Quay Dock No. 2 at Noumea and loaded aboard additional dry provisions, ship's store stock and clothing. It was, overall, an uneventful month. On 28 June, Riccardi tells his wife what he does aboard *Serpens*: "I guess I can tell you what I am doing. For awhile I have been maintaining deck winches that are used to lift cargo in and out of the ship's holds. Now I am working down in the engineroom, as auxiliary oiler, oiling the auxiliary steam engines, steering engine and the shaft. And what a shaft. I am hoping to get on as mechanic of the small boats soon. I don't know where you got the impression of us having cramped quarters, because we have plenty of room. About Lt. Alygood, yes, he is the same Lt. that was in charge of us in California, but I am not under him, we have engineering officers in charge of our line of work. The last time I weighed myself I weighed 162 pounds. I don't think it shows on me, not even my tummy, in fact, I haven't any to speak of."

MoMM2c Riccardi's letter to his wife dated 30 June 1944 includes the mentioning of the ship's orchestra:

> "I know you would like to have some idea when [I'm coming home], but that's impossible to say. I do know some of the boys are going home after a year out here. I am going to see if I can go to Diesel Advance School, but I think I better wait a little while first and get some time on this ship. Before I forget, I want to tell you that we are trying to get some sort of an orchestra together. We have the musicians but not all the instruments. We need a guitar and violin, we have an accordian(sic), mandolin, coronet and piano. The boys are always asking me to play the mandolin, they like it very much. I wish I had my banjo here. My fingers are finally getting limber and tough after the long time that I haven't played. Yes, honey, we get ashore once in awhile but as yet I can't tell you anything about it, one place in particular where there was civilization, the others are just islands, not much to talk about. So,

you're getting to drink a little beer? I think it is much better than the beer we get, I can hardly drink it and like it, it tastes so green. I did forget to tell you of the show or party, didn't I? Well, we had singers, musicians, the Captain spoke to us, and they told some pretty raw jokes. I'll give you an example of one. A woman visitor was watching a baker making dough for bread. He didn't have a shirt on and was perspiring which was running down his belly. He would knead it for awhile then slap it with his belly and knead it again. He did that for awhile then the lady remarked that she never saw bread made that way and that it was terrible. Then the sailor said, Lady, that's nothing, you ought to see me make doughnuts. Get it? Dirty, huh!?"

At 0405 on 1 July 1944 loading was complete and at 0607 *Serpens* got underway to Havannah Harbor, Efate Island. At 1545 on the following day they were standing into Hilliard Channel and at 1638 they were moored to Buoy #15. At 1820 they were discharging dry provisions and general cargo ashore. Having completed unloading on 3 July, they loaded mail and 45 tons of canned butter for Espiritu Santo. On 4 July MoMM2c Riccardi writes his wife: "I weighed myself today, 165 lbs., pretty good, huh? Yes, today marks 18 months of service. It's hard to believe. But most important is tomorrow being our 19-month Anniversary. Today was declared a holiday so I'll have some time, I hope, for a little recreation. Maybe go to the beach and play ball, try some fishing. I'll let you know in my next letter. Maybe I'll get some sleep instead."

In his next letter he writes: "I promised to tell you what I was going to do on the Fourth. Two of the other boys and I got permission to use the skiff, so we lowered it over the side with the winch, we rowed in deep water, with our [fishing] lines in but nothing happened, so we went in close to shore over the coral reefs. One of the boys got a fish about a foot long. Never did see anything like it. It was brown with a sort of orange or red stripe around its mouth along its gills and side. Beautiful color. That's all we caught so we came back to the ship, had chow, took a shower and then a nap. If you want to see beauty, look down in the clear green water at the coral reefs. It looks just like jungle, little green bushes, trees without leaves, and all sorts of growth in different bright and dull colors, and all coral, just as hard as some of those pieces I sent you with the shells."

The holiday routine was cut short. Later, still on 4 July, they got underway at 1529 and at 0728 the following day they arrived, anchoring in Berth #32-1/2 in Segond Channel, Espiritu Santo, New Hebrides Islands. At 1630 a U.S. Army boat came alongside and took the mail. Receiving mail and running into old buddies was certainly a morale booster for these young men sent off to war. MoMM2c Riccardi was especially pleased to have run into several of his buddies now stationed on another ship also anchored in Segond Channel, as he writes to his wife:

"Remember Morgan? Well, I found out his ship was anchored near ours, so I got special liberty to go over there and visit. The whole crew on there left the States with me, and to see them after 7 months was really swell. I shook hands with about 15 of them before I seen Morgan. I went down to his quarters and when he seen me he let out a yell and put his arms around me. It was great seeing him. What surprised me was that he had a full growth of a beard on him, he looked like Robinson Crusoe, red beard. We sat and talked old times for awhile and he asked about you and said to say hello to you my sweet. Then he showed me around his ship (I like ours much better) and I kept seeing more fellows I knew. So I finally got him to come back with me to our ship. I showed him your pictures that you sent me. He thought they were very nice (of course). I played the mandolin for him, we had chow together, and he stayed for the movies (Buffalo Bill) of which he seen on his ship only two days before. I also showed him around our ship. He wished he could stay with me. Remember when I left the station with a Chief and Morgan? Well, the Chief is on the same ship too. He sure was glad to see me too. It certainly was a good day for me for a change, seeing all those boys and Morgan."

On 6 July the Army took the canned butter and on 7 July, discharging complete, *Serpens* departed at 1701, heading first for Guadalcanal, to be followed by Tulagi or Purvis Bay as needed. At 1710 on 8 July *Serpens* exchanged calls with USS *Spangler* (DE-696) upon passing. At 0700 on 9 July *PC-1228* joined up with *Serpens* as escort and stayed with them all the way to Guadalcanal. At 0600 the following day *PC-1228* departed company and at 0705 *Serpens* dropped anchor in Berth #23 off Tenaru Beach, Lunga Point. Some four hours later, at 1135, *Serpens* got underway for Purvis Bay, Florida Islands, British Solomon Islands. They anchored there at 1418 the same day, Berth #13. On 11 July they began discharging stores to forces afloat which included SS *Peter Burnett*, SS *Edgar Allen Poe* and the Purvis barge. The discharging of dry stores, ship's store stock and clothing to forces afloat continued through 22 July at which time they had a Change of Command ceremony.

On 22 July 1944 LCDR Peery L. Stinson, USCG, relieved LCDR Magnus J. Johnson, USCGR, as commanding officer of *Serpens*. MoMM2c Riccardi writes to his wife about the change in command: "Well, my beautiful wife, I don't ever have much to say as far as my self is concerned, because everything is the same old thing every day. Just the daily routine of which is natural in time to get monotonous, so I need your encouraging letters honey. Our skipper was sent back to the States for transfer, so we have a new one. Our old skipper was tops and will never be forgotten. As a gift from the crew we gave him a large hand-sketched picture of the ship with all our signatures on it. And in turn he gave us a swell farewell speech. Our new skipper seems to be a pretty good fellow, at least that's our opinion, and I hope it stays that way, because if they want they can make life pretty hard. Well, I don't care anyhow because I've had some pretty tough ones since I've been in and I get along alright."

From 23 to 30 July *Serpens* continued discharging their cargo while at the same time a 4-SF-1 radar was installed. The 4-SF-1 radar was being installed on small vessels and cargo ships throughout the fleet. It was used to detect surface vessels and aid in navigation. If the antenna height was 100' ASL (above sea level) it had an estimated reliable range of 12 miles on large ships. It is believed that the antenna height for *Serpens* was lower than that. The logbook states: "Installation made by Landing Craft Repair Unit 1, *Carter City*. The mast installed extended 30 feet above the hurricane deck, instead of 47 feet as required." It came packed in 19 units for shipment, weighing a total of 3,300 lbs. The largest of the 19 units was 55" x 42" x 64" and weighed 510 lbs. Packing material set aside, the actual components weighed a total of approximately 2,770 lbs. The antenna assembly weighed 280 lbs. and measured 58-1/2" x 48-3/4" x 26-1/2". To be efficient It needed to be installed as high as possible on the ship. It was not.

For the young *Serpens* crew, no matter how hard they worked or what beautiful South Pacific island they were anchored at, a wave of homesickness was being felt. On 28

July 1944, while once again anchored in Purvis Bay on the southern central coast of Florida Island in the Solomon Islands, S1c Murray Caldwell Flowers, USCGR, wrote to his aunt:

"Dear Aunt Bessie & family: I have been intending to write you for some time but haven't gotten around to writing. I guess you have your hands full with Sammy and Cloud while they are sick. Sure hope they are both well and able to be out now. It looks like mother has had a bad time of it, first with her leg and now her hand. I wish she would be careful. I hope it's nothing to serious wrong with her. If it is I want you to tell me. I have been worried about her. She won't write me if there is any thing wrong. I know you will tell me. Daddy seems to be doing fine. I think he must enjoy the dog. How is Elsie and Carolyn? The last time I heard from mother she was doing fine. I don't get mail very often now. I bet Uncle Sam is very busy now with the cotton. I sure hope they have a big crop this year. When I get home I am going to bring Sam and Cloud some souvenirs from over here. I have lots of things that I have found. I hope to get a lot more before I leave from over here. I wrote mother and dad today so you both should get the letters the same time. I don't have much to write about. I can say one thing – it looks like now this war will soon be over on both sides. Write real soon, All my Love, Murray."

At 0600 on 31 July *Serpens* got underway with escort USS *Osmus* (DE-701) for Noumea, having discharged approximately 1100 net tons of dry provisions, ship's store stock and clothing at Purvis Bay to forces afloat. At 0735 the 4-SF-1 radar went out of operation due to rain leaking down the radar's wave guide into its transmitter. It could not be repaired.

USS Serpens crewmember S1c Murray Caldwell Flowers, USCGR. Photograph courtesy Sam Neilson, first cousin to Murray.

Serpens continued underway until 4 August, anchoring in Fisherman's Bay, Noumea, at 1330. MoMM2c Riccardi writes to his wife the same day: "I didn't write before this, if I did, you wouldn't have gotten it any sooner, because we were underway, in short notice, and during that time, I am sorry to say, I lost my sea legs again. I can't understand it. I thought I was over it or have gotten used to it but I really felt terrible. I am so sorry to have to tell you this because it makes me feel like a big baby, but that's my excuse and there is no sense in my pretending to be salty. And when you feel that way it is useless to try to write."

At 1400 the following day they shifted over to Dock #3, Grand Quay, and began loading additional stores and clothes until 9 August. During this time MoMM2c Riccardi writes to his wife on 6 August about his visit to another ship in port and the movies he's been watching:

> "The other night after I wrote to you we had a very good picture for the movies, it must have just come from the States, and in Technicolor. Gary Cooper in [The Story of] Dr. Wassell – maybe you heard of it? It was a 15-reel picture, lasted two hours and 15 minutes. Last night a few of the boys that came with me from California and I went to visit some of the boys I haven't seen since we left California. It was nice to see them. They are on another ship so they invited us to stay for the movies and they also had a little entertainment. A couple of Army boys did the entertaining. It was pretty good, one fellow passed out a magazine, late issue, then he asked anyone in the audience to give him any number of the pages. He would tell you what was on that page, there were 78 pages in the magazine. He must have had a very good memory because he would even tell you some of the jokes that were on that page. And he only missed one. One of the fellows was a good whistler, another a singer, and they also told some jokes. Then we seen the picture, Kay Kyser in 'Swing Fever.' I didn't think much of it. As a movie actor I think he is terrible."

Another letter dated 8 August from Riccardi says "I just got through seeing a movie. Barbara Stanwyck in 'Double Indemnity' with Edward G. Robinson. Well darling it will be a little while before you get the next letter after this one because I won't be able to mail another again until we drop anchor again, so don't be too impatient, it won't be too long.

The fellow sitting across from me keeps picking up the envelope of your letter up, and smells it. He says hello and thinks your lovely. He's not telling me anything I don't know."

Serpens unmoored from the dock at 0700 on 10 August and headed for Espiritu Santo, New Hebrides Islands. At 1037 on 12 August they anchored in Segond Channel at Espiritu Santo where they first unloaded general cargo before loading deck cargo for Guadalcanal. MoMM2c Riccardi finally gets permission to tell his wife he had been to Auckland, New Zealand:

> "We are anchored at the same place Morgan is anchored again, so I hope to see him again. I was supposed to go on the recreation liberty party but instead I took a shower and then sat down to write to you my dream girl. I found out that the boys are writing home about the place they were at, remember? I said I couldn't tell you yet? It's been so long since we have been there, I won't say as much as I would if I wrote you then. We were at Auckland, New Zealand. If you look on a map you will see that's quite a ways off. Well, to begin with, it certainly was good to see civilization, street cars, buildings, stores, theaters, etc. The whole trouble is, or was, that they pulled the sidewalks in about 6 o'clock. Most of the people have false teeth at about 18 years old and look like 25 or 30 years old. It's on account of some sort of protein or something they lack. I think it is in the water. The first thing we did was went to a restaurant and ordered steaks. Boy were they good, they serve them with French fries and an egg sunny side up, and it cost only two shillings and a sixpence, that's a little better than 40 cents. When you go to a show you have to buy a reserve ticket in advance, so if you get a ticket you get a seat. All the drinking you can buy legally is beer, and what beer. I couldn't drink it, they sell it in a bottle like our gingerale

bottles. If you want liquor it would cost about 20 dollars a quart and that's mostly rum. I tried it, not so good, nothing like our own whiskey. We went shopping for souvenirs and walked all over town looking it over. I bought a few things, every thing is too expensive. I did manage to get something for you, I think you will like it. It cost me 1 pound and 10 shillings, about 5 dollars. I hope I don't lose it before I get home with it. It is a small heart with silver background and mother-of-pearl set in and it hangs on a little silver bar pin. They have a lot of things hand-made by the Maori tribe. They sure do beautiful work. The original people were the Maori tribe, now they are pretty well mixed, married into different races. They think a lot of the Negro and mix well with the white people. I have seen a lot of them but never spoke to any. I guess when the servicemen came there they sure woke the people up because it must have been a lot worse before, it is so dead now, no place to go and nothing to do. From what I heard they don't have heat in their homes and go to bed early."

MoMM2c Riccardi's movie theater ticket stub mentioned in his letter to his wife. Photo courtesy Douglas Campbell.

Secured from loading at Espiritu Santo, *Serpens* got underway at 1633 on 14 August.

At 0714 on 17 August *Serpens* anchored off Tenaru Beach, Guadalcanal, and began discharging general cargo. They shifted position at 1727, tying up to Pier #6, Tulagi Harbor. After unloading some general stores at the pier over the next three days, they again repositioned – this time to Purvis Bay, Florida Island, arriving in Berth #26 at 1032 on 20 August.

On 21 August LCDR Stinson ordered the reorganization of the crew by establishing a "Cargo Division". This Division included the winchmen, checkers, hatchmen, boat personnel and deck engineers, all now coming under the direct control of one officer, the Cargo Officer. The result, as stated in the *Serpens* logbook, was "a notable increase in the speed of provisioning."

On 22 August MoMM2c Riccardi writes his wife:

"I just seen a spooky movie, 'The Uninvited,' that's the first ghost picture I've seen in a long time. It certainly was spooky. It must have been, to make a chill run up my spine. The fellows thought so too.

Bob Hope was at the place I was stationed at for 5 months, with his whole show. We got there after he had left. The boys I went to visit said he was swell. They also have the best outdoor theater of all the islands.

Well, I had two more shots the other day, and it certainly surprised me. I didn't get sick from them like I did in boot camp. I must be getting used to them.

I hear they are getting ready to celebrate the end of the European war and have the police on a twenty-four hour standby just in case. That really is good news, then we can really go to town and wipe up the yellow rats. I don't think it will last much after that. I won't be able to celebrate much here, but boy I'll sure make up for it."

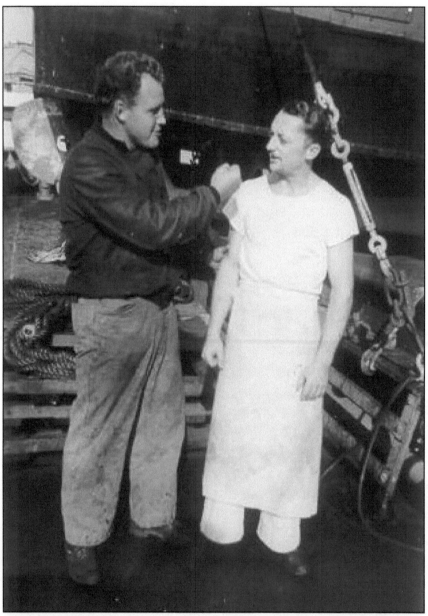

Unidentified crewmen from USS Serpens (AK-97). Photo provided courtesy of CAPT James D. Ellison, USCG (Ret.), who served aboard Serpens as a LTJG.

On 23 August 1944 Fireman Second Class (F2c) Gerald "Jerry" C. Breen wrote to his wife Myrtle and his 2-year-old son Robert about his upcoming tour of duty aboard *Serpens* and that he was expecting to be home for Christmas 1944 – he was one of the some 250 killed aboard *Serpens* 29 January 1945. He writes:

"Dear Myrt, Bobby: Well today I went to the Personnel Office and found out where I am going. I got a good break too for I am going on the ship with a fellow who shipped out of here a couple of weeks ago. He is Kiley, [Seaman First Class Ralph Dana Kiley, USCGR], the guy from Boston who just got married before we left N.J. Now this ship is a cargo ship and the name of it is the Serpent(sic), it is A.K. 97. It just carries supply to small places. Supply that consists of clothes and canteen supplies for the fleet. It travels from island to island and it brings troops back and forth among the islands. It has been down there for a long time and is due back in the States and I think that its home port is N.Y., but I am not sure. Now I think that this is the best job that you can get here. It's a lot better than most of the duty down here. The only thing is that it goes out for 4 or 5 days at a time and I won't be able to write every day. However, I will write every chance that I get. When you don't get any mail from me for a few days I don't want you to get the blues or get discouraged for every thing will be alright and there will be no need for you to worry. What ever happens you mustn't lose faith in me nor about my coming home.

"Like I told you before, these ship jobs are better than shore duty because you don't have any disease to worry about when you are on a ship. There is plenty of diseases on these islands down here too. In fact that's our biggest enemy down here. The Japs don't mean anything, it's just a matter of time and they will be all through here. The way these Marines go after them it isn't even funny.

"Well hon, I didn't get any mail from you today but I guess I will get it tomorrow. In fact no mail came in at all today. You keep writing to this same address until I tell you different. I don't want you to send any Christmas presents down here to me (I was looking at a paper the other day and I saw where they are sending Xmas presents overseas already) for I expect to be home by Christmas. If I am not home I will be somewhere in the States anyway.

"I know that you are having a hard time bringing up Bobby, but you just keep on being a good mother to him and you can rest assure that it won't be all in vain, for I will soon be home to give you a rest, while I rule him under the iron fist. Now you just keep your chin up and keep smiling.

"I think this long, long, long letter's going to surprise my wife no end and maybe she will write me a long letter too, soon.

"Well, I guess that this is just about all the news for one day. I want to save some for tomorrow or I won't have nothing to write about as usual. I hope that this letter finds you safe and sound, home from the beach, and I hope that you and Bobby had a nice vacation. With All My Love, Jerry."

Another morale booster was the constant stream of motion pictures that made their rounds between ships. On 23 August MoMM2c Riccardi tells his wife about another one he watched:

"I seen the picture finally of Gary Cooper in 'Pride of the Yankees.' That picture certainly was good. Their love affair was beautiful, she reminded me so much of you, the way she acted. I can't say that about him, with me, because that would be your point of view. But I do love you like he did her. And I still say the same thing he told her, before he died. That you gave me so much to make me happy, and still, do. They sure had a beautiful romance as long as they knew each other. It was too bad he died so young.

Well, I am going to start reading. I mean books instead of magazines. Did I tell you we have a library on our ship? Well we have any how, my first book is, A Night in Bombay. It is supposed to be good according to some of the boys. I think this is the type of both you would read. I did read a lot of Readers Digest, I think they are interesting, they cover so many different and interesting things. I think the more you read the better your knowledge. So I hope to better mine. Don't you think I need it?"

For the week running from 20 to 26 August 1944, *Serpens* issued nearly a quarter of their dry stores, ship's store stock and clothing to forces afloat in Purvis Bay. For cargo that wasn't being winched over from *Serpens* directly to other large vessels, five landing craft were assigned to *Serpens* and they carried cargo to others in Purvis Bay. On Sunday, 27 August, *Serpens* moved to Hutchinson Creek, Florida Island, and discharged 306 tons to an LST flotilla with other floating units. They returned to Purvis Bay the morning of 28 August and continued the issue of dry provisions, ship's store stock and clothing to forces afloat. By the end of August, a little over one-third of the current cargo had been discharged.

MoMM2c Riccardi writes to his wife on 2 September about his friend Morgan stationed aboard another ship: "I received a letter from Morgan today. He said he couldn't get the skipper of our ship to transfer anyone to exchange for him, and he is getting to be a nervous wreck. For one reason his ship don't go any place, to sort of take the monotony out of the routine life. I don't blame him. I'd hate to be stuck in one place especially where he is, if he does go ashore there is nothing to do. So he is being patient, the same as I, and waiting for our time and turn to go home, and hoping and praying it won't be too long. It makes me feel miserable just thinking of waiting, waiting." On 9 September he writes: "I seen Morgan's ship pull in the same harbor we are in. I certainly was surprised to see it, that's the first trip they took in months. I thought he might come to see me today, but he didn't. I'll have liberty tomorrow maybe, I'll go visit him. One of our officers is on his ship as Executive Officer and he sure is a swell fellow." On 11 September he mentions his friend Morgan once again: "I guess Morgan must be pretty busy because I didn't see him and I didn't get a chance to go over and see him. The day I did have liberty I was too tired to leave the ship, so I took a nap. It certainly is surprising how much work there is on a ship besides standing your regular watches."

Serpens remained in Purvis Bay until 15 September and continued to issue provisions to forces afloat. Much of this period, as stated in the *Serpens* logbook, was "waiting for customers." At 0633 on 16 September *Serpens* moved to Tulagi Harbor where they discharged 51 tons of provisions and took aboard 53 tons of general cargo. They returned to Purvis Bay the next day, arriving at 0630, where they continued discharging cargo. On 20 September MoMM2c Riccardi writes his wife:

> "Sweetheart, I did get that grass skirt I told you about, but it cost me a couple of weeks work in my spare time. Yes, I made a ring, all by hand, I even set a mother-of-pearl shell in it. I hated to give it up but I was bound to get that skirt for you. So now I will have to get busy and make a wooden box so I can send it to you. I am going to put the rest of the things in it and

send it together. I'll try to get it done very soon. I will feel better to know that it will be on its way. I hope I am not too optimistic but I feel like I may have a chance to leave, around the first of the year, at least a little before or after. I hope I am not making a mistake by telling you this, because, we will both feel bad if it don't work out that way. Nobody told me that but I just figure it that way, and also hope it to work that way, although I would like to be with you for the holidays. Another bunch of boys is getting to leave very soon, so you can see why I feel that way. I also am trying to make 1st Class before then. The four of us that came on together, with the same rates, will be on top of the list of Motor Machinists after the next draft goes. Boy does it make me feel good to think that it won't be long and I'll be back with you."

At 0659 on 21 September *Serpens* shifted again to Tulagi for a day and then at 1240 on 22 September steamed to Lunga Point, Guadalcanal. By this time nearly 90% of all their cargo had been discharged by the newly-formed Cargo Division, possibly at a faster rate than anticipated – 179 tons that had been offloaded had to be restowed back aboard *Serpens* on the night of 22 September and the following morning at the request of the Army loading officer.

On 24 September MoMM2c Riccardi writes to his wife about life aboard ship and coming home:

"My darling wife, I am sorry that I was not able to write you as soon as I said I would. Things have changed considerably on here, although I did not mention it before. Sometimes I put as many as 17-18 hours in, so that don't give me much time to do any thing. I didn't hit the sack until 12:45 last night, from 6 in the morning. I'd better quit beefing because you have enough trouble of your own. I do want to get off this work ship, and bad too. You say you feel blue because you don't know when I am coming home. Well honey, I could say the same for myself but I try to think I will be on my way before or after Christmas, but I am not sure. That's as close as I can figure, one way or the other. I just hope I am right. When we get the new replacements or reliefs I will be able to tell much better. If they would send a few Motor Machinists that had no sea duty, I should have a swell chance of coming home soon. I hope this helps you some. One of the boys that got off about 3 weeks ago is going to try to stop and see you although he is still waiting for transportation home. It will be about a month more before he gets there. He is a Gunner's Mate First Class and his name is Kelsey. A nice kid. I hope he makes it so you can have a nice talk with him.

The "Kelsey" whom MoMM2c Riccardi was referring to was GM1c Walter J. Kelcey who had reported aboard *Serpens* on 23 April 1943. On 25 September Riccardi writes his wife about LT Alygood: "Do you remember me telling you of having an officer on here that was in charge of us in Alameda, Cal? Well, well, he was transferred to another ship. His ship was docked at the place where I stayed for five months, so we took him over in one of our boats. I had to be engineer. It took us two hours and fifteen minutes, we left about five in the evening so we stayed all night and slept in the boat on cots. The mosquitos kept me awake all night. We got back to our ship about 8:30 next morning. Had pancakes and ham and coffee, then I got permission to sleep in. I took a nice shower then slept until 11:30, had chow again, and here I am writing to you." On 28 September he adds: "Well honey, I am on another job now. I have three boats to maintain and keep running, so I am back at my line of work again."

Serpens was anchored off Lunga Point for the rest of September, being loaded by the Army. For September, *Serpens* had only been underway for a total of 7 hours and 42 minutes. Although she was in full active commissioned status for the entire month of September, no availability was requested or granted. Marine growth was found to be developing rapidly on the ship's bottom.

On 4 October MoMM2c Riccardi writes to his wife about the two mascots *Serpens* has on board: "Summer time is coming around here now and the heat is certainly terrific. I do mean hot. I'd give anything to be back home in that weather. I didn't tell you that we have two dogs on here that we bought in New Zealand as pups. We have had a lot of trouble with them. One time the female took a fit and ended up falling into the cargo hold about 30 feet but she survived. Another time she tried to jump from one ship to another alongside, and missed, falling in the drink between ships. She swam to the fantail and one of the boys picked her up. During that time the other, a male, was too small and sick to do anything. He finally snapped out of it, the two of them together really put on a show sometimes. Today the male dog got sick and has been yelping with misery. One of the boys gave him worm pills and what not. If he lives through the night he should be alright in the morning. I guess it is too hot for the dogs but they are a lot of fun and we hate to lose them."

Serpens would continue being loaded by the Army at Lunga Point until 7 October. During that time two incidents occurred aboard the ship which resulted in minor damage, both caused by the Army loaders. The first incident occurred when an Army winchman lowered the No. 2 jumbo boom onto an open door attached to the boom table locker. This bent the watertight door out of alignment. The second event occurred when an inexperienced Army winchman "froze" while maneuvering the No. 3 winches with the throttles wide open, resulting in a broken guy tackle and preventer. While there were no injuries to personnel it was enough to have been noted in the logbook and may have reflected on the overall inexperience or indifference of the Army stevedores. Most accident investigations have usually concluded in their Report that an accident was attributed to a lack of training, the absence of direct supervision, and/or no method in place to determine personnel qualifications prior to being authorized to handle the situation or machinery.

The more serious incident which occurred during this same time was when, at 1410 on 7 October, the loading had been completed and for the first time, *Serpens* was carrying explosives. The logbook states: "…completed loading, 2472 tons general cargo and explosives." The explosives were loaded into a ship whose holds were not compatible for holding explosives. These were general cargo holds, not magazines. The holds did not even have carbon dioxide (CO_2) systems installed in them; the release of carbon dioxide would help in extinguishing any fires. It is believed that *Serpens* carried the explosives on board for nearly a month - until 5 November.

Serpens left Guadalcanal at 1600 on 7 October and arrived in Espiritu Santo at 1215 on 10 October where they discharged over 2,000 tons of general cargo. If was rough sailing as mentioned in MoMM2c Riccardi's 10 October 1944 letter to his wife: "We sure had a rugged trip. I don't think I'll ever get away from being seasick. This time I seen fellows get sick that never were before. Some more of the boys are going home and packing up and making a rumpus. Lucky group. There still is quite a few old fellows yet, but it brings it closer every time a bunch leaves."

On 14 October Riccardi tells his wife more about his new job and what happened to the male dog:

> "Hello my sweet, I finally managed to get a little time tonight to write but I must explain. I have been put in charge of the small boats, which means that I am on call at all hours now, rain or shine, day or night. I say that because I was called last night at midnight and it was raining like the devil. One of the boats were out on a run and stalled about a mile away. So this job is going to keep me plenty busy, besides keeping five other men on the ball. It isn't so bad when one goes bad but when all of them do then I don't know where to begin.
>
> I was going to tell you about our dog, the one that was sick. He was taken to a vet. He said there was no hope for him so we had to destroy him. Now our female looks pretty lonesome without him.
>
> I have been so busy and the boats in such a bad condition that I couldn't go over to see Morgan. I guess he will be kind of peeved but I wonder why he didn't come to see me? So I'll write and explain. I hope he will understand.
>
> One of my shipmates worked for General Motors as a tool buyer and was offered a job after the war in China, as a personnel manager with a salary of 15 thousand a year for three years. Boy isn't that swell. I used to work for them back in '28 so he said he would see if he could get me in. They wrote back and said they couldn't find my record, so I am going to give him a little more data to help them find it. The company is going to put up three new plants there. But I don't think I'll get a break like that. If I get any more information

on that I certainly will tell you. You want to live in China?

Yes, it's been a whole year since I've been away from you. At times it seems like years and then again it don't seem that long. But it is so good to know that I have most of my time in out here. So now I am hoping we get some rated men in the next couple of drafts. Because the other two Motor Machinists that came on with me are the top-rated men and can't be relieved until we get me of the same rate. So honey cross your fingers and pray."

Serpens then sailed for Noumea at 1200 on 16 October, anchoring there in Great Roads at 1155 on 18 October. There they discharged 1,076 tons of general cargo and loaded 635 tons of vehicles destined for Bougainville, Munda, Russell Islands, Tulagi and Guadalcanal. In previous letters MoMM2c Riccardi had been promising his wife a photo of him in full beard. In his letter dated 18 October he breaks the news to her:

"Hello darling, I am so sorry that I was unable to write before this but I do every possible chance I get. This new job changes my routine a bit. I did manage to see Morgan the night before we left. I visited him for about four hours, took in the movie on his ship. Dorothy Lamour is some South Sea island picture. It would really be something if the islands were like they show in the movies, they certainly make it look extremely good. I guess that's where the people at home get the impression of the islands being so beautiful. They might be to look at but that's all.

I didn't take liberty today because I took the time to make a box to put the grass skirt and things in. I think when you get it you will get a kick out of going through the things I sent you. When I come home I'll tell you all about them.

Well, it looks like I won't be able to take a picture with my beard because the officers on the beach won't let us on unless we shave them off. Can you beat that? They can think of the damnest things sometimes."

On 22 October MoMM2c Riccardi writes: "I am feeling pretty good, the weather being cool where I am now. I am pretty well caught up with the serious work on the boats, so now I can see things more clearly. They sure were in poor shape when I got them, but they will be still better when I get through with them."

Riccardi's letter to his wife on 25 October breaks the news that his beard is now gone: "We took some more pictures yesterday and they should be very interesting because we had a lot of fun getting fixed up for them. I am going to try to get the negatives as quick as possible so I can send them to you. So after all that picture taking, today I shaved my Van Dyke and it sure felt funny when I put my hand on my chin. It seemed as though my chin was gone, but it feels good to have a nice smooth face again. One of the boys said 'Now I see why you have such a beautiful wife. You look pretty sharp with the beard off.' Was he kidding honey?"

Before departing on 27 October, a chaplain came aboard to hold confession and communion. At 1531 they departed for Cape Torokina, Bougainville Island. While underway MoMM2c Riccardi writes his wife:

"Hello darling, it's been a long time since I have heard from you. In fact, 11 days. And it will be at least another 5 before I do. But I can take it pretty good now, I just make up my mind that it is no use grumbling or complaining. I have been pretty fortunate, or we have, we have been under way three days and the water has been calm, that's the way I like it. I can go about my work without any trouble. I just hope it stays that way.

This is the first time I really felt good under way. I always dreaded to see the anchor come up.

The news told about a hurricane hitting the state that Turner lives in but it wasn't near his home town, so that was good. Turner is the tall fellow in the picture with me. He is dying to meet you and always talks about the good times we are going to have when we come home. He was stationed in Cleveland where I had boot training and he was crazy about it. He talks about it like as though it was his home town. He is a swell fellow. He is First Class and in charge of the deck engineers. Him and I used to work together. We are always together and always arguing about machinery or engines."

The "Turner" mentioned was MoMM1c Hubert Turner who reported on board *Serpens* on 30 May 1944.

Serpens anchored at Cape Torokina at 1105 on 2 November 1944. On 3 November Riccardi writes:

"Hello Lovely, we finally dropped the hook and I must say I did pretty good, not getting seasick in all that time. But of course it was considerably calm water although it did get rough toward the end, but I guess I got used to it gradually with an easy start. Well, I seen the first volcano, something I thought I would never see with my own eyes. I thought it was hot where I was before, but it certainly is much hotter here. Your skin gets as red as a beet in fifteen minutes. So I stay out of the sun as much as possible because it just draws the strength out of you.

Here is a little more dope on that China business. This fellow's father is still going through the records trying to find mine. If he finds it there will be a good chance of us living aboard for a few years. I don't know yet where, but France is one place. But any how, when I get back I am supposed to call his father long distance and make an appointment for an interview. There is a possible chance of a position as superintendent. I think if I get that break it will be a good start for both of us."

At Cape Torokina U.S. Army working parties came aboard and unloaded 667 tons of general cargo and rolling stock until 0030 on 4 November. At 0732 that same day, *Serpens* got underway for Sasavele Anchorage, New Georgia Islands, arriving at 1202 on 5 November. While in Sasavele Anchorage the ship's crew discharged 345 tons of general cargo from Hold #5, exercising under "Battle Condition." The term "Battle Condition" is a modified General Quarters also called Condition One ABLE or 1A. It calls for all battle stations to be manned by the crew even though any working party may continue loading or unloading the vessel. After the general cargo had been unloaded, a working party of Seabees unloaded an additional 68 tons of cargo. At 1555 on 6 November they departed Sasavele Anchorage and at 0728 on 7 November dropped anchor at New Georgia Island in the Russell Islands chain. The next two weeks reflected the mission of a cargo ship during World War II – to sail between islands loading and unloading cargo. MoMM1c Riccardi wrote to his wife on 9 November, acknowledging all the recent travel to distant islands and that he made First Class:

"Hello my peach, it's been a long time since I heard from you. In fact to be exact it is 15 days. That is a long time but it can't be helped, we are making stops but there is no mail. It is held up at another place so I am expecting to be there at least in two days." The same letter continued on over to 11 November: "Sorry honey but I was called off and couldn't finish last night. I thought sure I would be able to finish. I was even hiding in the carpenter shop thinking that nobody would find me. I think it will be a couple of days yet before I will hear from you, so that's not far off, though it is a terrible long time. You asked me How things look for my coming home. Well, right now things are at a stand still. In fact an order came through that there would be no more transfers until the 23rd of December. That means things didn't work out the way I expected with none going before then. Still have quite a few old timers on here.

Well my darling wife, I made First Class. Not bad for 22 months in the service starting as apprentice seaman. What do you think honey? I guess that's as far as I want to go."

By 0440 on 11 November, 1,187 tons of general cargo and rolling stock had been discharged by Seabee working parties and at 0915 *Serpens* got underway for Guadalcanal. At 1501 the same day they anchored off Kukum Beach. Here everyone's mail caught up with the ship – MoMM1c Riccardi receiving six letters and two packages from his wife and packages from his relatives containing mixed nuts, dates, hard candy and a picture album to start putting all the photos in that he had been receiving over the months from everyone back home.

On 14 November MoMM1c Riccardi received two more letters from his wife. In his 14 October reply Riccardi wrote about a tragedy concerning some *Serpens* crewmembers: "Most all the boys sure got some bad news today. We heard that three of the boys that went home took a plane from Frisco to Los Angeles and the plane crashed, killing all three of them – 2 cooks and an electrician. They were on their thirty-day leave. Isn't that terrible? Two of them had brothers killed in action. After all the time they had out here, just going back to see their love ones. It certainly was a shock to us."

Research by the authors found it to have been an aircraft accident occurring on Saturday, 3 November 1944, as found in this article entitled "Midair Blast On Luxury Liner Kills 24 Persons" published on the cover page of *The Petaluma Argus-Courier* (Petaluma, California) newspaper dated 6 November:

HANFORD, Nov. 6 (AP)—A wide area near here was searched here today for evidence to piece together the mysterious mid-air explosion late Saturday of a Transcontinental Western Air luxury liner in which 24 persons perished.

The big San Francisco-Los Angeles bound plane appeared to explode at great height, flinging bodies and hundreds of pieces of the plane "like birds" over the central valley farmside. The disaster occurred at the height of a rain and electrical storm, but company officials doubted that the ship might have been struck by lightning.

"Lightning dissipates and comes off in the form of static," L. Flanigan, TWA operations manager at Burbank, explained.

Army, Navy, Civil Aeronautics authorities and TWA officials are investigating the crash.

Twenty of the dead, whose names were withheld pending notification of next-of-kin, were military personnel. There was one civilian passenger—Dr. B. D. Saklatwalla, Pittsburgh, Pa.

[The pilot] had called Burbank control tower on landing conditions a few minutes before the explosion was reported by a farmer, H. Anderson.

Eye-witnesses said an explosion rocked the neighborhood and a huge flash rent the sky. A piece of the plane fell and shorted a highpower line. Mail sacks were scattered over a wide area.

"It looked like a battlefield," a newsman reported.

At Kansas City, TWA officials said they had been authorized to announce the names of the Coast Guard passengers killed aboard the big air liner."

Of the five Coast Guardsmen who were killed, three were from *Serpens*: Seaman First Class Kenneth L. Zook, of Kingsford Heights, Indiana; Electrician's Mate Second Class Gerald E. Land, of St. Louis, Missouri; and Seaman First Class James K. Deans, of Tilden, Illinois.

By 0700 on 18 November, all cargo destined for Guadalcanal, a total of 949 tons, had been discharged and 221 tons of general cargo had been loaded. At 0859 they got underway for Tulagi Harbor and at 1226 anchored there. By 1505, 26 tons of cargo for Tulagi had been discharged. At 0704 on 19 November *Serpens* got underway for the Russell Islands, mooring to Tillotson Dock at 1316. For the next 26 hours the ship was loaded with 641 tons of repairable vehicles; the work ceasing at 1510 on 20 November. At 0645 the following day she got underway back to Guadalcanal where she anchored off Lunga Point at 1304 the same day. There she loaded 11 more tons of repairable vehicles. MoMM1c Riccardi writes his wife on 21 November: "Remember the place I told you about, that I couldn't tell you where it was until a long time after that? Well, that's where I'm going again." Departing Guadalcanal at 1303 on 22 November, *Serpens* got underway for Auckland, New Zealand.

Riccardi writes a letter to his wife on 23 November:

"Hello sweetheart, Thanksgiving Day and under weigh, the same as a year ago today. For dinner we had a regular Thanksgiving dinner. Turkey and dressing, cranberry sauce, plum pudding, lima beans, creamed peas and carrots, pumpkin pie, shrimp salad, shelled mixed nuts and a menu with greetings. Not bad, hey? But it is never like home. I'll be so glad when this trip is over.

We got rid of some of my boats, only leaving me a couple. I guess they will take a couple of my men too, because I won't have enough work for them. Do you note how small I am writing? Well, it's the cold climate that's causing it. The sudden change sure can be felt. I am sleeping with blankets now.

I started the jeep up today and tried to put it in gear, but it was pretty hard because the oil was pretty stiff from the cold. Yes, we have a jeep on board. We use it on shore for the boat master and officers and so forth. My men did a nice job of fixing it up during the trip and it sounds so quiet. One of the men made a muffler for it out of a five-inch shell and it really is good.

I finally finished that book 'Out of the Night.' I never knew a man could stand so much torture and live. I hope you don't read it, it's not your type. I also finished a western novel 'A Little Different.' Now I am reading 'The Dry Guillotine.' It's another like 'Out of the Night.' I mean, it talks a lot about torture in prisons, etc. I am getting tired of it so I'll have to find something better. I would like to be reading your letters instead, that's what I really like."

It was an otherwise uneventful cruise that put her back into Auckland at 1645 on 30 November. At 2300 a civilian working party began discharging 221 tons of cargo and by 2055 on 1 December they had completed their task.

At 0705 on 2 December *Serpens* got underway for Wellington, New Zealand. In his letter dated the same day, Riccardi writes: "Here I am underway again. There was nothing of much interest that happened. I did do a lot of walking around alone, and did some window shopping, of which don't cost much. I did take in a show. It sure was beautiful inside and they had an organ that came out of the floor and it certainly sounded beautiful."

Serpens arrived at Wellington at 1153 on 4 December where at 0020 the following day they began discharging more than 600 tons of repairable vehicles. On 5 December Riccardi celebrates his 2-year Anniversary by writing a letter to his wife reminiscing about that day. The following day they completed unloading the vehicles by 1015. From 1740 on 7 December to 0715 on 10 December repairs, alterations and additions to ship and ship's equipment were made by civilian workers and ship's crew. Part of the work was to convert three of the ship's five holds to hold explosives. On 10 December the entire crew was given a 24-hour pass while the ship was fumigated. No personnel were allowed back aboard *Serpens* until 0815 on 11 December.

Work then resumed on repairing and altering parts of the ship and at 1752 on 15 December *Serpens* was placed in a floating drydock to enable the scraping of its sides and bottom.

On 15 December MoMM1c Riccardi writes his wife and comments on the nightmares she has started getting:

> "Hello lovely, I finally hit the jackpot, seven letters and four cards. I don't know where to begin. The letters were wonderful honey and the cards very nice, especially the Anniversary card you sent me, I am crazy about it.
>
> So my poor darling is getting nightmares too now? Honey I wish I could be along side of you to comfort you when you get them. They are bad, I know. Honey you're getting nervous from something or you wouldn't

have them. Please take it easy and get all the rest you can."

Hull work was completed in drydock at 0950 on 19 December; the drydock was reflooded and *Serpens* refloated – moving over to Aotea Quay. On 20 December MoMM1c Riccardi writes to his wife about his whereabouts, getting ready for Christmas and the Ship's Dance:

"Hello darling, you didn't do so good in guessing where I was, but you were pretty right when you said maybe in the Solomons. But that takes in a lot of islands, in fact we were in the top end of them. I guess you know where we are now. You should anyhow because I sent you some pictures and things from there, and the little book telling about it. I don't know about staying where we have been before. I think things will be different. But don't worry honey, I'll be alright.

You know what I did today? I was selected to go in the country and buy some Christmas trees. I bought two and the skipper wants me to get some more tomorrow. We are putting them in different parts of the ship with lights on them. We also have a big star on top of our mast, about 5 feet with lights on each point. But to me it will never be like Christmas until I am home with you.

I don't seem to say much about what I am doing, but really, I never thought there would be so much work to do. I did manage to take in the sights which are quite different from our home surroundings. I finally got a chance to get enough to drink, but I didn't get plastered and I behaved like a gentleman. We had a Ship's Dance and it would look bad if I didn't go, so I did. I know you trust me and I can say truthfully, I have no guilty conscious. I did dance with the girl friends of some of the boys. In fact, the boys asked me to because I was alone and, too, some of the boys couldn't dance. I had a nice time, but when I danced honey, I pretended it was you in my arms. We had a group picture taken. I am going to send it to you if possible. I am in the front and look pretty good. They certainly play old-fashioned music here, even on the radio. Some songs are 15 and 20 years old."

The "little book telling about it" as mentioned in MoMM1c Riccardi's letter above was a 36-page booklet handed out by the New Zealand Department of Internal Affairs specifically written for Americans about their history, culture, liquor laws, night life, etc. The Introduction reads:

Welcome! When we say that, we mean it. Those of us who have met Americans before have liked them (or most of them), and we hope you Americans will like us (or most of us). We know you're here to do a job of work and that you want to get on with it, but when you get liberty we want to meet you and know you and we want you to meet and know us; and not merely on the streets but in our homes. You won't find subways, skyscrapers or night-life. You will find that when you break the crust we're much like the folks back home. New Zealand is a small country, but we like to think our hearts are reasonably big.

And that job of work. We're on it too. We don't like war, and we don't enjoy reading our casualty lists, or anybody else's for that matter, but we feel, like you, that our way of life has got to be fought for and we're glad that we're fighting together side by side. That's something worthwhile.

We know about the United States. Some of us have been there, most of us have read American books, all of us have seen American movies; our children learn about George Washington and Abraham Lincoln, and we listen to Franklin D. Roosevelt over the radio. We think you might like to know a little about New Zealand, so here's this booklet.

Haeremai, haeremai! e Te Hokowhitu-a-Tu! Haria mai te whakairo papatahi kia mate te hoariri mo ake tonu atu! "Welcome, Welcome, fighting men of the warrior god Tu! With minds as one let us defeat the enemy for ever!"

Repair work continued until the ship's availability was completed at midnight on 23 December. The following important repairs, alterations and additions were completed during this period:

Construction and repair:

1. No. 1 hold, No. 4 hold (lower) and No. 5 hold (lower) converted into "Magazine A" stowage.
2. CO_2 system partially installed in No. 1 hold.
3. Two (2) new 5-ton winches installed at No. 2 hold to handle single whips or jumbo guys.
4. Swapped 50-ton winches at No. 4 hold with 30-ton winches at No. 2 hold. 50-ton winches are now with 50-ton boom at No. 2 hold.
5. Installed mail locker in No. 4 tweendeck.
6. Cleared, wire-brushed and painted whole hull.
7. Sealed and oiled main deck.
8. Numerous minor repairs and improvements.

Engineering:

1. Rewooded rudder post and pintle bearings.
2. Repacked stern tube gland.
3. Overhauled and inspected all sea valves.
4. Made major repairs to main engine, intermediate valve and valve bridle.
5. Set main engine valves to proper clearance.

The "little book telling about it" as mentioned in MoMM1c Riccardi's 20 December 1944 letter to his wife Sylvia. It was a 36-page booklet handed out by the New Zealand Department of Internal Affairs specifically written for Americans about New Zealand's history, culture, liquor laws, night life, etc. Photo of booklet courtesy Douglas Campbell.

Now it was Christmas 1944 in Wellington, New Zealand. Riccardi writes home: "Christmas was nothing out of the ordinary. I went to church and prayed for you and us."

The *Serpens'* Executive Officer, Lieutenant J. Gayle Aiken, III, wrote to his mother on Christmas Day 1944: "This is one of the windiest cities in the world. You can tell a [CENSORED] man anywhere in the world, because as he turns a corner he will instinctively clutch his hat. It rarely ever snows here, but now in midsummer, it is chilly enough to wear topcoats. It seems strange to hear people speaking of 'Christmas lilies,' which are blooming in profusion outdoors. The good ship *Serpens* has lighted Christmas trees on her foremast and mizzen, and a large lighted "Star of Bethlehem" at the main truck. This is about the only Christmas flavor here. All decorations have been prohibited for the duration, and Christmas trees in private homes are the exception rather than the rule. A favorite Christmas pastime in this part of the world is to go cruising in a sailboat."

On 31 August 1945 the New Zealand newspaper *Evening Post* published a Letter to the Editor written by Charlotte Aiken, the mother of *Serpens'* Executive Officer, Lieutenant J. Gayle Aiken, III. The Letter, titled "Lost Naval Men: Memories of a Visit," was mostly about Christmas 1944 in Wellington. It reads:

> "Sir,--Several very interesting and pleasant weeks at Christmas time, 1944, were spent by the U.S.S. *Serpens* AK 97 in your port. This ship was completely destroyed on January 29, when loading ammunition at Guadalcanal, with only two men on board being saved.
>
> "As the mother of the executive officer, who was lost, I have been writing as many of the families (over 150) of the men as possible. Some write, 'Our son told me he would write us all about those wonderful weeks

as soon as he could, but he never did." I quote the letter of our son, Lieutenant J. Gayle Aiken, III, December 25:-- 'The ship is docked in one of the most beautiful ports of the world, a large harbor entirely landlocked, ringed around with green hills that rise steeply from the water, with mountains receding into the misty distance.'

I quote from a letter of Fred Eckart, coxswain, of Glen Ellyn, Illinois, dated January 3, 1945: 'All of a sudden we hit a civilized port, and it was great. We had a four-day leave, and after that two nights' liberty, and one night duty—you can't beat that. I had Christmas dinner in a private home, and it was a great dinner. Roast chicken and all the trimmings. I also had a nice girl with me—her name was Margret. I really had a nice Christmas—after all it was the next best thing to being home for Christmas. These people were really nice. I never felt more at home than I did there. I did everything from raiding the ice-box to starting the fire in the fireplace, and what a time we had! We went to church first and then to their place for dinner. It was really great and I only hope you enjoyed your day as much on your side of the world as I did on this. We are still going strong—beach parties and dances. It is hard to explain how good all this seems after being away from it so long. We don't miss a thing and nothing is too good for us.'

"Mrs. Eckart, Fred's mother, writes me they wish they could hear from this family, and from 'Margret.'

"It is not surprising that five of this crew of men (all volunteers, none drafted) became engaged to your New Zealand girls, who my son wrote were so splendid.

"Many of your hospitable, kindly people knew the men of this ship. If they will write letters to the parents of the men they knew, I will forward all letters, and I believe such a kind act on their part will be deeply appreciated.

"Thanking you for just being a delightful city and such a splendid place—I am, etc., Charlotte Aiken (Mrs. Gayle Aiken, Jun.)"

Although out of chronological sequence with the rest of this book, some 50 people from Wellington, New Zealand, responded to that Letter to the Editor and a sampling of those replies are mentioned here:

William McLelland Loudon wrote:

"I worked aboard the *Serpens* all the time she stayed here. I have worked on lots of American ships during the war. But of all the ships, I never got to know and like such a large number as I knew on that particular vessel."

An anonymous person wrote: "Always I will remember when we in New Zealand were praying and working to defend ourselves from the fast-coming Japs. Picture our joy and relief when the city was flooded with your American sons. We owe them undying gratitude for the sacrifices they have made for us."

Shirley P. Brien from the Masonic Hotel on Cuba Street in Wellington wrote about Radioman Third Class John Clifford Dedmon, Jr., USCGR:

"John was very happy when he was here in New Zealand, as I'm sure all the rest of the crew were. I first met John in my father's hotel. He always stayed here with the rest of his shipmates, and we all came to know each other very well. John also became a very good friend of the family, so on his leave – he had five days – Dad took both John and his closest friend Ray Waddel [Coxswain Delos Ray Wardle, USCGR] out in the car golfing and swimming. In fact there was nothing they missed.

About fifteen miles out of town we own a Stud-Farm where Dad keeps and breeds his racehorses, so on many occasions a few boys from the ship, including John, went horseback riding, so you can see they had as good a time as our little country could show them. At nights there were always cabarets to go to or movies to see. Now and then someone had a party we were usually invited to, and went.

Then last but not least there was a skating rink where the best time of all was had.

You know I could go on telling you of all the good times John had here for hours, but I know the main thing you require to know is "was he happy". Well, once again, I'll tell you he was.

We had a Mass offered up for John's safety. I hope you don't mind as our religion is Catholic and I know yours is not, but I'm sure it makes no difference."

Janet Washburn (Mrs. Charles Washburn) wrote:

"In last evening's newspaper was your letter calling for news of the boys off the U.S.S. *Serpens*. Well, I knew dozens of these boys. We have a Riding Academy in Wellington, and they spent many of their leisure hours there – many of them used to ride early in the morning, fairly early anyway, and then used to spend the whole day there just filling in the time talking and helping us with the horses. Of course I can't remember all their names. There was Les Chambers [Seaman Second Class Leslie Earl Chambers, USCGR] from California – he was very proud of his wife and young baby, a boy I think, back in the States. I have a little girl 2 years old and his baby was about 3 weeks younger so he often used to come up home after the Riding Academy was closed to have a look at my little girl. She is also an American, I am married to an American Marine from South Bend, Indiana.

Three boys who spent a lot of time with us during their leave were Perry Headrick [Seaman Second Class Perry Paul Headrick, USCGR] from Dallas, Texas, Elmer Hagmire [Water Tender Second Class Elmer Pratt Hagemeier, Jr., USCGR], Houston, Texas, and Bob Harrington [Fireman First Class Robert Allen Herrington, USCGR]. They were always welcome to bring girl friends if they wished and they used to make themselves really at home. Perry Headrick cut down our Christmas tree for us and we all had lots of fun decorating it and putting on the Christmas presents. Thanks to their splendid efforts it was the lovliest Christmas tree we ever have had.

Others I remember were Les Diehl [Seaman First Class Lee Henry Diehl, USCGR], I believe his wife was living in California, and Ray Masonnic [Coxswain Raymond Gregory Mazzanti, USCG] but he was always called "The Professor." He was very proud of his lovely wife, who, I think, lived in New York.

All the boys used to show us photos of their folks back home and we used to love to see them. I met most of the lads off the *Serpens* but don't remember the names of any others now."

At 1330 on 27 December 1944, impregnated sand bags were being loaded aboard *Serpens* when, at 1920, one net full of bags caught fire inside the No. 3 hold. The net load was immediately deposited back onto the dock where it was extinguished by the ship's crew and the Wellington Fire Department. Damage occurred only to the cargo in the net. The Commanding Officer deemed that this particular cargo, as a whole, was unsafe for stowage aboard his ship and the 111 tons of sand bags that had already been placed in the hold was discharged back onto the Dock. At 0335 on 28

December all the impregnated sand bags had been removed from the ship. It turned out that the bags had been treated with a chemical to prevent rot and it was this chemical that reacted with the bags and caught fire. Similar sandbags were loaded aboard USS *Cetus* (AK-77) while at Aotea Quay, Wellington, and they caught fire as well. Also on 28 December MoMM1c Riccardi writes to his wife, having read that she had received the wooden box with the grass skirt and other items he had mailed home:

> "So you finally received the box I sent you. I am so glad you enjoyed it so much. I think it is interesting. It will be more so when I can tell you about them in person. As for the sweater, I just thought that being made by a native, and the design of the knit so different, that you would like it. It just needs cleaning after handling so much. Yes, I did want you to give the bottle openers away, but I hope you give them to some one close to us. But do as you please with them honey. So you can't figure out what that waterproof thing was? That should be simple honey. Just put your head through the hole in it. Then snap the sides up shut, then put your hands through the top of the sides and you have a poncho. See? That writing you see in back of the rosettes of the grass skirt is probably French. That skirt came from Tonga Tabu. I never was there but the boys that were before I came aboard said the girls were pretty and that they have a Queen of the whole island. Now I will explain the ring. It is a Tiki (TEE KEE). Every native wears one, either around the neck or arm or finger. Without it they will not go to battle or on dangerous missions, like hunting, etc. It is supposed to give them strength, courage and luck. And they are made of all different materials like rosewood, shells, silver, gold, etc.
>
> And honey it's past Dec. 23rd and I am sorry to say nothing doing yet so please don't be impatient and bear

with me. It will be awhile yet before anyone gets transferred. I can't even say what the chances will be for me when it does come, that's how quiet things are, as far as that is concerned."

At 0611 on 30 December *Serpens* got underway from Wellington and arrived back in Auckland on New Year's Eve, 1944. Before arriving in Auckland on New Year's Eve, MoMM1c Riccardi writes his wife: "I wish the *Serpens* would say put, but after all there is a war on. We are underway right now. My boys and I just finished working. It is 9 o'clock. After I cleaned up and took a bath I am up on my bunk, writing to you darling. I sure had a busy day. Tomorrow will be another, trying to put the boats in to running condition. The time certainly goes when you're busy. So honey, I'll write you soon next year."

The explosion of *Serpens* on 29 January 1945 destroyed her January 1945 War Diary so ship movements could only be culled from other sources. We do know the *Serpens* completed a full reload of provisions at Auckland and departed on 6 or 7 January and returned to the Solomons on 15 January 1945.

On 4 January 1945, still in Auckland and not having received any letters from anyone, MoMM1c Riccardi writes to his wife about the ship's band: "Some time ago I was assigned to go to town and buy some string instruments. So I bought a tenor banjo and a fiddle. Some of the boys bought their own, so now we have the banjo, fiddle, two guitars and two mandolins, an accordian and piano. In awhile, getting together, we will have some sort of an orchestra. I hope, in good time, I'll have their picture taken and send it to you. At least we will have some other amusement or entertainment that I think the boys will enjoy, especially when we lay around the islands where it is so quiet at anchor." Riccardi also talks about the boats he is responsible for: "Everything is running smooth again for a change. After having three of my boats broke down at a serious time, it sure had me going for awhile. Getting into tough spots like that doesn't do one much good, but we came through in pretty good shape, considering what we have to work with."

On January 6, still in Auckland, Riccardi writes: "My precious wife, I was hoping I would receive a letter from you before I wrote this one but no soap. But I must write something because if I am not mistaken this will be the last for a while. I should have an awful lot of mail when I do get in."

While at sea, MoMM1c Riccardi writes a letter that begins on 10 January 1945 and ends on 14 January. The envelope is postmarked on the morning of 16 January. In the letter he writes:

"My darling wife, I know that you have waited a long time for this letter, although I have written it in plenty of time for you to receive it. It was just impossible to send it off to you. The time between the last letter and this one is the time I have been under way. So you see, add another week to that and you will know how long I have been without a letter from you. But no one is to blame honey, we have to expect these circumstances.

I guess we will lose quite a few of the boys at our next stop. I don't know who or how many, but I guess most of the old ones will get off. It's been some time since the last transfer. Boy wouldn't it be something if I was one of them. If I don't honey it won't be long after that because I have most of my time in. So keep plugging with me, my peach, and it won't be long I'll be on my way to you.

> Here I am back to finish this letter. Of all the trips I have made this is the best so far. I could just barely feel the ship move. But we still have a few days to go yet and it can change. But I doubt it. I can hardly wait to get there because it means mail. And from you honey, it's been so long."

With *Serpens* back in the Solomon Islands, we hear again from MoMM1c Riccardi as he writes to his wife on 16 January:

> "My adorable wife, we finally dropped the hook, that sure was a long one. What a day I just put in. Our ship got 69 bags of mail, so you can imagine, mail was sorted pretty late last night. I was opening packages and reading letters until 1:30 last night. I was so glad to get your letters honey, I read all of them last night. 23 letters from you alone. In all your letters your main question is, How long will it be, or when? So I am going to try to tell you all I know, of which isn't definite, so you will have to try to understand the way I do. We expected a lot of reliefs but only 7 came aboard, and only 5 are going home. Some of the boys that have 19 months on here are so mad and disgusted and Babcock is one of them. It really is something to be that way about, so you see honey, I haven't got that much time in. So all I can do is hope and pray for a possibility of getting off before my time is up. And when (in case I don't make it) my time is up then a certain somebody is going to have me in the office every day until I do.
>
> It seems as though they are not sending as many men here from the States like they used to. They should go to the Coast Guard garage downtown in Cleveland and clean out about 150 Motor Machinist's Mates that are there with a pretty snappy life, and send them out here.

As I said before, I think there is a chance for me to get off before then, but I am just guessing or hoping that a rated Motor Machinist's Mate comes in one of the relief gangs. I hope honey that this will help you understand the situation and have a little more patience.

I received the stationery, lighter, cigarette case, fruit cake, joke books, dress uniform and all your lovely cards. I am hoping I can get another letter to you before we move again, but the next move will be short, I hope. Things are different now, we will move more often now. I'd like to see one move in particular and that's heading to Frisco. You can never tell though. Nobody knows. Strange things do happen.

One of the boys is going to be stationed in Cleveland. I am going to see him tomorrow and tell him to get in touch with you, then you can get all the information first-hand. I'll let you know more about it.

Honey, here is some good news for our future. Babcock's father just wrote and said he found my records finally and said I am in. He said he has a position for me as superintendent, I forgot of what, anyway, at a truck plant in Czechoslovakia, at around 9 thousand dollars a year. I wonder if you would like it there? But a couple of years there would sure get us started."

The "Babcock" who Riccardi is referring to is GM3c Woodward Solomon Babcock, USCGR. GM3c Babcock's father was Irving B. Babcock. As a bit of background, on 1 September 1925 the Yellow Cab Manufacturing Company merged with General Motors Truck Corporation (GMT Corp.) to form Yellow Truck & Coach Manufacturing Company (YT&CMC). GM acquired a controlling interest of 57% in that new company and made it an affiliated subsidiary of GM. Ten years later, on 1 September 1935, Mr. Babcock became

President and General Manager of YT&CMC. He started by revising the 1936 GMC Truck program. He wanted trucks to look as up-to-date as passenger cars with new colors and features. Most importantly, he decided to have GMC enter the half-ton light truck market, competing with Chevrolet, Ford and Dodge. On 1 September 1943 Mr. Babcock became General Manager of GMC T&C and then was elected Vice President of GM. On 1 February 1945, upon hearing of the death of his son, Mr. Babcock resigned. He died on 6 February 1964 of a heart attack at his home in Bloomfield Hills, IL. He was 72 years old.

When being transferred back to the States, a lot of military personnel volunteered to go around and meet with wives and girlfriends of their other crewmembers to let them know what was going on that was otherwise censored in the mail. On 18 January MoMM1c Riccardi writes to his wife:

> "I must first tell you that I did talk to the fellow that left for the States and to be stationed home near you. He is an awful shy or quiet fellow. I don't know him very well, he is a quartermaster 2nd class. I didn't see him much or have any contacts with him on board. His name is John Adsit. He don't know anyone in Cleveland and was glad to know he could get in touch with you, because he intends to bring his wife with him, so see if you can make him some sort of connections. I think he will be looking for a place to live. Some of the things you want to know from me, that I couldn't tell you, you can ask him.
>
> And about that position I wrote about yesterday. The information I got was brief, but positive inasfar as being 'in' is concerned. I am pretty sure that the location can be changed or will be changed to another country, maybe one more suitable to both of us. It will be contracted as to salary and time and position. He

said close to 9 thousand dollars a year for about three or four years. I sure would like to take it, it will mean so much. And once I get in something like that I can keep going after we get back, and settle down to a good position in the States, and really have what we want – a beautiful home, beautiful clothes and all that goes with it."

The 'John Adsit" that MoMM1c Riccardi referred to in his letter was Quartermaster Second Class John W. Adsit who reported on board *Serpens* on 21 April 1943.

On 20 January Riccardi writes that he watched the ship's movie - Bing Crosby in "Going My Way" – and that he "almost dropped tears in the last part. It was very good." He went on to mention the heat: "It seems to me it's getting hotter every time we come back here. I have to keep wiping my hands while writing."

In a typical letter being written by a single young man to his friend back home in Detroit, Michigan, *Serpens'* Steward's Mate Third Class (StdM3c) Frederick Edward Adolph Qualmann writes in a letter postmarked 21 January 1945 to Richard Muzinski: "Dear Richard, Well, how's the boy? Good I hope. I am going pretty good myself. How's the old gang coming along? Morris still go around with Jean? If you see either of them tell them I said hello for me. Do you still play the drums? I hope so because you were pretty good at it. Sorry I didn't write sooner but we were at a liberty port the month of December. And I had a five day leave. And I had liberty two out of three days. And lots of drinks and girls. So I had a pretty good time. Well Kid that's all for tonight. Please answer soon. Your old pal Fred."

On 22 January MoMM2c Riccardi mentions the heat again to his wife: "It is summertime here as you can imagine. What terrific heat we are having. Doc gives me hell because I don't take enough salt tablets, but I catch up and am OK."

Also on 22 January, at 1817 local time, the War Diary for USS *Tutuila* (ARG-4), moored in Purvis Bay, Tulagi (just north of Lunga Bay, Guadalcanal) reports: "The Commander, Naval Base, Tulagi, ordered the net guarding Purvis Bay closed on receipt of warning that a possible enemy submarine was sighted in waters south of Songonangona Island."

On 24 January Riccardi writes his wife: "A person would think that after 15 months one would sort of get used to the fact [of being apart], but it isn't true with me. Because now more than ever I keep saying, even out loud, 'I want to go home' and 'I want my wife.' I just can't get used to living this way and never will. I often think of the complete difference in the way I am living compared to living your own life, and again I am hoping it won't have any affect on my personality whereas it will have an affect on me going back to normal living again. And never again have anyone around to even suggest things to me of what to do. I have had my fill of that so I pity anyone trying to order me around. I am going to try to get another letter to you before another delay because this trip is going to really be different. I guess you know what I mean, but don't worry honey, I'll be alright."

On 25 January MoMM1c Riccardi writes his 88th and final letter to his wife since being stationed aboard *Serpens*. The letter is postmarked 27 January 1945. In its entirety, it reads:

"Hello darling, I did receive another of your swell letters and I am more than satisfied because, again, you tell me how much you enjoy and like your typewriter. I really was in doubt when I ordered it as to whether you would like it so I guess you know how happy it makes me. It must be awful not being able to get the right food when you want it, and the cigarettes being so scarce. I wish I could help you honey. As for so much snow, you really are getting more now than there ever was in many a year. Keep yourself warm honey and take care of yourself.

Yes we have a radio speaker in the mess hall and recreation room but I don't get much time to sit and listen to it. It's too warm inside anyhow. I have heard the song "I Walk Alone." I don't know the words but I play the melody on the banjo. The other songs I never heard I don't think.

Yes honey you are absolutely right about us being sweethearts. I want us to be sweethearts always. I know we will be happy that way and it is so nice to look at it that way. To me darling you are even more than a sweetheart. You're my ideal in every respect, no matter what happens, nothing could change it, because my love for you is so deep in my heart. To lose your love would be to tear my heart out. Believe me honey, it's true. And I agree with you again, about living just as man and wife. In other words, making it a routine and doing things not because you feel you have to, because that way you don't really enjoy doing things.

You say "Why don't you write a book?" I have thought of that often, from reading your letters, and I think it a very good idea honey. Why don't you try it honey? Your thoughts are beautiful and I know your heart is in them. So honey here is your title 'True Love."

You say "Do I mind your long letters?" Honey I could read them forever, so please keep it up. The longer the better. That way you tell me what is in your heart and I understand every little thing. I used to say so very often that I wish I could write letters like you do and make my heart talk the way you do, that's what I tried to tell you.

I am afraid I cannot write lying on my stomach. I just put my pillow up against the bulkhead and rest my back on it, stretching my legs out with a light over my right shoulder, and your letters scattered all over the sack and your picture on the wall to my right. I keep looking at it while writing. See? I am afraid I haven't the will power to read one page of your letters a day. If I start to read one I finish it, no matter what. Because when I read your letters I absorb every word and it just carries me away with you, just like a dream. If it's a blue letter, I am blue. If it's a happy one, I am happy, so you see what you are doing to me honey?

So you don't know what kind of boats they are? Well, a couple of them are landing boats and a couple are the old type, personnel, double-end round bottom Navy boats and a headache, see?

No, I didn't wish I was anywhere getting pie-eyed on New Year's Eve. I just wish I were with you. The rest would take care of itself. I guess you know what I mean. So I didn't mind, as long as I had to be away from you. To me it was just another day.

I received a Vee Mail from Sophie today. Everything is ok at home but that Mickey is taking overseas training. That's not so good is it? I sure would like to be with him and see him before he goes, so I hope and pray he won't leave soon. I'll bet mother is something awful, he is the baby of the family. I guess you know that though. Well my sweet little peach, my next letter will be a few days longer in getting to you but not too long. So don't worry about me, I am feeling fine. Except for the heat and missing you. I love you my lovely sweetheart as much as ever because I don't think I could love any more. You have every bit of it. Hugo"

On 27 January 1945, S1c Ralph Dana Kiley, USCGR, wrote to his mother saying that "he was well and everything was quiet" from his post on the USS *Serpens* in the South Pacific near Guadalcanal. Two days later Kiley, Qualmann, Breen, Riccardi and some 250 other men would instantly die in the explosion which disintegrated USS *Serpens* and cut short the dreams of those aboard her.

29 January 1945

USS Serpens (AK-97) exploding in Lunga Bay, Guadalcanal, British Solomon Islands, on 29 January 1945, as depicted by artist and retired Coast Guardsman Dick Velesque. His work can be found at http://dick514.tripod.com/index.html.

Late in the evening on 29 January 1945, *Serpens* was still anchored off Lunga Beach, Guadalcanal, a port she knew well by this time. The commanding officer - Lieutenant

Commander Peery Lamar Stinson - along with one other officer and six enlisted men, had gone ashore. As standard operating procedure the loading continued late into the evening. This practice was to allow the men to work at night, away from the heat of the daytime sun while still keeping to a war footing schedule. This also left a well-lit target against the backdrop of a darkened town. The remaining 198 members of *Serpens* crew and 57 members of an Army stevedore unit were on board the ship loading such goods as ammunition, depth charges and general cargo supplies into her holds as she had done many times before. It was during this time that USS *Serpens* was suddenly ripped apart by two explosions.

The two explosions were nearly simultaneous. The smaller initial explosion was witnessed and reported by many; the second explosion atomized most of the ship and crew and probably took 1/15th of a second (faster than the blink of an eye) to erupt. Only two sailors aboard survived the incident - S1c Kelsie K. Kemp and S2c George S. Kennedy - escaping from the Bosun's hole in the remaining bow section. The force of the second explosion was so great that it supposedly killed an Army soldier situated on the beach although while repeated in many articles has not been independently verified by the authors. After the explosion, only the bow of the ship was visible. The rest of the vessel had completely disintegrated and the bow sank soon afterward.

What exploded was the majority of the 3,399 aerial depth charges that had been placed three to a pallet and loaded inside Holds No. 4 and 5. Each depth charge weighed 350 pounds and each carried 252 pounds of the explosive material called Torpex (short for 'torpedo explosive' and known to be 50% more powerful than TNT). All but a few detonated. Had 3,300 exploded, the amount of Torpex would have been 831,600 pounds, or roughly the equivalent of 1,247,400 pounds of TNT (623.7 tons). To put that in perspective, the yield of a current-day Tomahawk cruise missile is equivalent to 500 kg (roughly 1,100 pounds) of TNT, or approximately 0.5 tons. *Serpens* would have suffered the equivalent of being hit by some 1,250 Tomahawk cruise missiles all having struck the ship at the same time.

Motor Machinist's Mate Third Class Robert Allen Easterday, USCGR, born 21 September 1921 in Columbus, Ohio, was one of the casualties of the Serpens explosion. Photo courtesy www.ancestry.com.

Eyewitness reports stated hearing shells exploding and the sky filled with tracers. Parts of the ship landed in waters throughout the harbor and on shore, nearly a mile away. Boats searched for any survivors besides Kemp and Kennedy but found only debris, body parts and dead fish. Fire and oil covered the water, an oily mist hung in the air, and all were horrified at the shock and sight of the bow of the *Serpens* slowly sinking.

In the Fall 2018 issue of The Quarterdeck Log (Volume 33, Number 3), the official publication of the Coast Guard Combat Veterans Association, author William H. Theisen writes in his article entitled "USS *Serpens*: The Coast Guard's Greatest Loss":

The night of 29 January 1943 was a peaceful one. USS *Serpens* lay at anchor about a mile offshore in 19 fathoms with a smooth sea, a light easterly breeze, clear sky and bright moon and a steady easterly current. In other words, a perfect night for an enemy submariner looking for a target. Seventy-five enlisted personnel had just returned to the ship after enjoying some well-earned liberty ashore at Guadalcanal's base. A short time later, ten officers returned from a party aboard another Coast Guard-manned attack cargo ship (AKA). The commanding officer, Lieutenant Commander Peery L. Stinson, USCG, was ashore along with eight(sic) others from USS *Serpens*. [Note: 8 total, but 7 others]

At 2318 hours, two explosions were heard, the first one dull sounding, like a "thud", followed by a bright flash and very loud blast a second later, loud enough to be heard 70 miles away. The explosion disintegrated everything aft of Hold 2 of USS *Serpens*, instantly killing everyone aboard and those on the loading barge, save two Coast Guardsmen who were asleep in the forward Bos'n Locker. George Kennedy and Kelsie Kemp made their way out of the bow which remained afloat for a short period of time. Kennedy and Kemp were quick thinking enough to grab battle lanterns during their escape which they used to signal rescuers as they clung to the floating bow.

Thirty minutes after the sinking of USS *Serpens*, a Japanese submarine was located three and one-half miles away. Navy crews dropped depth charges for three hours with undetermined results. Tokyo Radio reported the explosion at Guadalcanal before any communication had gone out over official U.S. Government channels. But what really happened to USS *Serpens*?

A report was made by Colonel T. L. Dunn from information gathered from LCDR Stinson and submitted to the Field Inquiry Hearing at Guadalcanal. In it Dunn states, "It is believed that the original blast was caused by enemy action, probably by an enemy submarine, since Tokyo radio boasted of the explosion before they possibly could have learned about it from us."

What made *Serpens'* ammunition cargo so dangerous? Author John U. Bacon, in his 2017 book entitled The Great Halifax Explosion, talks about "high explosives."

"All explosives require two components: a fuel and an 'oxidizer,' usually oxygen. How destructive an explosive is depends largely on how quickly those two combine. With 'low explosives,' like propane, gasoline and gunpowder, it's necessary to add oxygen to ignite them and keep them burning. If a fire runs out of oxygen, it dies. Another factor is speed. The rate of the chemical reaction, or decomposition, of low explosives is less than the speed of sound, or 767 miles per hour. In contrast, a 'high explosive' combines the fuel and the oxidant in a single molecule, making each one a self-contained bomb, with everything it needs to create the explosion. To ignite, a high explosive usually requires only extreme heat or a solid bump. Once started, the dominoes fall very quickly, ripping through the explosive material faster than the speed of sound. When detonated, a high explosive produces a flash of light, a sonic boom, incredible heat from the rapid chemical decomposition, and immense pressure caused by the instantaneous production of gas and the expansion of hot air, creating the kind of airwave [now] associated with nuclear weapons. A high explosive releases these forces in spectacular fashion and that is what makes them so dangerous."

And that is what those in and around Lunga Beach witnessed:

From the War Diary of USS *Mintaka* (AK-94)

25 January 1945 (Zone -11)

0512 Departed Espiritu Santos Island having loaded cargo and embarked 6 troop officers and 25 enlisted troops. Enroute to Guadalcanal Island in accordance with orders from Port Director, without surface escort. Speed 11.5 knots, 68 rpm.

27 January 1945 (Zone -11)

1350 Arrived Guadalcanal Island. Disembarked 6 troop officers and 25 enlisted troops. Commenced discharging cargo.

29 January 1945 (Zone -11)

2325 U.S.S. *Serpens* destroyed by explosion. All ships in area ordered underway by C.T.U. SOSOLS.

While the War Diary of USS *Mintaka* (AK-94) was sparse about the event which unfolded before them, a letter written by Mrs. Mary Elsasser [related to Seaman First Class Sylvan Bernard "Bill" Elsasser, Jr., USCGR, who was lost aboard

Serpens] of South Gate, CA, after the war provided some additional details. She wrote:

"John Millhorn, a signalman of the AK-94 which was anchored that day near the *Serpens*, came to see me recently. He told me that the AKA-94, his ship, traveled always in convoy with the AK-95, -96 and the *Serpens* (97). They picked up most of their cargo at Espiritu Santo, New Hebrides, and had been in most of the islands that came under heavy attack, to unload their cargo. That dear, lovable Captain Johnson, who had been skipper on the *Serpens* before, had then command of AKA-94. He said there was no finer man in this world than Captain Johnson, and when he heard the *Serpens* was in the harbor, he asked John Millhorn to signal an invitation to the crew of the *Serpens* – all of whom Captain Johnson always referred to as "my boys", to come over to their ship and have dinner that night and see the picture that was being shown. John said he knew practically all the boys on the *Serpens* because they had been in so many ports together. John told me that Bill (her son) was looking wonderfully well and that he was happy and in high spirits over the wonderful leave the crew had had in Wellington such a short time before. He said that about 10 p.m. the *Serpens* crew went back to their ship. John was at his post when that terrific explosion occurred. He saw the *Serpens* go up in one terrific flash. For 3 hours afterward it literally rained oil in the whole vicinity. DEFINITELY it was torpedoed. By what they called a miniature Japanese sub. John had been in combat long enough (3 years) to be able to differentiate between an explosion caused by an accident and that caused by a direct hit. Had it been caused by accident he said it would not have blown up as it did. Only part of the ship would have been damaged, as they were trained for such emergencies. Only a direct hit could have sent it up as suddenly and as completely.

Nothing was left of any of the crew by which anyone could be identified. One Army man was identified by his shoes, which floated to shore. He said no one could have possibly had a split second of comprehension. They never knew.

My oldest son, just released from the Navy, has an officer friend who phoned us a few days ago. He had just returned to this country in company with several officers who were on ships at Guadalcanal on January 29th. They all said that no one doubted that it was a Jap submarine attack. He said that destroyers had searched for the submarine immediately, and thought they had destroyed it.

One observer said "the ship simply disappeared into the air." She did not sink. She vanished in the air. No one on board could have had a second's consciousness of what was happening. You can understand why no survivors, except Kennedy and Kemp, have been heard from.

Our men never told us the dangers they were often in. They were operating in waters under continuous Japanese attack. My son wrote us once of 9 successive nights of Jap air raids. The ship lay quiet and dark so as not to disclose its position in the harbor by firing. A fire broke out once. Carrying munitions was a most dangerous work. Our men knew they had no hope, if hit. You cannot be too proud of what they did. It is very surprising that no official recognition, such as Purple Heart, citations, etc., and even a Congressional Medal of Honor, which is well-deserved, has come. Surely it is just a mistake or error that something has not come. Perhaps you will want to write your Congressman and Senator, asking about it."

From the War Diary of USS *Zaurak* (AK-117)

26 January 1945:

0109 Underway for Guadalcanal Island in obedience to orders of Port Director, Russell Islands, of 25 January 1945.

0715 Anchored in berth No. 3, Kukum Beach, Guadalcanal Island of the Solomon Islands.

1025 Disembarked 37 U.S. Navy and 1 U.S. Marine Corps enlisted personnel.

27 January 1945:

Anchored as before.

28 January 1945:

Anchored as before.

29 January 1945:

Anchored as before.

1500 Embarked 9 U.S. Army enlisted personnel and 1 officer

2330 Terrific explosion in the vicinity of Lunga Point. Impossible to ascertain as to whether it was on the beach or a ship at anchor. The following is quoted from a statement made by Ensign Earl A. Clark, an officer on board this ship, who witnessed the explosion of the U.S.S. Mt. Hood at Manus island of the Admiralty Islands: "Similarity between this explosion and the explosion of the Mt. Hood in Larengen Bay, Manus Island, was distinct. Both explosions were concentrated in a small area, short in duration, and left no visible small fires in the surrounding area. The smoke fumes were identical." The explosion was subsequently reported as the U.S.S. *Serpens* (AK-97).

30 January 1945:

Anchored as before.

0025   Discontinued loading cargo.

0027   Underway in obedience to orders of Port Director, Guadalcanal, maneuvering off shore as a result of possible enemy submarine contact.

In the "Narrative War History of USS *Zaurak* (AK-117), March 17 1944 to January 30 1946," the unknown author writes: "On the 29th of January, the ship was at Guadalcanal. She had just completed loading ammunition consigned to Munda Bay, New Georgia. The U.S.S. *Serpens* (AK-97) was anchored nearby around a point of land, loading ammunition. At 2330 the U.S.S. *Serpens* was destroyed in a terrific explosion. As the cause of the explosion was not known, it was possible that there had been a submarine attack, the *Zaurak* got underway immediately. Since the *Zaurak* had been scheduled to leave for Munda at midnight, she set her course then, not waiting for her escort, which joined her two hours later."

From the War Diary of USS *Fond Du Lac* (APA-166)

28 January 1945: Completed loading supplies. In morning watch anchored in Berth 14, Segond Channel [Espiritu Santo]. In afternoon received the following ammunition: 2340 rounds 20 MM (AA) HEI. At 1630 underway in obedience of orders from the Port Director, Espiritu Santo, for Guadalcanal. Ship's position at 2000: 15^0-00'-9 S; 167^0-25'-8 E.

29 January 1945: Steaming as before in minus eleven time zone. Ship's position at 0800: 12^0-55'-0 S; 165^0-04'-0 E.

Ship's position at 1200: 12^0-04'-5 S; 164^0-30'-0 E.

Ship's position at 2000: 10^0-35'-5 S; 162^0-58'-5 E.

At 2315 observed two bright flashes off our port bow which were later identified as the explosion of the USS *Serpens* off Guadalcanal, some hundred miles distance.

From Ship's History, USS *Gendreau* (DE-639), submitted 15 November 1945, pages 4-5.

While returning to Port Purvis on the afternoon of 22 January after a day's tactical exercises with two other ships of the division, a report of a submarine sighting in the vicinity of Florida Is. was intercepted followed shortly by orders from ComSoSols to conduct a joint air-surface anti-submarine action in company with the other two ships and a PC. Air cover was provided by 2 RNZAF aircraft and CortDiv 73 in the *GENDREAU* was placed in charge of the operation. The whole lower Solomons area and New Georgia was searched thoroughly for the next two days with negative results and the search was broken off on the 24th.

On the evening of 29 January the ship was anchored off Lunga Point, Guadalcanal when, at 2314, two violent explosions were observed and felt directly astern followed by brilliant flashes and a column of heavy grey smoke several hundred feet high. Numerous pieces of debris, some apparently quite large and heavy, fell into the water in the vicinity of the starboard bow and port quarter. The U.S.S. *Serpens*, a Coast Guard manned AK, had exploded and been completely destroyed with the loss of nearly all hands, 1500-2000 yards astern of this ship. She had just completed taking on a capacity load of ammunition. Although considerable damage was done on the beach and many fragments landed near this ship, *GENDREAU* miraculously suffered neither damage nor casualties. At about this time U.S.S. *SC 1039*, patrolling off Lunga Point, reported a possible submarine contact in the vicinity of Koli Point and this ship [*GENDREAU*] got underway immediately and commenced an anti-submarine sweep of Lengo Channel. In the meantime, a joint air-surface anti-submarine action had been started and one

RNZAF aircraft reported to ComCortDiv 73 at dawn 30 January followed by the *DAMON M. CUMMINGS* (DE-643) about 1000. A search procedure similar to that followed 22-24 January was carried out with negative results and the search was broken off at dawn 1 February. The *SC 1039* had gone aground on Peri Pile Island near Sealark Channel during the night of the 29th-30th and *GENDREAU* stood by the following day until she was refloated by tugs from Guadalcanal and towed into Port Purvis."

From the War Diary, USS *Gendreau* (DE-639), submitted 1 February 1945, covering 1-31 January 1945, pages 6-7.

27 – 28 January 1945

Moored at Port Purvis, Florida, B.S. I.

29 January 1945 – 1 February 1945

Underway at 0628, 29 January in company with U.S.S. *William C. Cole, Paul G. Baker, and Damon M. Cummings*, guide and OTC ComCortDiv 73 in *Gendreau*, in accordance with voice radio dispatch of CTU 11.5.6 of 28 January and conducted tactical maneuvers in vicinity of Savo Island in simulated convoy escort procedure. At 1630 completed exercises and detached *Cole, Baker* and *Cummings* to proceed independently to Port Purvis. At 1635 proceeded to Guadalcanal Island and anchored in Berth 18, Lunga Roads at 1809.

At 2314, 29 January observed and felt two heavy explosions directly astern followed by brilliant flame like flashes and a column of heavy gray smoke several hundred feet high with numerous particles of debris falling in the water in the vicinity of the starboard bow and the port quarter. This proved to be the explosion and total destruction of the U.S.S. *Serpens* moored 2,000 yards astern in Berth 24. The *Serpens* was loaded with a large quantity of ammunition and casualties were later fixed at approximately 250. An immediate inspection of this vessel disclosed no material damage or personnel casualties. Immediately made all preparations for getting underway. At 2157 CTU 11.5.6 ordered all ships in Lunga Roads by CO message to get underway and maneuver off shore until dawn. At about this time U.S.S. *SC-1039* reported a possible submarine contact in the vicinity of Koli Point and this vessel was ordered by CTU 11/5/6 dispatch Number 291350 of January to proceed to her assistance with U.S.S. *PC-588* also in the vicinity. A Joint Air-Surface Anti-Submarine Action in accordance with Guadalcanal Island Command Secret Operation Memorandum Number 17-44 was started immediately. *Gendreau* made one eastward and one westward sweep in waters between Guadalcanal, Florida and Savo Islands throughout the night. The *SC-1039* had, in the meantime, followed her contact into Sealark Channel, dropping one depth charge pattern in the vicinity of the entrance. Shortly after this she went aground on a reef at Peri Pile Island about halfway through Sealark Channel and awaited daylight for assistance in refloating herself.

At dawn, 30 January one RNZAF aircraft reported to the OTC and was assigned a series of sweeps designed to cover the whole lower Solomons and San Cristobal area. During the 30th many floating objects were sighted some of which were sunk by gunfire. One badly damaged 15-man life raft, presumably from the *Serpens*, was picked up between Guadalcanal and Florida Islands. At 0950 U.S.S. *Damon M. Cummings* reported to OTC and was assigned to cover area around Savo Island. Shortly afterwards U.S.S. *SC-1048* reported to OTC and was assigned to stand by *SC-1039*. After searching Eastward through Lengo Channel, entered Sealark Channel and stood by until *SC-1039* was refloated at 1714 by U.S.S. *ATA-123* sent from Guadalcanal by CTU 11.5.6. At 1737 OTC detached *SC-1039*, *SC-1048* and *ATA-123* all of whom returned to Port Purvis.

At 1758 joined *Cummings* in vicinity of Savo Island and continued anti-submarine search until 0540, 1 February covering waters around Florida, Guadalcanal, and Savo

Islands, and New Georgia Sound to a distance of about 90 miles Northwest of Savo Island. RNZAF aircraft continued to give air support.

At 0540, 1 February broke off Joint Action by authority of CTU 11.5.6 voice radio dispatch. Detached *Cummings* to proceed to Port Purvis and *Gendreau* anchored in Lunga Roads at 0716. Conclusions were that no submarine were then present in the vicinity and that *SC-1039's* contact on the night of the 29th was probably false.

Admiral Chester W. Nimitz, Commander in Chief, U.S. Pacific Fleet and Pacific Ocean Areas, published a monthly classified [Secret] report called "Operations in the Pacific Ocean Areas." In his report for January 1945, on page 45, under the sub-section called "B. Anti-Submarine Activity," he writes: "There were no reported sinkings of United States naval or merchant ships in the Pacific Ocean Area during January, although the USS *Serpens* (AK-97) was sunk on 29 January off Lunga Beach, Guadalcanal, due possibly to an enemy submarine attack. An anti-submarine search was instituted immediately and SC 1039 obtained a sound contact between Lunga and Koli, dropping depth charges without results. The search was abandoned on 1 February without further contacts."

The War Diary of the Commander South Pacific Area and South Pacific Force for 1-31 January 1945, had a bit more detail in it: "At 2318 29 January USS *Serpens*, at anchor and loading depth charges off Lunga Beach, Guadalcanal, exploded and sunk. Commanding General Guadalcanal reported possible submarine contact coincident with explosion obtained. Guadalcanal Island Command initiated JASA [Joint Air-Surface Action] 17. GENDREAU (DE-639), DAMON M. CUMMINGS (DE-643), SC 1039, PC 588 were dispatched to search possible submarine. JASA 17 supplemented by 6 ships Guadalcanal screen. SC 1039 obtained sound contact between Lunga and Koli at 2340L 29 January and dropped depth charges without result. SC 1039 went aground at 1039L 30 January. At dawn 1 February JASA 17 was terminated with results negative. Among the survivors of the USS *Serpens* were two officers including the Commanding Officer and 8 enlisted men, two of whom received minor injuries. The remainder of the ship's complement, 13 officers and 193 enlisted men are believed lost. Also missing are 1 Army Officer and 56 enlisted men who were aboard at the time of the explosion. Injuries were also received by 6 enlisted men aboard the USS YP 514. The latter vessel received extreme damage to her superstructure. Minor damage above the water line was inflicted upon Q 400, PC 588, YMS 281, SC 1266 and SC 1039 but with no personnel casualties. A court of inquiry is now investigating the exploding and sinking of the USS *Serpens*."

The War Diary for January 1945 from the Commander Naval Bases, South Solomons Sub-Area (comprising Guadalcanal, Tulagi and Russell Islands), dated 1 March 1945, states the following summary on page 1: "A Court of Inquiry was convened 30 January to investigate the explosion which blew up and sank the U.S.S. *Serpens* (AK-97) at 2317, 29 January 1945, while at anchor off Lunga Beach."

Attached to the 1 March 1945 War Diary Report was the 11 February 1945 War Diary Report from Commander Naval Base, Guadalcanal, which stated: "At 2317 January 29th the U.S.S. *Serpens* (AK-97) blew up and sank immediately at anchor off Lunga Beach while loading airplane depth charges. A Court of Inquiry was convened 30 January to inquire into the explosion. To date the findings have not been published."

From the War Diary, *YP-514*, 1-31 January 1945, pages 2-4:

26-29 January 1945

"Shifted anchorage at 1843 on 26 January, 150 yards inboard of Berth 22. [On 29 January] At 2325, or thereabouts, the U.S.S. *Serpens* (AK-97), anchored 600 yards distant in Berth 24 and loading ammunition, exploded and sank almost immediately, severely damaging the U.S.S. *YP-514* and injuring personnel on board. Three men were on watch – gangway, engineroom and bridge, first two of which were injured beyond ability to give information, and the third also unable to give information contributing to the cause of the explosion due to momentary shock. All remaining ship's company were in their bunks. Damage to this vessel believed to be above water line and to hull and fittings resulting from concussion, large pieces of flying steel, which passed into the ship at vertical and oblique angles, piercing its wooden structures at numerous points. No fires were started and no ammunition on the ship was set off. One of the largest pieces was identified as a connecting rod approximately five feet long and four inches in diameter which lodged in the overhead of ship's magazine. Other heavy pieces demolished the bow, crow's nest and fore yard, broke all radio antennae, demolished large sections of rails, above deck frames, ruptured ready boxes and bent gun shields, blowing off and damaging hatch covers, doors, breaking glass, shorting out electrical circuits and rupturing numerous topside waterlines. Ammonia refrigeration lines remained intact. Large and heavy metal pieces hurtled through decks and overheads into compartments where officers and men were asleep, in four instances landing in bunks from which men had been thrown by explosion. No deaths occurred to members of ship's company. Muster was held at about 2335 and all hands accounted for. Casualties beyond treatment on board, or where any doubt existed as to extent, were dispatched ashore in boats which came alongside to assist immediately following explosion. Nine men were sent ashore, 3 of which returned to ship after treatment for minor injuries. Two of the remaining six in Fleet Hospital #108 were considered in extremely critical condition. A mangled torso beyond identification was removed from bridge deck and sent ashore. Numerous small bits of dismembered bodies were thrown overboard. The following personnel casualties occurred:

Abbott, W. G., S1/C, 721-71-26, wrenched back – returned to duty.

Appel, J. E., Cox, lacerations, feet – returned to duty (871-20-39).

Apperson, B. R., S1/C, 873-82-16, lacerations and bruised forearm – returned to duty.

Boy, H. L., BM2/C, 641-51-97, shock – returned to duty after one night of treatment at N.A.B. Dispensary.

Craven, Roy J., Sea2/C, 314-02-00, lacerations scalp – returned to duty.

Dishong, H. B., Sea1/C, 941-30-49, lacerations feet – returned to duty.

Gibbs, W. E., Sea2/C, 575-53-33, lacerations multiple – returned to duty.

Haarsma, H. J., MoMM3/C, 871-83-67, possible fractured skull, shock, Fleet Hospital #108.

Moorer, K. L., GM1/C, 274-17-55, multiple lacerations and bruises, bruised kidney – ship's binnacle list.

Music, L. S., Sea2/C, 945-45-44, concussion of lungs and shock – Fleet Hospital #108.

Rucki, S. F., (BM), 311-20-16, superficial burns, lacerated feet.

Serra, Vito, Sea2/C, 951-36-16, shock, Fleet Hospital #108.

Threlkeld, Budge, 618-12-78, multiple lacerations – returned to duty.

Wright, W. H., Ensign, 372999, superficial burns.

> Paine, G. P., Lieut., 201261, laceration, thigh – wound closed with two sutures at Fleet Hospital #108.
>
> 30 January 1945
>
> At 0130 got underway and moored to East Pier, Kukum Docks at 0230. At 0814 the ATA 123 took this vessel in tow and moored her to buoy in Govana Inlet, Florida Island, at 1228.
>
> 31 January 1945
>
> At 0953 got underway under own power and moored to Carter City Pier, Florida Island, for repairs to be effected by *LCRU 1*.

According to the Fleet Marine Force Reference Publication (FMFRP) 12-12 entitled "The History of the Medical Department of the United States Navy in World War II," Mobile Hospital No. 8 arrived in Guadalcanal in April 1943. It was commissioned August 1943 and designated as Fleet Hospital No. 108 in 1944. By December 1944 this hospital had treated 39,395 patients. During 1943, 2,208 patients were admitted for some form of psychoneurosis.

Alex Haley, later to become famous for his book *Roots*, was a Coastguardsman aboard USS *Murzim* (AK-95) during World War II. *Murzim*, a sister ship of *Serpens*, was reported by Haley to have also been at Lunga Point that fateful day. "Our principal cargo was 500-pound bombs destined for our South Pacific air bases. From those air bases, Allied aircraft would drop our cargo onto strategic Japanese targets about the area. When not delivering bombs, we transported shiploads of U.S. Marines and Army personnel to the fighting fronts. My shipmates and I realized how close death was one day as our bomb-laden ship sailed from Guadalcanal. We heard a strange giant whooshing blast, which the radio reported had been our sister ship, the *Serpens* (AK-97).

Somehow her duplicate cargo of bombs had detonated, and of her crew of about 250, only 10—eight of whom had been ashore—survived."

However, USS *Murzim* was at least some 600 miles away from Guadalcanal at the time of the explosion, according to her own war diary:

January 26 1945: Anchored in San Pedro Bay, Leyte, P.I. Discharged demolition gear.
January 27 1945: Departed Leyte, P.I. to Manus.
January 28 1945: Underway Leyte, P.I. to Manus.
January 29 1945: Underway Leyte, P.I. to Manus.
January 30 1945: Underway Leyte, P.I. to Manus. Detached from convoy and proceeded in company with USS *STAFFORD* and USS *APACHE*. Orders of Div. DE-76.
January 31 1945: Underway Leyte, P.I. to Manus.
February 1 1945: Underway Leyte, P.I. to Manus, Admiralty Islands
February 2 1945: Underway Leyte, P.I. to Manus. No events.
February 3 1945: Underway Leyte, P.I. to Manus. Transferred 5000 gallons of water to USS *STAFFORD* (DE-411) while underway.
February 4 1945: Underway Leyte, P.I. to Manus. 0858-Anchored in Seeadler Harbor, Manus.

The last time USS *Murzim* was in Guadalcanal was 24 November 1943, when she sailed from there to Auckland. Mr. Haley's account of sailing from Guadalcanal and hearing "a giant whooshing blast" was pure fiction.

From the War Diary, *APc-30*, 1-31 January 1945, submitted 2 February 1945:

1 January – 31 January

On guard mail run between Lyons Pt., Covana Inlet, Florida Is., B.S.I. and Kukum Dock, Guadalcanal Is., B.S.I. This mail run consists in stopping at Halavo Seaplane Base, Florida Is., B.S.I. and at Sturgis Dock, Tulagi Harbor, Florida

Is., B.S.I., carrying passengers, officer messenger mail, guard mail and ordinary mail.

On 29 January at 2325, a tremendous double explosion occurred in the vicinity of Lunga Pt., Guadalcanal Is. At the time the U.S.S. *APc-30* was moored starboard side to Kukum Dock, Guadalcanal Is., and the explosion caused the ship to vibrate in the water. At first, the commanding officer believed that the explosion was caused by an ammunition dump on Guadalcanal, but immediately after the explosion, small boats in the vicinity of Kukum Dock got underway in the direction of Lunga Pt., and it was then known that the explosion must have occurred on a ship anchored off Lunga Pt.

At 2347, the Duty Officer, Kukum Dock, requested that the U.S.S. *APc-30* get underway for Lunga Pt. to search for survivors of the U.S.S. AK97 which sank off Lunga Pt. and all preparations for getting underway were made.

At 250 got underway from Kukum Dock for Lunga Pt. with running lights and masthead light. All hands reported topside for lookout duty. All battle lanterns and search lights were manned and ready.

At 0020 maneuvering off Lunga Pt. in search of survivors. Received word by visual of submarine contact. Condition Red declared. Secured all navigational lights and darkened ship.

During the search for survivors, numerous life jackets were seen, but no survivors. Two empty 16-man life rafts were found and taken on board.

At 0605, having found no survivors, returned to Kukum Dock to resume regular guard mail duties.

From the War Diary, *APc-39*, 29 January 1945, page 5:

29 January 1945

1505 Arrived off Lunga Point, Guadalcanal, anchored in
        berth (20)

2320 U.S.S. AK 97 exploded off starboard quarter, distance about 1000 yards.

2325 Inspected ship, no damage to equipment or personnel. Only damage was to weather decks, amounting to three (3) holes.

30 January 1945

0025 In pursuant to all ships signal from (H1), Lunga Point, Guadalcanal, underway from Lunga Point, Guadalcanal, en route to maneuver off shore until dawn.

From the War Diary, USS *Effingham* (APA-165) for 1 November 1944 to 28 February 1945:

January 28 & 29:

At Guadalcanal, discharging cargo. 2320 – Observed U.S.S. *Serpens* then laying at anchor east of Lunga Point to explode. 2332 – Commenced launching boats for possible rescue. 2400 – 26 boats with full medical parties had been dispatched. Made preparations for getting underway.

January 30:

0115 – Underway in compliance with the Commander Naval Base visual dispatch, and maneuvered off Kukum Beach at 16.5 knots until 0720, when all boats were recalled and hoisted. (No survivors found). 0755 – Departed for Russell Islands ... escorted by the U.S.S. PC-588.

From the War Diary, Aircraft South Pacific Force (AirSoPac) for 1 January – 31 January 1945:

29 January 1945

The U.S.S. *Serpens*, partially loaded with miscellaneous aviation cargo (engines, centerline drop tanks) for discharge at Manus was completing its load of 350-pound depth charges (Torpex) while anchored off shore opposite the old Port Director's Headquarters. At approximately 2330, the ship exploded and sank.

From the War Diary, Aircraft South Pacific Force (AirSoPac), United States Pacific Fleet:

It was discovered that one (1) R-1830-92 aircraft engine [from AirSoPac] was lost on the USS *Serpens* (AK-97) [Having been loaded aboard *Serpens* before the explosion}. It has been stricken from the records, according to existing directives.

[Note: the Pratt & Whitney R-1830-92 *Twin Wasp* aircraft engine was typically used in the Consolidated B-24 Liberator, Douglas C-47 Skytrain, Grumman F4F Wildcat and the Consolidated PBY Catalina. Pratt & Whitney records show that 173,618 of such engines were built.]

Bill Hitt, LM, USCGR '42-'46, wrote in the Quarterdeck Log (publication of the Coast Guard Combat Veterans Association), Volume 28, Number 2 (Summer 2013), page 13: "I knew that ship [*Serpens* (AK-97)] well and had several friends in the crew, including one close friend, William H. Harlow. We planned a meeting in the Guadalcanal-Florida Is. for January 30 or 31, 1945. *Serpens* was to be at Lunga Point at that time and we were at Purvis Bay to top off and pick up orders. On pulling into the slot the morning of January 30th, we passed through a vast debris field. Our blinker to the *Serpens* was answered by the Navy Signal Station, informing us of the disaster. *Serpens* was not an ammunition ship, per se, but rather general cargo, Liberty. This could have been her first time carrying explosives. Needless to say, that debris field was the *Serpens*."

Later, the USS *Wateree* (ATA-174) would salvage some of *Serpens'* cargo from the bottom of the bay. *Wateree* was laid down on 5 October 1943 at Orange, TX, by the Levingston Shipbuilding Co. as the unnamed rescue tug ATR-101; launched on 18 November 1943; redesignated an auxiliary ocean tug, ATA-174, and commissioned on 20 July 1944, LT A. J. Vetro in command. On 9 January 1945 she departed Kwajalein Atoll, Marshall Islands, for Manus, Admiralty Islands. On 22 January 1945, she stood out to sea from Manus and set a course for Noumea, New Caledonia. En route, however, she received orders diverting her to Guadalcanal. The tug arrived at her new destination on 26 January, tying up to the starboard side of USS *Tutuila* (ARG-4) at 1430 for some small repairs. She served in the southern Solomons for almost two months. Early in February, she conducted diving operations on the sunken wreck of *Serpens* (AK-97) during the investigation of her explosion and sinking. In mid-February, she salvaged six bulldozers originally aboard *Serpens* from 110 feet of water off Lunga Point. Later, she pulled two grounded submarine chasers off reefs in Skylark Channel. She concluded her duty at Guadalcanal on 22 March when she took ARD-18 in tow for Hollandia, New Guinea.

From the Ship's History of USS *Las Vegas Victory* (AK-229): "On January 30 [1945] we left Ulithi, en route to Guadalcanal, on a special mission. When we reached Guadalcanal, we learned that an ammunition ship had blown up several days before, and we were as welcome as a plague. After a quick trip across Iron Bottom Sound to Tulagi, where, mission accomplished, we returned to Guadalcanal."

In an oral interview with "Buck" Sergeant (E-4) Daniel T. Mihuta: "My outfit was called the 492nd Port Battalion, and I was in a group called 231st Port Company. Basically, we were trained -- being trained – on how to load and unload cargo ships. And I was made -- because I had some schooling that they thought was good, I was made and called a 'super cargo.' I was in charge of weights and measures, how to load a ship, where to put all the cargo so the ship would stay in balance when it went on water. When we got to Guadalcanal, the island was still in battle, considered in battle. Most of the Japanese at that particular time had been chased into the mountains, and many others were pulled out and went up to some further islands up north, but none there. The only combat that we would say was ordered to us is that we were loading one ship called the USS *Serpens*. I closed the ship up at noon [on 29 January 1945], and about 2:00 in the afternoon they said they found some more ammunition that they needed to load in the ship, and they went and did that. At midnight, that ship blew up and 250 fellows were killed."

USS *Serpens* (AK-97) earned one battle star for her World War II service.

An aerial view of Lunga Point, Guadalcanal, during World War II showing the airfield captured by the U.S. Marines early in the campaign and later called Henderson Field in honor of United States Marine Corps Major Lofton Henderson, commanding officer of VMSB-241 who was killed during the Battle of Midway while leading his squadron into action against the Japanese carrier forces, thereby becoming the first Marine aviator to perish during the battle. The airport is today the Honiara International Airport. U.S. Navy photo.

AFTERWARDS

ABOARD USS SERPENS. FRONT ROW: (L to R) -- Dr. Schweigert, USPHS; LTJG Banach; LTJG George C. Auble, USCGR (Died in explosion). SECOND ROW: (L to R) -- unk; LTJG D. Palma; LT Elliott; Warrant Officer Palmer; LTJG Brown. STANDING: (L to R) -- LTJG William C. Kotkas (Lieutenant by loss date, died in explosion), USCG; LTJG James D. Ellison; unk; LTJG Carber; LT John G. Aiken III, USCGR (died in explosion). No date/photo number; photographer unknown. Photo provided courtesy of CAPT James D. Ellison, USCG (Ret.), who served aboard Serpens as a LTJG.

Personal letters written late in January 1945 by the wives, girlfriends, parents and family members, and hometown friends to those aboard *Serpens* were returned to them, the envelopes stamped "No Record of Unit." The finality of the event began to sink in to all the relatives and friends of those lost on 29 January. Silvia Riccardi, wife of MoMM1c Hugo Riccardi, had her last letter to Hugo postmarked on January 23 with a return postmark stamped on it "U.S. Navy, January 31, 1945." It was her 187th and last letter to her husband.

A Court of Inquiry was convened 30 January 1945 by the Commander Naval Bases, South Solomons Sub-Area, to inquire into the explosion. The Court would have interviewed eyewitnesses, collected weather information, and discussed possible scenarios as to *Serpens'* loss. A transcript of the proceedings, including exhibits, Findings and Conclusions, would have been sent to the Secretary of the Navy via the chain of command. Originating from the Court, the *Report on the Loss of USS Serpens* would have had its First Endorsement signed by the Commander Naval Bases, South Solomons Sub-Area, the Second Endorsement would have been signed by Commander Service Squadron, South Pacific Force; Third Endorsement signed by the Commander South Pacific area and South Pacific Force, and Fourth Endorsement by the Commander in Chief, United States Pacific Fleet. Over the ensuing years the Report was packed up and moved to the Federal Records Center in Suitland, MD.

A series of Freedom of Information Act (FOIA) Requests were pursued by co-author Robert Breen to obtain a copy of the Report. One FOIA Request was mailed to the Department of the Navy's Office of the Judge Advocate General (JAG) located at the Washington Navy Yard,

Washington, D.C.; specifically, to the JAG's General Claims and Tort Litigation Division (Code 15). Their response to the FOIA Request, dated 21 October 2015:

> "Code 15 searched its database which showed that a responsive file was maintained at the Federal Records Center in Suitland, Maryland. Code 15 then contacted the Federal Records Center to request the file. Federal Records Center records, however, indicate that the file was checked out to Code 15 in 2003 and never returned. After learning that the file had previously been checked out, Code 15 personnel searched the spaces of Code 15 and Code 11, which serves as the Office of the Judge Advocate General's Admiralty and Maritime Division. Code 15 personnel also searched historical files maintained by the Office of the Judge Advocate General and contacted a former FOIA employee employed at Code 15 in 2003. Neither the searches nor the personnel contact resulted in the location of information pertaining to USS *Serpens*."

The search for a copy of the Report continues. The two-page Summary of Findings usually attached to the end of Court of Inquiry Reports was located by employees of the National Archives and Records Administration (NARA) in College Park, MD. The two pages were discovered in Record Group 38: Records of the Chief of Naval Operations. The Summary of Findings were as follows:

1 On 29 January 1945, the USS *Serpens* (AK-97), an EC-2 Liberty-type vessel, blew up at 2318 local time, while moored at Berth No. 24, Lunga Point, Guadalcanal, British Solomon Islands. See Admiralty Chart HO, chart #1009.

2 The ship was in 19 fathoms in a smooth sea, with a light easterly breeze, clear sky and bright moon, and steady easterly current.

3 There were at the time of the explosion on board or on a barge moored alongside 3,399 bombs, 350# Torpex-loaded depth bombs Mk54. Those on board were all in No. 4 lower hold, stowed 660 bombs in a layer, with 3" lumber dunnage between layers. These bombs were unfuzed but contained two boosters. They were uncrated. Each bomb held 250# Torpex and probably over 800,000# of Torpex exploded.

4 The holds had been sheathed so that there were no projecting nails or other sharp corners with which the bombs could come into contact. There were, in a separate strong room in No. 1 hold, 1026 AN Mk 230 Mod 3 and Mod 4 bomb tail fuzes in boxes.

5 The method of loading the bombs were as follows: 3 of the bombs were placed on a pallet and 2 pallets with their 6 bombs were loaded on an amphibious DUKW [a DUKW, pronounced *duck*, was a 2-and-1/2-ton amphibious vehicle used during the war. The name DUKW comes from General Motors Corporation model nomenclature in which D stood for 'Designed in 1942;' U meant 'Utility;' K meant 'All-wheel drive;' and W stood for 'Dual-tandem rear axles.'). The bombs were transported to the side of the ship and placed, one pallet at a time, into a landing net, hoisted up and placed into a hold and then the individual bombs were rolled across dunnage to their final stowage point.

6 Arrangements were made for loading from both sides of the ship simultaneously, but precautions were taken to avoid collision during loading. Bombs were also loaded from a barge and one of these was alongside the ship at the time of the explosion.

7 Witnesses of the explosion reported 2 distinct explosions several seconds apart, the second one being much the larger of the two.

8 All of the Coast Guard officers and crew who were on board and all of an Army port battalion which was on board were killed except two Coast Guardsmen who were asleep in the bow of the ship. Total loss of life was 194. All of the ship disintegrated aft of No. 2 hold, while the bow of the ship settled to the bottom and gradually sank. Divers afterwards found some unexploded depth bombs on the sea bottom and also determined that the fuzes in No. 1 hold were undamaged.

9 It is believed that an enemy submarine was in the immediate vicinity of the ship at the time of the explosion, and was detected 3-1/2 miles away about 30 minutes afterward. It was followed and depth charged, about 3 hours later, with undetermined results.

10 There is a possibility that the explosion was due to rough handling and the court could not reach an agreement as to the probable cause. The majority of the court blamed it on enemy action, while a minority report blamed it on rough handling. There was, however, absolutely no evidence of rough handling and the minority report was obviously based on the bad reputation which Torpex has.

11 In addition to the complete destruction of the ship and of the DUKW and barge alongside, the following damage was done: USS YP 514, moored 650 yards away, was badly damaged, the bow and crow's nest being demolished by the blast, and considerable minor damage and missile penetration was suffered. Fourteen of the crew were injured. The body of one of the crew from the *Serpens* landed on this ship.

12 The USS YMS 281, moored 3/8 mile away, had its deck badly shattered and pierced by missiles, together with some minor damage.

13 The USS LCT 317, moored on the shore about 1800 yards away, had its deck pierced by missiles, and one man injured.

14 The HMNZS Q-400 at an unspecified location had its deck pierced by missiles in several places and suffered minor damage.

15 Steel Quonset huts on shore were badly damaged by blast and missiles at a distance of approximately one mile. Other buildings in the vicinity suffered broken glass and minor injuries. Witnesses on shore at a distance of over a mile were thrown to the ground by the blast, and debris from the explosion fell over at least a one-mile radius. A considerable tidal wave also hit the shore. A ship 3000 yards away was lifted a considerable distance by underwater shock and many missiles landed on it. Ground shock was felt as far away as 5 miles."

LT John Belcher was in command of Her Majesty's New Zealand Ship Q400 (HMNZS Q400) at the time Serpens exploded, its deck "pierced by missiles in several places" and suffered minor damage. Photo courtesy John Belcher, son of the former commander.

The Commanding Officer of USS *Serpens* at the time of her loss was Lieutenant Commander Peery Lamar Stinson, USCG. Most records note his first name as Perry but his actual given name was Peery. He was born in Morell, Chicot

County, Arkansas, on 19 April 1906. He was appointed to the U.S. Naval Academy in Annapolis, Maryland, on 2 July 1923 and was graduated and commissioned in June 1927. The Annual Register of the United States Naval Academy shows Ensign Stinson being ranked 426th out of 579 graduates in the Class of '27. As a newly-minted Ensign he reported aboard light cruiser USS *Memphis* (CL-13) on 26 August 1927 and later served aboard the destroyer USS *Borie* (DD-215). On 22 July 1929 he resigned from the Navy under honorable conditions. On 27 May 1931 he was appointed Ensign in the U.S. Coast Guard. He was promoted to Lieutenant (junior grade) on 7 June 1933, promoted to Lieutenant on 7 June 1935 and in June 1941, LT Stinson relieved LCDR Harley E. Grogan as commander of USCG Base 6 (covering the Bahia Mar and Ft. Lauderdale, FL, beach area). In April 1942 he became Captain of the Port of Miami in addition to his other duties and was promoted to Lieutenant Commander on 1 May 1942. He was detached from the Port of Miami in September 1943 and reported to the Navy's Sub Chaser Training Center (SCTC) Miami, where he received additional combat training. He later went on to command the 306-foot-long destroyer-escort USS *Harveson* (DE-316). The Coast Guard ultimately manned 30 such destroyer escorts during WW II. He also served aboard the Coast Guard-manned SS *Manhasset* on weather patrol in the North Atlantic.

On 22 July 1944 LCDR Stinson relieved LCDR Magnus J. Johnson, USCGR, as commanding officer of *Serpens*. Six months after taking command, and just two days after the explosion, in accordance with Article 841 of the U.S. Navy Regulations, LCDR Stinson had to write a letter to the Secretary of the Navy on the loss of his ship:

31 JAN 1945

From: The Commanding Officer.

To: The Secretary of the Navy.

Via: (1) Commander Task Unit 11.5.6.

           (2) Commander Service Squadron, South Pacific Force.

Subject: Official Report of Loss of Ship

Reference: (a) Article 841, U.S. Navy Regulations

1. At approximately 2317 on the 29th of January 1945, the U.S.S. *Serpens* (AK-97) was totally destroyed by an explosion of undetermined origin.

2. At the time of the explosion the U.S.S. *Serpens* was riding at anchor in Berth 24 as that berth is delineated on H.O. Field Chart 1009 at Guadalcanal, British Solomon Islands.

3. The ship was being loaded at the time by the 492nd Port Battalion, United States Army, located on Guadalcanal, British Solomon Islands, with depth bombs, plane parts, and general cargo.

4. The ship, all of its crew, with the exception of the ten survivors hereinafter referred to, and all of its cargo were lost. The cargo consisted of depth bomb fuzes, airplane wings, airplane engines, airplane belly tanks, and depth bombs and miscellaneous freight.

5. I am unable to state whether the explosion which destroyed the ship was due to enemy action and the explosion of the depth charges constituting its cargo or to the explosion of cargo alone.

6. At the time of the explosion I was ashore standing in the quarters of Captain Conklin, 319th Fighter Control Squadron, just preparatory to returning to the ship. I felt a shock and asked if it was an earthquake. Immediately following there was a great

glare in the sky followed by a tremendous explosion. I immediately set out for the dock and tried to determine from the position of the smoke whether it could have been the *Serpens*. Officers with me who lived in the vicinity did not think it could be, saying that it might be the ammunition dump at Henderson Field. Upon arrival at the dock I found that the *Serpens* had exploded and since the *Serpens'* gig had been wrecked by the explosion I commandeered a boat and in company with Lieutenant Commander Audrey A. Scott, U.S. Coast Guard Reserve, searched the area covered by debris along with many other boats until between 0100 and 0130, 30 January 1945. When I returned to the dock and reported to Captain Mark L. Hersey, Jr., Commander Naval Bases, South Solomons Sub-Area, I located Lieutenant John R. Clark, U.S. Coast Guard, Stanly M. Jones, 515-547, CCS, USCGR, Morris M. Houseknecht, 563-428, F1c, USCGR, William E. Hughes, 519-163, S1c, USCGR, Fidel O. Carmona, 676-292, S2c, USCGR, Robert J. Smart, 675-709, S1c, USCGR, and Richard M. Figgs, 7009-229, St3c, USCGR. George S. Kennedy, 587-983, S2c, USCGR and Kelsie K. Kemp, 599-922, S1c, USCGR, had been removed from the bow of the *Serpens* by Captain Hersey. All were quartered at Naval Advanced Base, Guadalcanal.

7. The search of the area disclosed only about thirty or forty feet of the bow floating keel up which sank in about two hours. Some of the belly tanks which were parts of the cargo were seen. Large patches of what appeared to be explosive residue were seen.

8. One body has been found and identified as CAMMARATA, Michael L., (685-177), S2c, U.S. Coast Guard Reserve. Portions of other bodies have been found but identification is impossible.

9. The following material of the ship was saved being ashore at the time of explosion: one ¼-ton

reconnaissance car, one 28' motor whale boat and one landing craft vehicle.

PEERY L. STINSON

cc: Commandant, U.S. Coast Guard

LCDR Stinson retired from the U.S. Coast Guard on 1 November 1948. Sadly, he died on 22 September 1952 at the age of 51 in Los Angeles, CA. His remains were buried in Arlington National Cemetery, Section 1, Site 450-D, on 30 September 1952.

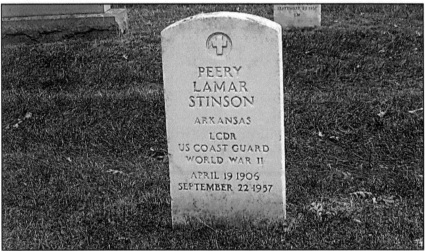

LCDR Peery Lamar Stinson, USCG, Commanding Officer of USS Serpens (AK-97) at the time of her loss, is buried at Arlington National Cemetery, although not with his shipmates.

Just days after the loss of *Serpens*, the two survivors sent Western Union telegrams to their family and friends, ensuring them that they were safe and sound. On 4 February 1945, S1c Kelsie K. Kemp, USCGR, sent his back home, stating "Am well and fit. Rumor not true. Regards to the gang."

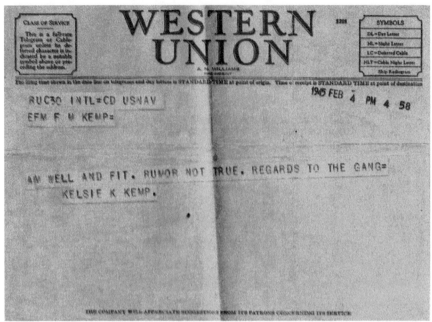

On 4 February 1945, just days after the loss of USS Serpens, S1c Kelsie K. Kemp sent this Western Union telegram back home. *Photograph courtesy of CAPT Chuck Polk, USCGR (Retired).*

On 10 February 1945 letters signed by Vice Admiral R. R. Waesche, Commandant of the United State Coast Guard, went out to those who lost their loved ones aboard *Serpens*. The parents of F2c Gerald C. Breen received this one:

My dear Mr. and Mrs. Breen:

It is with regret that I inform you that your son, Gerald Clement Breen, Fireman, second class, USCGR, is missing in the line of duty since 29 January 1945.

The anxiety this distressing report has caused you is fully realized. You may be sure that all officers and men in the active theater of operations exert their utmost efforts to learn the fate of their missing shipmates.

When additional information is received concerning him it will be sent to you promptly. I wish to convey to you my sincere sympathy in your anxiety.

Sincerely yours,

R. R. WAESCHE
Vice Admiral, USCG
Commandant

Nine days later, on 19 February 1945, the Acting Commandant of the U.S. Coast Guard followed up the original letters with a similar one. An example was one sent to the parents of Seaman Second Class Paul Robert Jaissle, USCGR:

My dear Mr. and Mrs. Jaissle:

It is with regret that I confirm the information sent you regarding your son, Paul Robert Jaissle, Seaman, second class, USCGR, who was officially reported missing in the line of duty on 29 January 1945. Just as soon as we are furnished the details you will be informed.

The anxiety this distressing report has caused you is fully realized. You may be sure that all officers and men in the active theater of operations exert their utmost efforts to learn the fate of their missing shipmates.

When additional information is received concerning him it will be sent to you promptly. In the meantime I wish to convey to you my sincere sympathy in your sadness.

Sincerely yours,

L. T. CHALKER
Rear Admiral, USCG
Acting Commandant

Nearly two months passed before additional information was formally passed on to the families. On 10 April 1945 letters from the Chief of the U.S. Coast Guard's Military Morale Division were mailed to parents or next-of-kin. An example of such a letter was mailed to the parents of Steward's Mate First Class George Lester Dickerson.

My dear Mr. and Mrs. Dickerson:

When you were advised that your son, George Lester Dickerson, Steward's Mate, first class, USCGR, was missing with his vessel the USS *Serpens* you were told that when sufficient information had been obtained to make a change in status you would be advised.

A Board of Investigation was convened to inquire into the loss of the vessel when she was torpedoed by the enemy. After careful consideration a determination has been made that the death of your son occurred at the time of the action, 29 January 1945. All pay and allowances continue to accrue to the date the determination was made 6 April 1945.

I wish to offer you my sympathy and assure you that in event I can be of aid I shall be glad to have you communicate with me.

The forms necessary to claim sums due will be sent to you under separate cover.

By direction of the Commandant.

Very truly yours,

C. A. ANDERSON
Commander, United States Coast Guard
Chief, Military Morale Division

A framed photo of Steward's Mate First Class George Lester Dickerson with his sister's photo in the corner.

Notwithstanding the formal letters sent from USCG Headquarters, and shortly after the loss of *Serpens* and her crew and Army stevedores, letters from concerned parents, wives, fiancés and various next-of-kin poured in to Guadalcanal asking for more information on how their loved ones died. Many such letters were responded to by the various Catholic, Protestant and Jewish chaplains attached to the base. Private First Class Edwin L. Boos, U.S. Army, was one of those killed aboard *Serpens* when it exploded. William W. Zundel, U.S. Army Captain and Chaplain of the 492nd Port Battalion, wrote this initial letter to the mother of PFC Boos:

> "My Dear Mrs. Boos, it is with deep feeling that I write you concerning your son, Edwin, of the 231st Port

Co., who gave his life for his country. Our hearts were indeed heavy at the news of his loss.

Most of the men of his company have been together for over two years and Edwin was regarded as one of the men who through training and experience could be counted on to do his share in our important but often routine work.

We do not sorrow as those who have no hope, for we believe in God's offer of eternal salvation for those who serve Him faithfully. I trust that you too believe in "Him who is able to do exceeding abundantly above all that we ask, and think, according to the power that worketh in us." In this the time of your great sorrow I know that you will draw closer to our Heavenly Father and His abundant love, to feel and know the serene companionship and tranquil comforts of God, who has called Edwin home. I am certain that through faith in Him your courage will be strengthened.

The entire Battalion turned out voluntarily at a very impressive Memorial Service held in the American Military Cemetery. In spite of its sad associations the cemetery is beautifully located between the ocean on one side and the green clad hills on the other. Standing in the middle of the cemetery is a lovely chapel of native construction.

Full military honors were rendered at the service, a firing squad from Edwin's own company fired three volleys and a bugler blew Taps immediately afterwards.

Words are so inadequate to express fully our sorrow for one so likable and trustworthy. May I express to you the sincere sympathies of all the many friends made by Edwin while in his country's forces.

Very sincerely yours,

WILLIAM W. ZUNDEL, Chaplain (Capt.) USA

The Army, Navy, Marine Cemetery at Guadalcanal, pictured in 1945.
"Standing in the middle of the cemetery is a lovely chapel of native
construction" as written by Chaplain William Zundel to Mrs. Boos, mother
of the deceased Edwin Boos of the 231st Port Company, who was aboard
USS Serpens when it exploded.

Several letters were later sent to Chaplain Zundel by Mrs.
Boos asking for more information on what happened. In what
was most likely the Chaplain's last letter to her, he replies:

"My Dear Mrs. Boos, your letters of inquiry have not
been forgotten. You will be glad to know that not only
the men and officers of this Battalion are anxious for
you to have the details but this anxiety extends to the
General and his Staff.

As you know our job as a Battalion is to load and
unload ships. On the night of January 29th, a working
party from the 231st Port Co., including Edwin, was
working aboard a ship (the Serpens) in a stream off
Guadalcanal. At a little after 11:00 there was a terrific
explosion on the ship. There were only two survivors

in the very front end of the ship who were miraculously saved. I saw and talked to these men. Their story, as given to the newspapers, gives all the details. I enclose it on a separate sheet.

My previous letters had to be short on details due to censorship regulations. But is has been established that this explosion was due to enemy action. Tokyo Rose (Jap radio) was bragging about the Jap Navy just after the explosion occurred.

Very few bodies were recovered, and very few of the bodies recovered were identified, this is the reason we had a Memorial Service. The survivors of the ship were there and the Captain of the ship, the General and his Staff, and all the men of the Battalion with others who came to pay their respects.

Every reasonable precaution is taken when our men are working the ships and you need have no fear that there was any carelessness. But we are at war against a cunning and ruthless enemy. The men of our Battalion fight the same as front line men when they perform their assigned tasks.

Every means of identification has been exhausted by the War Dept. Under the circumstances it is extremely unlikely that Edwin's body has been recovered or will be identified. I tell you this because it is the sad truth.

His friends in the Battalion have been unable to write due to censorship regulations. I am sure you will understand that they too, are sad and heavy-hearted. Captain Erwin J. Rybarczyk, Commanding Officer of the 231st Port Company, joins with me in sending you this detailed letter.

Our faith in God and the cause for which we are fighting gives us courage to go on even at bitter cost. On Christian Faith is our bulwark, in this our time of need.

Sincerely

William J. Zundel, Chaplain, USA, Battalion Chaplain

Private First Class Edwin L. Boos, U.S. Army, 231st Port Company, 492nd Port Battalion, at Guadalcanal, British Solomon Islands. Photo and letters courtesy Rick D. Boos.

Tokyo Rose was a generic name given by Allied forces in the South Pacific during World War II to any of approximately a dozen English-speaking female broadcasters of Japanese propaganda. The intent of these broadcasts was to disrupt the morale of Allied forces listening to the broadcast. American servicemen in the Pacific often listened to the propaganda broadcasts to get a sense, by reading between the lines, of the effect of their military actions. Farther from the action, stories circulated that Tokyo Rose could be unnervingly accurate, naming units and even individual servicemen. Several reports claim that Tokyo Rose was airing the loss of *Serpens* by a Japanese submarine hours after the incident although no transcript could be found collaborating that story.

Survivors were questioned by the Court of Inquiry and then sent to California, more than likely Alameda. While there they were photographed and interviewed by the Coast Guard Office of Public Relations, Twelfth Naval District, San Francisco, CA, for distribution to their hometown newspapers. While the short interviews were similar to each other, each placed the survivor in a specific location to see or feel the explosion.

Fidel O. Carmona, 22, Coast Guard seaman, of 817 Pioneer Avenue, Wilmington, California, was one of ten men to survive the explosion by enemy action on the Coast Guard-manned ammunition ship *Serpens* at a Southwest Pacific Base.

Carmona was a member of the crew of the captain's gig and had just taken the skipper, Lt. Comdr. Peery L. Stinson of Washington, D.C., ashore when a terrible blast killed about 200 men aboard the ship and sank the vessel about one-half mile off shore.

Describing the explosion, Carmona said: "I was standing by near the gig on the dock when I saw a blinding red flare and heard a great explosion. The concussion knocked me down, damaged the gig, levelled a fish shack nearby and damaged part of the pier. I ran for cover when fragments of steel started pelting me. Later I tried to help in rescue work but the gig would not start."

The 10,000-ton *Serpens* was blasted by Japs as a shuttle fleet of amphibious jeeps had completed loading the craft with ammunition in preparation for another invasion operation.

A friendly call on a Los Angeles neighbor serving with the Army saved Coast Guardsman Robert J. Smart, 21-year-old seaman first class, of 4514 Eagle Street, East Los Angeles, from death recently when his Coast Guard-manned ammunition ship, the U.S.S. *Serpens*, blew up at a Southwest Pacific Base.

About 200 Coast Guard shipmates of Smart perished in the blast, which Navy officials said was the result of enemy action. Ten survived, including two who were aboard the ship when the explosion occurred.

Smart, a signalman striker with 20 months of sea duty with Coast Guard combat vessels, had gone ashore for the visit and was returning to his ship.

"I was standing on the dock when I heard a muffled explosion. The lights on the ship anchored about a half mile offshore went out. Then came a blinding flash and a tremendous explosion—the whole works went."

I was knocked down by the blast and when I got up I had to seek refuge behind some palm trees because of the flying steel and debris coming down from the explosion," Smart said.

Later Smart went with the commanding officer of the *Serpens*, Lt. Comdr. Peery L. Stinson, USCG, to Washington, D.C., on a fruitless search for survivors.

Two Coast Guardsmen, George Kennedy of San Marcos, Texas, and Kelsie Kemp of Barren Springs, Va., were aboard the ship at the time of the blast, but managed to get free from the wreckage. All others on the ship perished.

The vessel, a Navy assault-cargo ship, manned by the Coast Guard, had finished loading several tons of ammunition and was preparing to sail.

Survivors were flown to the West Coast.

The dead were buried while natives, who knew the *Serpens* well, garbed in their ritual rainment, performed their own solemn services for the dead.

William E. Hughes, 42, Coast Guard seaman of 3920 11th Avenue West, Seattle, Washington, was one of ten men who escaped death when the Coast Guard-manned ammunition ship USS *Serpens* was blasted and sunk by Japs recently at a Southwest Pacific Base with a loss of 200 lives.

Hughes, Coxswain of the Skipper's gig, had just taken the commanding officer, Lt. Comdr. Peery L. Stinson of Washington, D.C., ashore. He was standing by at the dock where amphibious jeeps were shuttling from the ship to shore loading the *Serpens* with tons of explosives in preparation for another invasion operation.

"I first heard a thud and then a bright flash. A second later there was a very loud explosion. The blast knocked us down and damaged the gig. I heard later that it was so bad that it was heard 70 miles away. I was looking at the ship at the time, because she was signaling. She had just started to send a message with the blinker lights when the explosion happened."

Escaping with Hughes in the gig, in addition to the commanding officer, were Fidel O. Carmona of Wilmington, California, and Morris F. Houseknecht, 23, of Hazleton, Pa., other men in the small boat crew.

A Coast Guard negro steward's mate, Richard M. Figgs, 21, of 438 Bradley Street, Lexington, Ky., was one of 10 crewmen who escaped death when the Coast Guard-manned ammunition ship U.S.S. *Serpens* was blasted and sunk by Jap action recently at a Southwest Pacific Base with a loss of 200 lives.

Figgs had just gone ashore and was standing on the dock where a shuttle train of amphibious jeeps were loading the *Serpens* with tons of ammunition in preparation for another invasion operation, when the explosion occurred.

"First I was blinded by a bright light and then a big explosion noise deafened me. Those on the shore ran for cover because bits of steel and everything was raining down. I ran to the MP shack and knelt and prayed for the boys on the ship. I didn't know that it was my own ship."

Escaping with Figgs were: Lt. Comdr. Peery L. Stinson, the ship's commanding officer, of Washington, D.C.; and two men who were aboard at the time and managed to make their way through wreckage to the water and were later rescued. They were George Kennedy of San Marcos, Texas, and Kelsie Kemp of Barren Springs, Va.

Still visibly affected from the shock of seeing his ship—the ill-fated USS *Serpens*—destroyed recently at a Southwest Pacific Base, with a loss of 200 Coast Guard shipmates, Morris F. Houseknecht, 23, fireman, first class, is Enroute East for a thankful reunion with his family at 594 Peace Street, Hazleton, Pa.

One hour before the blast that blew up the *Serpens*, the captain, Lieut. Comdr. Peery L. Stinson of 3382 Stevenson Place, N.W., Washington, D.C., ordered his gig readied for a trip ashore, one-half mile from where the *Serpens* was being loaded with ammunition for another invasion mission.

Houseknecht was selected as the motor machinist mate for the skipper's gig because the regular third class petty officer was on duty elsewhere.

"That saved my life, all right," said Houseknecht. "My older brother Gilbert was killed in France last August."

Speaking slowly and with obvious effort, Houseknecht continued. "My buddy aboard the *Serpens*, Coxswain Eddie Durso, lived just a couple of blocks away from me on Peace Street. He was 22, just a year younger than me, and we were inseparable aboard ship. Eddie's folks will naturally want to see me. All I can tell them is that Eddie died without any pain and that he's buried with a lot of other heroes."

"I was working on the motor of the gig when I heard a booming sound," continued Houseknecht. "Before I could look up there was a violent concussion. I must have passed out for a couple of seconds. When I picked myself up there was a sheet of flame that seemed to reach the sky. Then it seemed to explode and hot pieces of steel seemed to fly all over. One fell just five feet away."

"The skipper, who had been ashore, came dashing up. I'll never forget that scene. He was crying. But I guess all of us were. There was no doubt which ship it was that exploded. Ours was the only large ship anchored in the spot and we were loading aerial torpedoes."

"An eight-foot tidal wave from the explosion lifted our gig almost out of the water and bent the screw. That kept us from going out to the *Serpens* but we really couldn't have done much. About 30 Higgins boats put out a few seconds after the blast but by this time there were only two men alive."

"Next morning the hospital was filled with around 70 bodies but we could only identify two."

"The following Sunday we shed some unabashed tears during burial ceremonies, conducted by three chaplains, Protestant, Catholic and Jewish. Eight riflemen fired a 3-gun salute."

Houseknecht had been overseas seven months. He enlisted on September 19, 1942, going into the service from his job as a steel worker for the A.C.F. Company of Berwick, Pa. He graduated from West Hazleton High. Houseknecht's parents live in Drum, Pa.

One of 10 survivors from the USS *Serpens*, a Coast Guard-manned cargo ship which blew up recently at a Southwest Pacific Base with a loss of 200 men, Chief Commissary Steward Stanley Jones, 26, of 927 Gladys Ave., Long Beach, California, told a graphic story of his experiences upon his return to the United States.

"We had gone ashore with the skipper (Lieut. Comdr. Stinson, USGC, 3382 Stevenson Place, N.W., Washington, D.C.), in his gig. The *Serpens* was standing one-half mile off shore. Suddenly we heard a rumble, then a blinding flash. I was knocked off my feet. A wooden fish house standing on the pier collapsed. The Fleet Post Office, almost two miles from the explosion, was blown down."

Jones sighed, shook his head wearily before he spoke again. "To see your ship and your buddies go down was tough but next morning I was given the hardest job of my life. About 75 bodies were picked up over a wide area. I tried to identify them but only recognized two men. One of them was Moose. He was big—6 feet 4—always good-natured, helpful and the most popular fellow on the ship."

"On the following Sunday burial services were held. Three chaplains, Catholic, Protestant and Hebrew—read the sermon. Natives, who knew the *Serpens* well, dressed in their tribal garments and performed their own special services. The chaplains all stressed the fact that here, in one cemetery, far away from their native land, rested men of different faiths who gave their lives for a common cause. You know, I don't often cry. I did then." Jones, eagerly awaiting a reunion with his wife Tessa and 2-1/2 year old son, enlisted on January 1, 1942.

Ship's Cook Second Class George Arthur "Moose" Henshaw, USCGR (right), as mentioned by Chief Commissary Steward Stanley Jones in his interview above. Standing with Moose is Ship's Cook Third Class David Fielding Lewis, USCGR. Both were lost in the explosion. Photo courtesy Henshaw family at www.ancestry.com.

Possibly as a way to exorcise his demons, in what is today called Survivor's Guilt, CCS Jones sat down and typed up his own personal story:

> Approximately 75 enlisted personnel of the U.S.S. *Serpens* cleared the gangway recently after enjoying several hours liberty ashore at a Southwest Pacific

Base. The *Serpens* was at anchor about one mile offshore.

A few minutes later 10 officers returned to the ship from a party aboard another Coast Guard-manned AKA.

Then there was an ear-shattering blast that was heard with extreme force 14 miles away. A huge ball of orange flame seemed to shoot miles into the air and there was no *Serpens*, except for 20 feet of the bow compartment.

The ship rode heavy with high-powered explosives. The Navy announced she was lost "as a result of enemy action." I don't know what happened, except that 193 of my shipmates and 13 officers are gone. Eighty-seven of them lost their lives by an ironic margin of three to seven minutes be reason of their return to the ship.

Only 10 of us, including the commanding officer and the supply officer, who was with me, were among the living of the USS *Serpens'* splendid crew. Four others were in a hospital at the time, of they, too, would have been numbered among the dead.

Thus occurred the greatest single loss of life to Coast Guard personnel in the history of this, or any, war. To me it was a nightmare of horrible magnitude. But I didn't realize just how terrible that tragedy was at the time it occurred.

The supply officer—Lieut. John R. Clark, USCG—and myself were visiting some Army Signal Corps friends at a camp two and a half miles away, up in the hills. We could have seen the entire harbor from there had it been daylight. I went there at Lieut. Clark's invitation, otherwise I still would have been aboard the *Serpens*.

We had our backs to the windows overlooking the harbor when we heard a slight explosion... just enough to make us turn around. We looked out of the window and saw a horrible sheet of flame towering thousands of feet in the air. Then the full force of the explosion hit us. The windows were shattered, glasses broke and screens fell out of their casements. We all dropped to the deck and tried to dig fox holes. We thought the world had come to an end... yet we were two and a half miles from the scene!

When we regained our senses, I remarked: "My God, that explosion came from our ship!"

"Don't be silly," someone said. "How can you tell where your ship is out there in this darkness?" But I had a premonition. Someone got on the telephone, then turned around with a frozen face: "I've got some bad news for you two fellows," he said. But already I knew the worst.

Lieut. Clark and I scrambled into a Jeep and tore down the roads to the harbor. Oil was still raining down like water and already the harbor was alive with small craft going out to the scene.

One of them, in which was riding Captain Mark L. Hersey, naval commandant, picked up two survivors... Seaman Second Class George Kennedy, of San Marcos, Texas, and Kelsie Kemp, Seaman First Class, of Barren Springs, Va. They were the only two members of the crew aboard at the time of the explosion who survived. Both were asleep in the boatswain's locker all the way forward in the bow. The 20-foot section in which they were resting floated for two hours. Kennedy had an emergency light, such as are used on life rafts, and that was the only way the rescuers spotted them.

Kemp was treated for a possible skull fracture and Kennedy for a broken collar bone and several bruises.

Both had only a faint idea that "something terrible must have happened."

The next morning, they found one body and I was called upon to identify it. They kept me at this job for the next three days. Sometimes the only clue was a laundry mark on a skivvy shirt. Most of the bodies had no clothes at all. Sometimes there were only parts of bodies.

A soldier on the beach was killed by a piece of fragment. Some Navy men in a nearby patrol boat were killed or wounded. Quonset huts were levelled to the ground. A chunk of boiler plate crashed through the roof of a hut and sliced a bed in half like a piece of bread. It was the only bunk out of 50 in that hut that was unoccupied that night. A warehouse filled with bottled beverages was a shambles of powdered glass and spilled soda.

On the following Sunday they held a mass funeral service, with Catholic, Protestant and Jewish Chaplains officiating. It was tremendously impressive... but except in a few cases we didn't know who—or what parts of whom—we were burying. Fifty-seven graves were prepared. The only possible consolation I can feel is that none of my shipmates—and we had been out there 21 months and had written our wives and sweethearts that we were coming home soon—none of my shipmates knew what had happened.

I can't tell all I know. I wouldn't want to. I would like to forget it, but I can't.

Those men died heroes. I hope they found a hero's heaven.

The San Francisco Coast Guard Office of Public Relations interviewed two other persons – S1c Kelsie Kemp and S2c

George Kennedy – the only survivors aboard *Serpens* when she exploded.

The 10,000-ton Coast Guard-manned cargo ship, USS *Serpens*, rode calmly at anchor in the "safety" of a Southwest Pacific Base. Coast Guardsmen were busily hoisting munitions aboard from a shuttle fleet of amphibious jeeps, preparing the gallant vessel for another invasion mission.

Then a terrific explosion and the *Serpens* was no more. In those fleeting seconds more than 200 American fighting men were blasted over miles of water and land. All that was visible in the misty night was part of the bow, jutting grotesquely out of the sea.

By morning, the bow, too, was gone.

Today, back in the United States are eight of the nine survivors. Seven of them, including the skipper, Coast Guard Lt. Comdr. Peery L. Stinson of 3382 Stevenson Place, N.W., Washington, D.C., were horrified spectators on the beach when their ship blew up in a mass of flame and smoke. The other two miraculously survived the holocaust.

None know the exact cause of the tragedy. It was probably the largest loss of Coast Guard life suffered from one ship in World War II.

The two who were aboard the *Serpens*—and lived—don't remember too much. Details are hazy. But they don't particularly care to remember.

George Kennedy, seaman second class of Martendale Star Route, San Marcos, Texas, who was aboard the ship with Kelsie Kemp, 19, seaman first class, of Barren Springs, Va., told his story.

"Kelsie and I were sleeping in the Bos'n locker, forward of the No. 2 hold, which was really an accident. Ordinarily I bunk on deck but I didn't that night because it looked like rain. Kelsie sleeps in the crew quarters but he felt sleepy enough to sack in right where he is normally on duty."

"Next thing I knew I was swimming in oil inside the Bos'n locker. No, I wasn't scared; just plumb startled. There was less than a foot of head space and my head was butting against the deck. I heard a sort of gurgling sound and knew water was coming in someplace. I dove toward that spot. I came out of the ship just below the port anchor. I climbed up the anchor and there I was on the bow, which was the only part of the ship I could see. A few minutes later a small boat came alongside and picked me up. Looking back, I was lucky in more ways than one. I had been sleeping under the 3-inch gun magazine which did not explode."

Kemp, who enlisted in the Coast Guard when he became 17 back in October, 1942, picked up the story. "I woke up with water up to my neck and blood pouring down my face. The hatch door was open. I climbed on top of it. I sat there for what seemed like hours but actually was only 15 minutes. A small boat pulled up and a Captain Mark L. Hersey, Jr., of the Navy picked me up. He visited me in the dispensary on shore next day. He said his rescue of me was the proudest job he had ever done."

Besides writing a letter to the Secretary of the Navy regarding the loss of his ship, LCDR Stinson had another obligation to fulfill: to write a letter of condolence to each of the families of those crewmembers that died. This one, dated 25 March 1945, was to the parents of S1c John Clifford Daly, USCGR.

25 March, 1945

My dear Mr. and Mrs. Daly:

It is with sincere regret that I write you concerning your son, John Clifford Daly, Seaman, first class, USCGR, who, along with others, was declared missing in the line of duty. I know that you are anxiously waiting word of him, but there is so very little that I can tell you. In the late evening of 29 January, 1945, an explosion occurred aboard the USS *Serpens* causing the complete loss of the vessel. The explosion was due to enemy action. As I had gone ashore a short while before the attack, I was fortunate to be one of those who survived.

I want you to know that your son's conduct and service was of the highest type. He was well liked and respected by his fellow shipmates and his record as a great credit to himself, his family, his ship and his country. His memory will give us all added determination to fight this war to a victorious end so that the world may again live in peace.

I fully realize that my inadequate words offer small, if any, comfort in your anxiety and sorrow. My thoughts and sympathy are most sincerely with you.

Very truly yours,

PEERY L. STINSON

Seaman First Class John Clifford Daly. Photo courtesy D. J. Carruth, www.ancestry.com.

Ripley's Believe It or Not! is an American franchise, founded by Robert Ripley, which deals in bizarre events and items so strange and unusual that readers might question the claims. Originally a newspaper panel, this particular panel appeared on 7 June 1945 and shows George Kennedy surviving the *Serpens'* blast.

This particular "Believe It Or Not" did not sit well with the families who lost loved ones aboard *Serpens*. The Executive Officer's mother, Mrs. Charlotte Aiken, wrote this: "Several have written me protesting at Ripley's Believe It or Not, giving

$100 prize for Geo. Kennedy's story of the *Serpens* explosion. The broadcast was even worse, as one parent wrote 'Mr. Ripley's comments made it appear somewhat a matter of jest, rather than what it was in reality, and the audience present echoed his comments with peals of laughter. It was also made to appear that George was the only survivor.' My husband thinks that we should all write our Congressmen, protesting at Robert Ripley's unkindness. Surely he can have known no personal loss, and he owes you all a public, and individual, apology. I intend to protest in every way I can, also to our newspapers, although an action so devoid of good taste and common humanity deserves not even a scornful recognition. I am sorry to mention this. The clipping appeared June 6 or 7. George could not have realized that his shipmates' sacrifices would be handled slightingly."

The dead were initially buried at the "Army, Navy and Marine Cemetery Guadalcanal," located slightly to the east and inland from Lunga Point near Henderson Field on the north coast of Guadalcanal. During the middle of 1942, this cemetery was initially called the "American Cemetery Guadalcanal." It was established as a cemetery for American casualties from the Guadalcanal campaign. By 1943 the cemetery was further developed with a chapel made using local materials and a large cross, surrounded by machine gun bullets and 37mm shells. The "American Cemetery Guadalcanal" was known by many different names, including the "Marine Cemetery at Lunga," "Lunga Cemetery," "Guadalcanal Cemetery," and "1st Marine Division Cemetery, Guadalcanal." Later, the cemetery also included a section for New Zealand personnel killed on Guadalcanal or in the Solomon Islands. Postwar, it became known as the "Army, Navy, Marine Cemetery Guadalcanal".

Seaman First Class Charles Edward Craft, USCGR. Photo courtesy www.ancestry.com.

POST-WAR AND ARLINGTON NATIONAL CEMETERY

Retired Coast Guard officer LCDR Richard Stoud plays "Taps" at the Serpens Memorial in November 2013. Photo courtesy U.S. Coast Guard.

The surrender of Imperial Japan was announced on 15 August 1945 and formally signed aboard the battleship USS *Missouri* (BB-63) on September 2, bringing the hostilities of World War II to a close. With that action also came the lifting of censorship and the termination of censorship activities in the U.S. Government's Office of Censorship. On 21 October

1945 the *Tampa Bay Times* (Tampa Bay, Florida) published an article about First Lieutenant Alfred M. Livingston, U.S. Army, and his narrow escape from the *Serpens* explosion entitled "Escapes Jap Torpedoeing":

"First Lt. Alfred M. Livingston, with the Army Transportation Corps at Guadalcanal since last November, now writes his parents, Mr. and Mrs. B. F. Livingston, from his new station at Noumea, New Caledonia. In a letter this past week he tells of his miraculous escape from death on the ammunition ship USS *Serpens*, which was blown up last January by a Jap sub in the harbor of Guadalcanal.

'I was the first officer to work her,' Lt. Livingston begins his description of the sinking, which can be told now that censorship no longer exists. 'We unloaded land mines off her for three days (a very ticklish job). Then we began taking aboard 500-pound depth charges. She had around 600 tons aboard when the explosion took place.'

'We changed shifts that day so I worked from 8 a.m. until 4 p.m. A fellow officer, Lt. McGrath, relived me until midnight. The ship blew up at 11:15 p.m. with the worst sound I ever heard. We lost Lt. McGrath and 53 men, plus 150 coast guardsmen. The blast also killed three Duck operators alongside the ship. If we hadn't changed shifts, I would have been aboard. It's something I'll never be able to forget.'

'The Navy says she was torpedoed by a Jap sub and it's official. Even Tokyo Rose said so the next night. Everyone was alerted right away. I had just hit the sack when she went up in one loud report with clouds of smoke and debris shutting out the full moon.'

'The blast and concussion blew in sections of our huts. I was reaching for my helmet and it threw me off my feet. We were 800 yards away. The water killed most of the shock or we would have been in worse shape. Pieces of ships, some the size of table tops, flew through the air and injured several men in the area.'

'I was anxious to see Bob (Robert Hawk, his cousin, star third baseman on St. Petersburg softball teams). I knew he had been on the ship three days before and was glad he also had come through safely. We both were mighty thankful.'

The officer's father had been traveling in the east when a brief account of the sinking appeared in Philadelphia papers. Mr. Livingston clipped out the article and sent it to his wife because of the reference to Guadalcanal. Mrs. Livingston, in turn, sent the clipping on to the lieutenant. It wasn't until this past week, however, that they learned how closely the fate of their own son was associated with the story"

As an aside, in November 1945 the U.S. Postal Service issued this Coast Guard stamp showing landing craft and transports to commemorate the service's role in World War II amphibious combat operations. Image courtesy of U.S. Postal Service.

After the war, every *Serpens* grave was exhumed from Guadalcanal and transported to Honolulu, HI, aboard the transport ship *Cardinal O'Connell* and then back to the United States for permanent interment.

While the remains of the crew still lay at rest in the Army, Navy and Marine Cemetery at Guadalcanal, many parents and next-of-kin of the deceased received an Accolade from the President of the United States in tribute of their sacrifice. One example was the Accolade received by the parents of Edmund J. Durso in Hazleton, PA, as printed in the 13 September 1946 edition of the Standard-Sentinel newspaper (Hazleton, Pennsylvania), page 15, entitled *"Local War Hero Given USCG Accolade by President Truman."*

"A letter from the office of the Commandant of the United States Coast Guard at Washington, D.C., to Mr. and Mrs. Joseph Durso of 805 Peace Street was received yesterday and included a letter from Admiral J. F. Farley which reads as follows:

Dear Mr. and Mrs. Durso:

It is my privilege to forward to you an Accolade from the President of the United States in memory of your son, Edmund Joseph Durso, Coxswain of the United States Coast Guard Reserve.

This award is made to you in tribute to your son's sacrifice in the service of his country, may it serve in some small measure as a lasting memorial and a tangible manifestation of the Government's grateful recognition of his faithful and unselfish performance of duty

Sincerely,

Admiral J. F. Farley, USCG
Commandant

Inscription on Accolade

The inscription engraved on the Accolade is as follows:

In Grateful Memory

Edmund Joseph Durso

United States Coast Guard Reserve

Who died in service of his country 29 January 1945 at Guadalcanal.

He stands in the unbroken line of patriots who have dared to die that Freedom might live, and grow, and increase its blessings. Freedom Lives, and through he lives—in a way that humbles the understanding of man.

Harry S Truman, President
United States of America

Killed on Ammunition Ship

Coxswain Durso was killed on the Pacific island when the USS *Serpens*, a Coast Guard ammunition ship, blew up while being loaded for an invasion.

He attended Hazleton High School and was a member of the Mother of Grace parish."

Families and friends of the deceased began paying tribute in any way they could. On page 51 of the January 1947 issue of Baltimore & Ohio Magazine it was printed:

"A most worthy gesture on the part of Mr. and Mrs. V. F. Jacobs and family is the neon cross they had placed atop the Trinity Lutheran Church in memory of their son, Vernard C., 25, a member of the Coast Guard who lost his life on January 29, 1945, when his ship, the U.S.S. *Serpens*, was blown up at Guadalcanal by a Japanese sub. V. F. Jacobs is a switchman in the local yards in service since September 3, 1942."

Also, the Veterans of Foreign Wars (VFW) Post No. 1826 in Buckeye, Arizona, officially changed their name in 1949 to the Joseph D. Faust Post No. 1826 in memory of Joseph David Faust of the U.S. Coast Guard. Faust lost his life aboard *Serpens*. His mother, Ida Faust, became the Post's Gold Star Mother.

Serpens crewmember Seaman First Class Ralph Dana Kiley, USCGR, had the high school he attended renamed after him and his younger brother, Corporal Roger G. Kiley, USMC. They were both graduates of West School in Peabody, Massachusetts. They were killed within a fortnight of one another; Corporal Kiley died at the age of 21 due to wounds received while battling on the island of Iwo Jima. Seaman Ralph, age 22, died aboard *Serpens*. The West School was renamed the Kiley Brothers Memorial School in their honor in May 1947. The Dedication Ceremony was attended by Mayor Leo F. McGrath, Mayor Edward A. Coffey of Salem, members of the school board and city council and representatives of every veteran's organization in the city. Superintendent of School William A. Welch was the principal speaker. Mrs. Mary McCormack, a lifelong resident of West Peabody, spoke of the boyhood days of the Kiley Brothers.

Cyrus Tenney, who designed and made the tablet upon which two bronze plaques were placed, presided at the exercises. The uppermost bronze plaque bears the inscription "Roger and Ralph Kiley Memorial School 1945." The lower one states: "This memorial is erected to the men and women of this community who served in the armed forces of this country in time of war." The plaques were unveiled by George Goldsmith and Arthur Parrish, friends of Roger, and by John Rosa and Roland Kelley, friends of Ralph. The plaques originally stood mounted on a rock in front of the old school. On November 7, 1997, after a new school was built, the Kiley Brothers Memorial School was rededicated and the stone and markers were placed at the front of the school's entrance. At the Re-dedication Ceremony, Mayor Peter Torigian said "It makes us ever mindful of how lucky we are to live in a free country that was made free for us by people who are sitting here and people who are not here because of making the supreme sacrifice." Superintendent Louis Perullo added: "I think one of the most important things we could possibly do is to reaffirm the naming of this school. It is most important because what you have is really a direct result of the sacrifice all the veterans made. The sacrifices the Kiley brothers made were really supreme. They could give no more. They gave their lives...Always remember this school is named after two great people, two common people, two young boys, 22 and 21 years old."

Principal John Murtagh then read a letter sent for the occasion by a former classmate of the Kiley brothers, Theodore R. Stocker, who is a veteran of WWII serving in the U.S. Navy on the USS Bradford in the Pacific. He wrote, "I grew up with the family, attended school, enjoyed their company in local school plays and all the West Peabody activities of the late 1920's. The very ground that this Kiley Brothers Memorial School is built on was farmed by Roger and Ralph who toiled, weeded, gathered crops on this land. When Pearl Harbor occurred both boys, as well as all us other young fellows, joined the war effort." Shortly after changing the school's name from West School to the Kiley Brothers Memorial School in May 1947, plans to bring the remains of Kiley and the 250 others home were taking shape.

The bronze plaque bearing the inscription "Roger and Ralph Kiley Memorial School 1945" at their old school   Photo courtesy Douglas Campbell and Kiley Brothers Memorial School alumnus Eric Black.

The effort for the *Serpens'* exhumation from the Army, Navy, Marine Cemetery began with the establishment of the 9105th Technical Service Unit (TSU) in the Spring of 1947 and the American Graves Registration Service-Pacific Zone (AGRS-PAZ) in late 1947. The experiences from handling the remains of personnel in Hawaii came from the need for a clear understanding of conditions peculiar to each cemeterial area and for advance arrangements before disinterments. In addition, repatriation activities now included cemeteries and other areas on foreign soil, so it was also necessary to inform all governments concerned and to obtain their permission as well before proceeding with the work at hand.

In October 1947 a detail of four officers departed Hawaii for Guadalcanal and Australia to prepare for the arrival of the 9105th TSU. Two of those officers left Honolulu on 17 October and arrived at Guadalcanal three days later. Shortly thereafter they were joined by the other two who were already in Guadalcanal, attached to the Search and Recovery Expedition, combing the area for bodies in shallow graves or bodies simply left where they died.

Two of these four officers went on to Australia; the remaining two began preparations for the arrival of the 9105th TSU. They arranged for officer and civilian housing, for headquarters, unit supply, motor pool equipment, and for shipment of fresh meat and other perishables by air from Australia. An agreement was also entered into with the British Resident Commissioner for the diversion of local laborers from cemetery maintenance to final preparations for repatriation. Their work was to include reconditioning of the Processing Center and other operational buildings and provision of storage facilities for caskets. This was all laid out in a letter from AGRS-PAZ to AGRS Guadalcanal

Detachment dated 24 October 1947, entitled "Plans and Preparations for Arrival and Operations of 9105th TSU at Guadalcanal."

The AGRS-PAZ Operations Directive No. 1, dated 9 September 1947, called for the exhumation of all remains in Australia and Guadalcanal. In Guadalcanal the initial number given for exhumations was 3,346.

In accordance with American Graves Facility Headquarters Pacific Zone, Movement Order No. 2, dated 24 October 1947, the 9105th TSU was to set sail from Oahu on 31 October aboard USAT *Goucher Victory*. Troop strength aboard the ship should have been about 33 officers, 2 enlisted men and about 500 civilians comprising seven Field Operating Section (FOS) teams; however, some 17 officers, including the Commanding Officer, flew to Guadalcanal instead. *Goucher Victory* arrived at Guadalcanal on 9 November 1947 after an uneventful voyage. There they disembarked four of the seven FOS teams, a nearly complete mobile port company, and equipment for exhumation operations. Over the next week they off-loaded and began preparing the supplies and equipment for the formidable task that lay ahead. After off-loading, *Goucher Victory* departed for Australia with the three remaining FOS teams and the remainder of the mobile port company. Those in Guadalcanal were now looking at disinterring, processing and either temporary or final casketing of more than 3,300 remains, including those of the *Serpens'* crew. During the worst of the rainy season.

Exhumations in the Army, Navy and Marine Cemetery began on 27 November 1947 and by working six days each week the men disinterred and removed all remains to the Processing Center by 20 December. The remains of the

Serpens' crew were now in the Center, comprised of two large huts with a passageway separating the huts. Each hut contained three processing lines, with two embalmers in each line, and one officer in charge. The number of remains handled daily about equaled the exhumation rate. Since the Center became intensely hot during daylight hours under a tropical sun, all work soon took place at night between 11 p.m. and 7 a.m. The *Serpens'* crew, placed in shipping cases during the night, were held in the Center and transferred during the day to the custody of the port unit. Normally, the remains of all those disinterred, processed in the Center and turned over to the port unit would have been placed in one of three separate lots awaiting placement into transport ships.

The first lot were those remains placed in temporary containers (shipping cases), destined for the Central Identification Laboratory (CIL) at Schofield Barracks, Hawaii. These temporary containers were all stored in Quonset huts at Guadalcanal. Great care was exercised to make certain that all clothing, equipment, personal effects and other items of possible identification were placed with the remains in the temporary containers. The second lot were those who had been placed in final-type caskets destined for the Hawaiian Distribution Center. It was normal to give next-of-kin the option of having their deceased buried in Hawaii or transported back home for burial in, for example, the family cemetery. The third lot were those in final caskets whose family had already determined that their loved one was destined for the mainland and local burial. All *Serpens* crewmembers were placed in temporary containers and assigned to the first lot.

The system was used to facilitate unloading of the ship upon arrival at Honolulu. The port unit maintained a complete locator card system for each of the three lots. As a further precaution against error, an additional inspector was assigned to each processing line to double-check the regular inspector. The second man examined the remains after they had been placed in the final-type caskets before sealing. He also checked tags and markings on the caskets and shipping cases to be sure they were in agreement with the disinterment directives.

After all the remains had been processed and stored pending shipment, a complete check of the deceased against disinterment directives was made. There were no discrepancies. When the USAT *Cardinal O'Connell* arrived at Guadalcanal during December 1947, loading operations began and proceeded in an orderly manner. The master of the ship assumed responsibility for the caskets and shipping containers as they reached the pier and placed all of them aboard ship before work ceased at any given time.

When the USAT *Goucher Victory* returned to Guadalcanal from Australia bearing the remains of U.S. personnel buried in cemeteries at Ipswich and Rockwood, the USAT *Cardinal O'Connell* moved away from the dock and anchored in Lunga Bay. The *Goucher Victory* then unloaded its dead. Upon completion of this operation, it pulled away and the *Cardinal O'Connell* returned to the dock, where it received the remains from Australia. This method of shifting the deceased was adopted because the hatches of the two ships did not permit a direct transfer. After this operation has been completed, the supplies, equipment and personnel of the 9105th TSU were placed aboard the *Goucher Victory*, which sailed from Guadalcanal on 12 January 1948 for Saipan. The *Cardinal O'Connell*, carrying the remains of 3,358 deceased service members from both Guadalcanal and Australia, headed for Hawaii. The vessel arrived in Honolulu on 21 January.

USAT Cardinal O'Connell pictured here bringing the remains of the Serpens' crew back home. Here she passes under the San Francisco-Oakland Bay Bridge on 12 February 1948. Photo courtesy BMCS Richard Miller, USNR (Ret.).

Back in Hawaii, the remains of the *Serpens'* crew were turned over to the Schofield Barracks Central Identification Laboratory (Schofield CIL), located at the AGRS Pacific Zone Headquarters, in order to better effect or confirm identifications and return the men to either their next of kin for burial or for the mass burial planned at Arlington National Cemetery.

The Schofield CIL finished processing the large set of mostly unidentifiable remains from the USS *Serpens*. In this instance, 52 sets of unsegregated remains were approved by the Office of Quartermaster General (OQMG) Board of Review to represent the more than 250 casualties that resulted when the USS *Serpens* exploded in Guadalcanal. Loaded back aboard Cardinal O'Connell, the remains of the *Serpens'* crew passed under the Golden Gate Bridge after dark on 11 February. Cardinal O'Connell then anchored off the San Francisco Marina until daybreak on the 12th. At the first streaks of dawn the Army transport, its flag at half-mast, passed under the San Francisco-Oakland Bay Bridge and moored to Pier Three, Oakland Army Base. The memorial service was open to the public with next-of-kin of deceased servicemen provided a private area to sit.

Chaplains representing each of the three major faiths, Catholic, Protestant and Jewish, participated in the services. After making the opening remarks at the memorial service, Brig. Gen Neal H. McKay, commanding general of the San Francisco Port of Embarkation, introduced Lieut. Gen. E. K. Smart, the Australian Consul General in San Francisco, who was the principal speaker. Chaplain (Major General) Luther Miller, Chief of Chaplains for the Army, who was in the area on an inspection trip, offered a prayer during the service. Rabbi C. Mour J. Stern, chaplain at Letterman General Hospital, offered the invocation and Rev. John R. Boslet, Navy chaplain, offered the benediction.

Detachments from the Navy, Army, Marines, Coast Guard and Air Forces acted as honor guards during the ceremonies. Attending the services were Gen. Mark W. Clark, Sixth Army commanding general; Rear Admiral D. B. Beary, 12th Naval District commandant; Rear Admiral W. K. Scammell, 12th Coast Guard District commandant; Brig. Gen. John E. Upston, Fourth Air Force commanding general; Maj. Gen. W. M. Robertson, Sixth Army deputy commander; and Maj. Gen. Leroy P. Hunt, Marine Corps commanding general of the Department of the Pacific.

Following the ceremony, and after the area had been cleared, debarkation of the caskets began. After the flag-shrouded caskets had been unloaded, inspected and their identification checked, they were moved to special mortuary trains which moved them to distribution centers throughout the United States.

The Army dispatched the first rail cars in this unique troop movement at Oakland, CA, on 13 October 1947, attaching U.S. Army Transportation Corps mortuary cars to civilian passenger trains bound for five of 15 distribution centers serving the continental United States. For four years in that pre-television era, mortuary cars, sometimes making up an entire train, reminded Americans of the price that their compatriots had paid to maintain freedom.

Public Law 383, enacted 16 May 1946, authorized the U.S. Army to spend $200 million to repatriate GIs, sailors, and Marines, as well as civilian federal employees who died abroad between 3 September 1939 and 30 June 1946. Reminiscent of a post-WWI effort, America's post-WWII repatriation of remains was unusual. Most nations buried their casualties where they died. The United States offered next of kin the option of bringing their dead home. Of 279,867 American war dead, relatives requested the return of 171,539. Those not repatriated were moved from temporary graves to private cemeteries or national cemeteries overseas maintained by the American Battle Monuments Commission. Remains that could not be positively identified, except for one Unknown Soldier and the majority of the *Serpens'* crew interred at Arlington National Cemetery, were buried in those 15 overseas national cemeteries.

The Army regarded service personnel remains not as cargo, but as passengers whose names appeared on a

"Passenger List, Deceased" aboard Army Transportation Corps ships that brought the dead from overseas. That status also applied aboard mortuary rail cars. The Army paid railroads a special reduced fare for each repatriated casualty and, for guards and military escorts, as with any troop movement, the regular fare.

Preparing to lift casket containers out of a ship's hold at Oakland Army Terminal. Photo courtesy U.S. Army Signal Corps.

Serpens crewmember S1c Lorren Edward Grisamore, destined to remain in California, was not placed on one of those trains. Rather, on 20 February, he was sent directly from the Oakland Army base to the Mira Loma quartermaster depot, accompanied by a Coast Guard escort. On 27 February 1948 he was laid to rest at Hillside Cemetery, Redlands, CA.

Not all of the ship's deceased were buried at Arlington and, thus, not all names of those who died on *Serpens* was later etched into the granite monument at Arlington National

Cemetery. Of the few who could be identified, some of their next-of-kin wanted them buried near them. Such was the case with S1c Lorren Edward Grisamore, as mentioned earlier and in the following two newspaper articles:

From the *San Bernardino County Sun* (San Bernardino, CA) dated 21 February 1948 (Page 12):

Body of Redlands Man Killed in Action Returned

"The body of Seaman 1/c Lorren E. Grisamore, killed in action in the Pacific theater of war, arrived at the Mira Loma quartermaster depot yesterday. Returned aboard the transport Cardinal O'Connell, the Redlands seaman is the son of Elza Grisamore, 611 West Fern Avenue. Emmerson's mortuary will be in charge of funeral arrangements."

From the *San Bernardino County Sun* (San Bernardino, CA) dated 26 February 1948 (Page 16):

Rites Planned for War Hero: Services Tomorrow for L. E. Grisamore

"S1/c Lorren E. Grisamore, killed in action in the Pacific war theater Jan. 29, 1945, will be laid to rest in his homeland tomorrow in graveside services to be held at Hillside cemetery, at 2 p.m.

"Redlands post of the American Legion will be in charge of the reinternment services, assisted by the Rev. Frank E. Butterworth, pastor of the Grace Methodist Church, of which Grisamore was a member.

"Grisamore was 22 years old at the time of his death. He was born in Trenton, Mo., but had lived in Redlands 18 years when he enlisted for service in the Navy(sic). He was the son of Elza H. Grisamore, 611 West Fern Street, Redlands, and Mrs. Gordon Bowman of Alhambra. He is also survived by two brothers, Gerald and Ralph, and two sisters, Mrs.

Geraldine Green and Marjorie Grisamore, all of Redlands.

"Seaman Grisamore was serving aboard the U.S.S. *Serpens*, a navy cargo vessel, when she was sunk by enemy action at Guadalcanal. He had been in the Navy two years."

S1c Grisamore's name does not appear on the granite monument dedicated to the men who died aboard USS *Serpens* on 29 January 1945. Another name that does not appear on the monument is S2c Michael Louis Cammarata, USCGR. In the Commanding Officer's letter to the Secretary of the Navy regarding the loss of his ship, LCDR Peery Stinson says: "One body has been found and identified as CAMMARATA, Michael L., (685-177), S2c, U.S. Coast Guard Reserve." Cammarata's body was removed from USAT *Cardinal O'Connell* and transported by mortuary train to his hometown just north of Boston, MA. He was given a High Mass and buried at St. Anthony's Church in Everett, MA, on Friday, 12 March 1948.

Fifty-two remaining caskets, representing the vast majority of some 250 crewmembers and Army stevedores aboard *Serpens* at the time of the explosion, and whose remains were mostly unidentifiable, were transported by mortuary train across the United States and, on June 15, 1949, interred in 28 graves at Arlington National Cemetery. There were 30 grave sites set aside for the burials, arranged in five rows of six graves each. Two were set aside for the *Serpens* monument which was dedicated 17 months later.

On 10 June 1949 the U.S. Coast Guard released a memorandum to the press and photographers interested in attending the event. It read:

For Your Information

The unidentified remains of 250 servicemen killed January 29, 1945, when the Coast Guard-manned cargo ship USS *Serpens* was completely destroyed by explosion (since determined not the result of enemy action) off Lunga Beach, Guadalcanal, B.S.I., will be buried in committal services at 1:00 o'clock Wednesday afternoon, June 15, in Section 34 of Arlington National Cemetery.

Section 34 is located at MacArthur Circle, intersection of Grant and Jessup Avenues.

The remains of 196 Coast Guard, 56 Army and 1 Public Health Service personnel will be buried in group graves.

Ceremonies will be simple. The Coast Guard, Army, Navy and Marine Corps will participate. Fifty Coast Guardsmen will act as escorts to families of the deceased; these families will be seated in reserved chair sections on both intersecting avenues. A large headboard, upon which the names of all victims appear, will be displayed. Chaplains of all faiths will officiate. The Marine Corps Band will play "Taps." Two hundred and eight casket-bearers will distribute Flags to next-of-kin.

The *Serpens* explosion was the largest single disaster suffered by Coast Guard in World War II. One hundred and ninety-six Coast Guardsmen were killed, three later being identified.

A 14,250-ton ammunition ship, the *Serpens* was loading depth bombs at the time.

The remains of these 250 victims originally were buried at the Army, Navy and Marine Cemetery, Guadalcanal, with full military honors and religious services, and have been repatriated under the program for the return of World War II dead.

The press and photographers are invited to attend on their own initiative, although representatives of the Public Information Divisions of the U.S. Army and U.S. Coast Guard will be available at the ceremony for any required assistance. Owing to the anticipated traffic congestion, it is recommended that travel requirements be considered in advance.

Names of the 248 victims are to be made available in list form Monday morning, and thereafter, at Room 5B45, Pentagon Building.

USS Serpens crew's caskets arrive at Arlington National Cemetery from Guadalcanal in 1949. Photo courtesy U.S. Coast Guard.

Approximately 1500 people attended the reinternment ceremony on Wednesday, 15 June 1949 at 1:00 p.m., but there were no speeches made. Catholic, Jewish and Protestant chaplains officiated. The U.S. Marine Corps Band played Pasternak's arrangement of Taps. A bugler echoed

Taps in the distance. The U.S. Navy also participated. To conclude the service, a Gold Star Mother escorted by an American Legionnaire placed a white carnation on each casket. A witness at the ceremony described it as "one of the most elaborate military services accorded our fallen heroes in appreciation of a grateful nation. Words would have been inadequate to express the deep gratitude and admiration for the men that welled up in the hearts of everyone who witnessed the service."

The following day, 16 June 1949, in the morning edition of the *Washington Post* newspaper, *Post* reporter Robert P. Jordan wrote this fitting tribute on the reburial services, entitled *1500 Attend Reburial Services for 250 War Dad in Arlington*:

> "It was hot and still that quiet night off Guadalcanal's Lunga Beach. Of the few ships there, only a 14,250-ton cargo ship, the USS *Serpens*, was busy. For hours she had been taking depth charges aboard.
>
> "The scuttlebutt was that she was taking all the ammunition off Guadalcanal," John P. Cosgrove, 30, of 5009 7th pl. nw., recalled yesterday. Cosgrove, then a yeoman first class, was on a ship 2000 yards away.
>
> At 11:30 p.m., January 29, 1945, the Coast Guard-manned *Serpens* exploded with a blast heard and felt for miles. For short seconds, night was turned into day. Streaks of orange light shot far into the night, and shrapnel rained on Lunga Beach.
>
> The blast killed 250 servicemen, blowing them to bits. The *Serpens* was completely destroyed.
>
> They read the roll call of the dead yesterday at Arlington Cemetery, the names fading away into the sound of rustling trees standing above a gently sloping hillside. In their shade, placed in 52 flag-draped coffins

awaiting reinternment, lay the mortal remains of those who died that night off Guadalcanal.

At each coffin stood four soldiers, sailors or Marines. Seated or standing in a huge semicircle about the burial plot—24 double graves—were the next-of-kin of the deceased. Their number was estimated at about 1500 by a Coast Guard officer.

They sat or stood there, many moved to tears, all straining to catch each word, as services were held. Their eyes seldom left the long rows of caskets—dully-gleaming, sun-dappled receptacles with a tin tag at the head of each…"Unknown."

In this largest group reinternment at Arlington since the war, services were held for Catholic, Protestant and Jewish dead. A Greek Orthodox and a Christian Scientist intoned burial rites for deceased of those faiths.

"Let our hearts, we pray thee, be deeply moved at this sight of death," said the Catholic chaplain. "Let us be mindful of our own frailty…"

The Protestant chaplain said: "I will lift up mine eyes unto the hills…"

The Jewish chaplain said: "Teach us to emulate their trust in Thee…"

Then came the sounding of Taps. At stiff attention stood members of the Armed Forces. Openly weeping were many relatives of the 195 Coast Guard, 54 Army and one Public Health Service dead whose remains soon were to be consigned to the soil of their native land.

When the echo died away, a lone carnation was placed on each casket, and then the next-of-kin walked among them, fixing the scene in their memories.

Many carried in their arms the United States flags that had earlier been folded on each bier's top—one for each of the dead. The flags were presented to the next-of-kin by the Coast Guardsman or soldier who was assigned to serve them."

The extraordinary nature of the catastrophe that claimed their lives made identification of the majority of the individuals aboard *Serpens* impossible. Two additional gravesites in the middle of the group were set aside for an octagon-shaped monument. This monument, constructed of Georgia granite, has inscribed upon it an alphabetical listing of the deceased serviceman's names, their rank/rate and branch of service. Those remains who were identified and sent back to their families are not inscribed on the monument. A temporary monument was prepared for the ceremony, listing the names.

The original but temporary USS Serpens memorial at the 15 June 1949 reinternment ceremony. The permanent octagonal granite memorial was dedicated on Thursday, 16 November 1950 at 2:00 p.m.

The USS *Serpens* Monument was dedicated on Thursday, 16 November 1950 at 2:00 p.m. The octagonal monument occupies two grave spaces in section 34. About

100 relatives and 200 others attended the dedication. Participating units included a color guard from the U.S. Coast Guard Cutter Duane (WPG-33), a color guard from The Old Guard at Fort Myer, Catholic, Jewish and Protestant chaplains, and The United States Army Band (Pershing's Own). Vice Admiral Merlin O'Neill, Commandant, U.S. Coast Guard gave a brief address.

USS SERPENS MONUMENT DEDICATION SCENE: Vice Admiral Merlin O'Neill, Commandant of the U.S. Coast Guard, delivers a dedication address prior to the unveiling of an octagonal monument in Arlington National Cemetery in memory of the 250 men who lost their lives in the USS Serpens disaster off Lunga Beach, Guadalcanal, on January 29, 1945. The dedication took place on the grave site November 16, 1950, with chaplains of Catholic, Jewish, and Protestant faiths participating. Approximately 300 people were in attendance. Directly behind the speaker are (left to right): Rear Admiral Alfred C. Richmond, Assistant Commandant of the Coast Guard; Lieutenant Colonel James B. Murphy, U.S. Army; Commander Joshua L. Goldberg, U.S. Navy, and Captain Paul G. Linaweaver, U.S. Navy. A Coast Guard color guard from the USCGC DUANE stands at the extreme right, with a platoon from the ship in the background (center). The U.S. Army color guard is at the left. File Date: November 1950; Photo No. 917446-3; photographer unknown.

ADDRESS OF VICE ADMIRAL MERLIN O'NEILL

Commandant, United States Coast Guard

Given at Dedication Ceremony

November 16, 1950

At the Monument to Victims of USS *Serpens*

Arlington National Cemetery, Virginia

Mr. Chairman, Honored Guests and Friends:

More than a year ago...in June of 1949...I came to this hallowed ground with a heavy heart...here to witness, with many of you, the recommittal services for many victims of a bitter war.

Now we gather again...in sorrow and deep humility...to pay all the homage within our power to shipmates and members of fellow services who met death in a great disaster.

The loss of the United States Ship *Serpens* on the night of January 29, 1945, was one of the greatest single ship casualties suffered by our armed forces during World War II. And it claimed not only Coast Guardsmen, but soldiers of our Army and a member of the Public Health Service, for in such fashion were we integrated as we fought shoulder to shoulder against a common enemy.

Today we meet to dedicate a memorial...a perpetual reminder to the generations which will follow us of the grim price that has been paid so that our country may remain free, and the rights of its citizens held inviolate.

In fact, this memorial was dedicated a little over five years ago by those men to whom we pay tribute now.

But it does present an opportunity...feeble and inadequate as this effort may be...to insist that their sacrifice, and the sacrifices of their loved ones, shall never be forgotten.

We cannot undo the past, because we are only human. The days of our lives, too, are numbered. But we can insure, when the passage of time has mercifully dulled our grief, that we can be intensely proud of what they did and that their memory shall be respected and honored forever.

The memorial reflects the collective set of graves near the intersection of Jessup and Grant Drives, Section 34, in Arlington National Ceremony. The epitaph above the names reads:

Herein Rest Those Who Lost Their Lives In The Sinking of USS Serpens, World War II, Jan. 29, 1945

ENS Howard L. Schlise was a PT Boat commander during World War II. He was a schoolteacher in Kaukauna (Wisconsin) in 1942 when he received his draft notice for the Army and decided to enlist in the Navy instead. Upon completion of his naval education at Princeton University, he was commissioned an Ensign and sent to the Third Fleet in Guadalcanal. His first assignment was a maintenance officer in the boat pool, responsible for increasing the number of available small boats. He was then assigned to the PT boat base at Tulagi and was given command of a PT boat. ENS Schlise (1914-2006) served in the Navy from 1942 to 1946. After he was discharged, he worked as a partner in his father's construction business, and as a teacher for a few years. He was interviewed by Terry MacDonald on 21 May 2005 at approximately 10:20 a.m. on 761 Jefferson Street, Sturgeon Bay, Wisconsin. Side 2 tape 1 is Howard Schlise talking about taking his PT boat out and picking up pilots and crew of planes that crashed in the water nearby. And then his thoughts turned to *Serpens*...

"The other thing that happened out there was the USS *Serpens*, [I] remember when she was torpedoed at the base there; not on the base but when she was out in the anchorage, anchorage around Guadalcanal. There were all these different ships that came in and they went in through locations and they were supposed to anchor. It's called the anchorage and they kept these screens going around it all the time of PC's [Patrol Craft], Destroyers and Destroyer escorts just to keep so the Japs could not get in there. Well, somewhere or another they had gotten in and they torpedoed this boat, the ship, and she was loaded with ammunition to the top. The USS *Serpens* was her name. Everybody on the boat was killed, everybody. The funny thing was it wasn't too long before that happened the officers went in to get their orders from the port directors and they had gone back and they were back out there. When it blew up there was only one person that was saved on the whole ship and he was the man that was in his bunk and he was blown out. Whatever happened he didn't have any idea but he, he was located on the bow of the ship and all he had was a broken collarbone we brought him back. He was the only man of that whole ship that was saved. They took him to a hospital, hospital 108 I think they called it; field hospital 108. Anyway, I went to a PT [boat] reunion and there were 500 people there. But of the 500 people there were only 12 officers of the wartime. They were all children of those officers and the families and the parents, aunts, uncles and so on. They called them, um, chips off the old block. My daughter took me out there. So, there was a lot of people there. One of the fellows there asked me if I had been at Guadalcanal with the ship had blown up. I said, 'Yes.' Well he said 'The fellow that was saved', he said, 'I was at the hospital there when he was brought in. He was in the next bunk from me.' He was talking about this fellow [inaudible]. Just one man out of the whole ship."

The *Serpens* Memorial Monument has been the backdrop for other commemorative memorials as well. For example, the American Veterans of World War II used it to commemorate the 10th Anniversary of the Japanese attack of Pearl Harbor.

On December 7, 1951, Corporal Eaton Rockwood, of Fanwood, NJ, played "Taps" as the flags waved in the breeze and a general saluted at the Arlington National Cemetery. The occasion was an observance of Pearl Harbor Day by the national headquarters of the American Veterans of World War II. Lt. Gen. Anthony McAuliffe (left), hero of Bastogne, Belgium, laid a wreath at the mass burial site memorial for 253 victims of the torpedoing of the USS Serpens in the Pacific. The Amvets' national commander, John Smith, stood with him. Photo No. 36960 and caption courtesy Associated Press (AP) Wire Service.

A year later the Memorial was again the backdrop for the 11th Anniversary of Pearl Harbor Day.

On December 7, 1952, Frank Wirtz, 81, of Ionia, Michigan, played the bugle at Arlington National Cemetery services marking the 11th Anniversary of the Japanese attack on Pearl Harbor. In front of Wirtz are (left to right) Rear Adm. George C. Wright, USN, main speaker, and Rabbi Morris Adler, National Chaplain of AMVETS which sponsored the observance. The monument (left) is in memory of 253 victims of torpedoing of the USS Serpens. Ionia citizens sent Wirtz here after he disclosed a life-long desire to serve as bugler at Arlington. Photo and caption courtesy Associated Press (AP) Wire Service.

The following year the AMVETS again used the *Serpens* Memorial as a backdrop, this time for the 12th Anniversary of the attack on Pearl Harbor.

On December 7, 1953, a bugler sounds "Taps" at the wreath-decked USS Serpens Monument in Arlington National Cemetery as a Color Guard stands by during an AMVETS memorial service today in observance of Pearl Harbor Day commemorating the Japanese attack on the U.S. Pacific base December 7, 1941. Photo courtesy AP Wirephoto 1953.

On 27 November 1954, Donald McLean spoke over the radio on the Australian Broadcasting Commission's show called *Weekly*:

> "You know, people say 'Americans are purely materialistic.' Some say 'There is no real democracy in America.' Well, now that I have spent a couple of months among the people of the United States, I know that we Australians can learn from them a good deal about their democracy. I know that their term 'Grassroots Democracy' has real meaning. Far from being materialistic, their work benefits the whole world. As to materialism, listen to this story…

Among the Americans who came to fight in the South Pacific during World War II was a Lieutenant Gayle Aiken, second-in-command of the U.S.S. *Serpens*, a munitions carrier operating in the forward area. Once, when a two-inch hawser fouled the ship's screw, young Gayle volunteered to free it; he worked under water most of the time...and in spite of sharks, undertow and cramping cold, cut away that hawser.

On January 29, 1945, the U.S.S. *Serpens*, while loaded with 14,000 tons of ammunition, was torpedoed off Guadalcanal. Of the 257 men onboard only two who were thrown into the sea when the torpedo struck, survived. Gayle Aiken was among those killed.

One of the survivors told his parents that their son had made many friends while the ship had been refitting in New Zealand. The parents wrote to some of these and traced, with New Zealand help, other friends of the men who had been on the *Serpens*. They wrote 250 letters to parents of Gayle's shipmates and their friends in Auckland.

In the course of this correspondence they learned that infant mortality is lower in New Zealand than anywhere in the world; they learned about baby care and systems of education that make childhood happier, so, with a momentous decision, they decided to found a magazine as a memorial to their son.

They put all their capital into the Lieutenant Gayle Aiken III Memorial Foundation. In memory of their son and his shipmates, they founded *Child-Family Digest* which reprints from other magazines any article likely to help children have happier lives.

The Digest makes no profits and accepts no advertisements. The parents, Gayle and Charlotte Aiken, do all the work associated with editing and publishing and that involves an incredible amount of work. All their money and all their time is devoted to the magazine which spreads ideas likely to help parents, teachers and others who work with children."

On Saturday, 28 February 1995, a day before the 50th Anniversary of *Serpens'* loss, the *Enterprise* newspaper (Wytheville, Virginia) ran an in-depth article on Kelsie K. Kemp, their local hometown hero, knowing he had been invited to participate in the 50th Anniversary Memorial service at Arlington National Cemetery. The article was of particular interest as Kemp talks about the *Serpens* being followed by a submarine – something he would have mentioned when interviewed under oath at the Court of Inquiry. The article is entitled *"Survivor of WWII tragedy remembers fateful night."*

Fifty years ago Sunday a sudden explosion ripped apart the USS *Serpens* (AK-97) claiming the lives of 250 United States servicemen—most of them U.S. Coast Guardsmen.

It was the greatest single disaster sustained by the Coast Guard in World War II.

Miraculously, though, two men on board the ammunition-supply ship survived the blast. Kelsie K. Kemp of Barren Springs was one of those men.

This weekend, Kemp is flying to Washington, D.C., to attend a special wreath-laying ceremony at Arlington National Cemetery commemorating the tragedy.

It took some prodding to get Kemp to attend the event, according to his wife, Elsie. Even today, it's difficult for the Coast Guard veteran to talk about the events of that ill-fated night off the coast of Lunga Beach, Guadalcanal in the Solomon Islands—the site of heavy fighting during the war.

A quiet, balmy day

It was around 11 p.m. Jan. 29, 1945, when Kemp, then 19, bedded down in the ship's boat and locker room on the second deck. Kemp worked in the locker room issuing tools and work supplies to other crewmen.

Earlier in the day the crew had loaded ammunition onto the USS *Serpens*. Kemp said rumor had it that the crew would pull out the next morning with the cargo. He had been stationed on the Coast Guard ship for nine months—his first sea duty since joining the service at age 17.

That night, Kemp's assistant and friend, George S. Kennedy, had also ventured into the locker room to sleep. Both men were either asleep or on the verge of sleep when a deafening noise interrupted the quiet, balmy night.

At approximately 11:15 p.m., the 14,250-ton ship exploded sending ammunition and hunks of steel in every direction. Reportedly, the sound of the blast was heard 60 miles away and flying debris damaged several nearby vessels.

"I think part of a shaft hurled over on the island (a mile away) and landed in a tent," he said. "Somebody said that the guy went as crazy as a bed bug. He knew the Japs had hit again."

Rescue crews survey the damage

When rescue crews finally ventured out to look for survivors, Kemp was found clinging to debris surrounded by a mixture of oil, death and destruction. The first thing he remembers seeing after the blast were the search lights of the approaching rescue boats.

"After they picked me up and I got to shore, I thought I was a loaf of bread going in a bread truck," he said. "I thought I was going to freeze to death (despite the fact that it was probably 100 degrees). I was so cold. I guess it was shock coming on."

Members of the rescue crew gave Kemp, who was only wearing a pair of shorts, a shirt to warm him up.

"It was three days before I ever knew what was going on," he said, "The fellers that had picked me up asked me 'don't you remember me?' and I said, 'no.' When they asked, I gave them ball scores or something. My brain was jumbled up pretty good."

Rescue crews took Kemp and Kennedy to a hospital in Guadalcanal. The explosion fractured Kemp's skull, injured his knee and left him with cuts all over his body. Kennedy suffered a broken collarbone, Kemp said.

To this day, Kemp doesn't know how he and Kennedy survived the blast. Two officers and six other crewmen were on shore during the explosion and also survived the incident. Due to the severity of the explosion, only a minority of the dead servicemen were ever positively identified.

Explosion theories abound

Several theories as to what caused the blast have been offered down through the years. Apparently, the official ruling cited the cause as "accidental."

Kemp, however, believes the USS *Serpens* fell victim to a Japanese submarine. According to Kemp, the ship's radar had apparently picked up a submarine following the same course as the *Serpens* sometime before the explosion. In addition, Kemp remembers seeing a Japanese weather plane flying near the ship preceding the disaster. Gunners were ordered not to fire at the plane, which Kemp believes was tracking the *Serpens'* movements.

"I never could understand one thing," he said. "That little plane came out buzzing like a skeeter and we couldn't do anything. There's probably a picture of me in Japan looking up with my mouth gaping open."

Whatever caused the Coast Guard ship to plunge into the watery depths, the loss of life was irrefutable.

Kemp still vividly remembers leaving the hospital and hobbling down to the Army, Navy and Marine Cemetery at Guadalcanal to attend the funeral services of his fallen comrades and friends.

The remains of the servicemen were later moved to Arlington National Cemetery where a monument was erected in their honor.

"I can't stand them ("Taps") today," he said. "It's just something you don't get over."

Word of the tragedy soon spread around, and Kemp's family realized that something was wrong. Soon after the explosion, someone sent a telegram to Kemp's family in Barren Springs. It read, "Am well and fit. Rumor not true. Regards to the gang."

Kemp didn't send the telegram, however. He said his family knew something was amiss since he never referred to his family as "the gang."

Kemp's brother, John Kemp of Wytheville, was also in the service during World War II.

"He heard about it and said 'good gracious! My brother was on that ship,'" Kemp said. John then attempted to find his brother and check on his welfare.

"We just missed," Kemp said. "When he came to Guadalcanal checking on me I was already gone."

Oil and skin don't mix

After about two months in the hospital, Kemp and Kennedy flew back to the States together. Kemp immediately wired his family and asked for $100. All of his belongings, except for a pair of shorts and wristwatch, were destroyed in the blast.

Placed on indefinite sick leave, Kemp eventually made it back home to Barren Springs. He was discharged from the Coast Guard June 8, 1945.

Kemp and Kennedy were awarded the Purple Heart, but it wasn't until a few years ago that Kemp actually received the medal. It and his service photograph now hang in a frame above the television.

When Kemp finished up his military career and reunited with his family, one of the first things his mother did was "sand" the ship oil off his face.

"She used plain ol' soap, a washcloth and elbow grease," he said. "She said that she just couldn't stand to see that no more." Even after several months, the oil from the sinking ship hadn't left his pores, serving as a physical reminder of his survival.

Life goes on

After leaving the Coast Guard, Kemp ironically landed a job at the Radford Ammunition Plant. He soon quit, however, and enrolled in barber school. Kemp cut hair for 28 years until he retired about 10 years ago.

While he was trying to move on with his life, Kemp kept in pretty close contact with Kennedy through Christmas cards and letters. The two eventually lost touch, however, and Kemp hasn't heard from his friend since the 1950s. Kemp was hopeful that the Coast Guard could track down his fellow survivor and the two could reunite in Washington.

"Some on the ship said that we looked like brothers," he said. "He was a good ol' boy."

Kemp has been asked to speak at the ceremony Sunday, but it's doubtful that he will. The emotional strain would be too much to handle, he said.

Kemp's wife has witnessed first hand the emotional scars that a tragedy can leave behind. Still, she believed the trip would be good therapy for her husband.

I think all and all he'll be glad we went," she said.

Sunday, the 29th of January 1995, marked the 50th Anniversary of *Serpens'* loss and at 2 p.m. there was a Memorial and Wreath-laying Ceremony at the USS *Serpens* Monument at Arlington National Ceremony. Introductory music was performed by the United States Navy Ceremonial Band, followed by the Parading of the Colors by the United States Coast Guard Ceremonial Honor Guard. The Navy's Ceremonial Band played the National Anthem and then Commander Timothy J. Demy, CHC, USN, the Chaplain at Coast Guard Headquarters, gave the Invocation.

The Opening Remarks and Introduction of VIPs was provided by the Command Enlisted Advisor, Reserve Forces, Master Chief Petty Officer William C. Phillips, USCGR. His remarks included the following:

"Commissioned as a military ammunition supply ship in August, 1943, the 14,000-ton USS *Serpens* operated in the Pacific Theater and had a mixed crew of 203 Coast Guardsmen, 56 Army soldiers, and 1 Public Health Service physician.

"On the evening of January 29, 1945, the *Serpens* was anchored one mile off Lunga Beach at Guadalcanal in the Solomon Islands. Nearing completion of a full day of loading munitions, the ship suddenly and inexplicably exploded and rapidly sank, taking with her 250 of the 252 crewmen aboard. Of the 193 Coast Guardsmen who perished, 176 of them were Reservists who served side-by-side with their active duty counterparts.

"The destruction was so swift and so complete that only a miracle could explain the survival of two of its seamen.

"Initially interred at the Army, Navy and Marine Corps Cemetery at Guadalcanal, the remains of the lost crew were repatriated and reinterred here on this site on June 15th, 1949.   1500 family and friends attended the service in silence.

"On November 16, 1950, the Monument you see here was officially dedicated with full military honors by Coast Guard Vice Admiral Merlin O'Neill.

"Today we pause in our busy lives to remember the deeds of these brave men who took the final measure of devotion in the victorious Allied effort to preserve the Free World.

"At this time I would like to present to you our Guest Speaker, representing the Commandant of the Coast Guard, Rear Admiral Richard M. Larrabee."

The Keynote Address was presented by Rear Admiral Richard M. Larabee, USCG, Chief, Office of Readiness & Reserve. His remarks included the following:

"On November 16, 1950, the Commandant of the Coast Guard, Vice Admiral Merlin O'Neill, led more than 300 mourners on this site to dedicate the granite memorial that stands before us today. In his words, 'Now we gather again . . . in sorrow and deep humility . . . to pay all the homage within our power to shipmates and members of fellow services who met death in a great disaster.'

"He went on to say that, 'The loss of the USS *Serpens* on the night of January 29, 1945 was one of the greatest single ship casualties suffered by our armed forces during World War II. And it claimed not only Coast Guardsmen, but soldiers of our Army and a member of the Public Health Service, for in such fashion were we integrated as we fought shoulder to shoulder against a common enemy.'

"Admiral O'Neill's remarks at the original dedication ceremony still ring true today, 50 years after that terrible night in the waters off Guadalcanal. Five decades have not diminished the impact that this disaster had on our nation's Coast Guard. In that instant, the explosion onboard the *Serpens* took the lives of 250 of our shipmates, Army and Public Health Service brethren. It remains one of the worst disasters in our history. In fact, in the 132-year history of this world-famous cemetery, a span that has included six major wars and numerous conflicts, the 28 sites that mark the final resting places of our fallen mates represent the second largest mass interment at Arlington.

"More than the effects that this tragedy has had on our Service, we must remember what brought us back to this hallowed site. We are here today to simply offer our special appreciation on behalf of the Coast Guard family for the supreme sacrifice that was made that fateful night.

"The years that have passed have naturally diminished our ability to reach all of the surviving families of the lost crewmembers. We are indeed fortunate to have with us today the families of three of them:

"First, Mr. Ed Stillman, son of Chief Pharmacist's Mate Washington Edward Stillman, USCG. Tragically, Chief Stillman's widow had planned to attend today's ceremony but passed away unexpectedly and was laid to rest this past Friday here at Arlington. Her son wanted you to know that, during the half century since her husband's death, she never remarried. To the Stillman family, please accept my deepest sympathies.

"Also here is Mrs. Rachel Esqueda and her family. Mrs. Esqueda's brother was Seaman 2nd Class Emelio Cruz Gonzales, USCGR.

"Finally, Mr. and Mrs. Joe Burke. Mr. Burke's brother was Seaman 2nd Class Leo Henry Burke, USCGR.

"To you, I offer the Coast Guard's solemn condolences and heartfelt gratitude. Your loss has helped preserve the freedoms we all enjoy today.

"When the *Serpens* went down, two Coast Guard seamen were thrown into the waters off Lunga Beach and miraculously survived the ordeal. Those men were Seaman 1st Class George S. Kennedy of San Marcos, Texas, and Seaman 1st Class Kelsie K. Kemp of Barren Springs, Virginia. I am pleased to say that Mr. Kemp along with his wife and several family members are with us here today. Mr. Kemp, thank you for making the long trip to Arlington and thank you for your contributions to a grateful nation.

"On behalf of Admiral Robert A. Kramek, Commandant of the Coast Guard, who sends his regrets on not being able to attend, and the Chief's Association, I would like Master Chief Lackey to join me in presenting Mr. Kemp and chosen members of the deceaseds' families a meaningful remembrance of this day.

"As Admiral O'Neill said in closing those many years ago, 'We cannot undo the past, because we are only human. The days of our lives, too, are numbered. But we can ensure, when the passage of time has mercifully dulled our grief, that we can be intensely proud of what they did and that their memory shall be respected and honored forever.'

"To the officers and members of the Capital Chiefs Chapter of the Coast Guard Chief Petty Officers

Association, to Command Sergeant Major Johnson, Admiral Manley, Chaplain Demy, the members of the U.S. Navy Ceremonial Band and to all of you who are here today, let me thank you for helping to carry on the memory of the USS *Serpens* and its crew.

"Thank you."

At the conclusion of his address, RADM Larabee and Seaman First Class Kelsie K. Kemp, USCG (one of the two survivors aboard *Serpens*), along with the USCG Ceremonial Honor Guard, placed a wreath at the base of the *Serpens* Monument. Afterwards the USCG Honor Guard performed a Rifle Salute, followed by "Taps" played by the Navy's Ceremonial Band. CDR Demy then gave the Benediction and the Navy's Ceremonial Band played "Eternal Father." The USCG Ceremonial Honor Guard then Retired the Colors and Master Chief Petty Officer Phillips made the Closing Remarks. As the guests departed they heard the Navy's Ceremonial Band play "As the Caissons Go Rolling Along" and "Semper Paratus". A reception immediately followed at the Fort Myer Community Center Ballroom.

Several inches of fresh snow surround members of the U.S. Coast Guard Honor Guard's Rifle Squad in preparation for the USS Serpens 50th Commemorative Ceremony at Arlington National Cemetery on 29 January 1995. Photo courtesy USCG.

CDR Timothy Demy, USCG Chaplain, delivers the Invocation at USS Serpens 50th Commemorative Ceremony on 29 January 1995. From left to right: MCPO Timothy Lackey, USCG; CDR Demy; RADM Richard Larrabee, USCG; and Command SGT MAJ Edwin Johnson, U.S.A. Photo courtesy USCG.

U.S. Navy Ceremonial Band plays patriotic music prior to the USS Serpens 50th Commemorative Service at Arlington National Ceremony on 29 January 1995. Photo courtesy USCG.

RADM Richard M. Larrabee, USCG, Chief, Office of Readiness and Reserve, delivers the Keynote Address at USS Serpens 50th Commemorative Ceremony at Arlington National Cemetery on 29 January 1995. Looking on is Command SGT MAJ Edwin Johnson, USCG. Photo courtesy USCG.

The U.S. Navy Ceremonial Band looks on as the wreath was laid at the USS Serpens Monument in Arlington National Cemetery at the 50th Commemorative Ceremony on 29 January 1995. Photo courtesy USCG.

US Coast Guardsmen, Serpens family members and other interested parties pause at the Fort Myer Community Center for the USS Serpens Reception following the 50th Commemorative Ceremony for the lost ship and crew at Arlington National Cemetery on 29 January 1995. Photo courtesy USCG.

The *Pentagram* is a weekly newspaper serving the Department of Defense in the DC Metro Area. On 3 February 1995, the newspaper published an in-depth article on the 50th Anniversary honors, written by Pentagram staff writer S. H. Kelly:

"For the first time in 50 years, a survivor of the Coast Guard's biggest disaster got to visit with the families of some of his former shipmates.

Former U.S. Coast Guard Seaman First Class Kelsie K. Kemp, one of only two survivors of the explosion and sinking of the USS *Serpens* off Guadalcanal Jan. 29, 1945, was a guest at a ceremony Sunday at Arlington National Cemetery honoring those who perished in the explosion.

Families of four sailors who served aboard the *Serpens* were also among the guests at the ceremony conducted at the *Serpens* Monument.

At the Fort Myer reception that followed the ceremony, Kemp explained why he had not contacted the families over the years. "I wanted to," he said, "but I didn't want to be the one to have to explain how their loved ones died."

The Barren Springs, Va., native said he had enlisted in the Coast Guard about three years before the *Serpens* sank. "I enlisted when I was 17—third year of high school," he recalled. "I had tried to enlist in the Navy and Marine Corps first, but they wouldn't take me."

He said that for the nine months he served aboard the *Serpens*, he worked in the "bosun's locker," issuing tools to the rest of the crew. He credits the locker's position near the bow of the ship with being instrumental in his survival and that of the only other survivor, Seaman 1st Class George S. Kennedy.

Kemp said that he and his good friend Kennedy bunked where they worked. "I don't know if I was asleep or awake" at the time of the explosion, he said, "but I guess I was asleep, because it was 11:25 at night."

He said the explosion caused him to see "nothing but a big red ball." And then he was picking himself off the deck. Contrary to the historical accounts, he said, he and Kennedy were not thrown from the ship by the blast.

"I don't know why, but the first thing I did was run my tongue round and round my mouth to see how many teeth I had lost." The search turned up no missing teeth, but he said he had searched so diligently he cut his tongue on his teeth.

His next order of business was to get out of the quickly flooding locker. "I guess air pockets in the bow kept the bow afloat," as the stern of the ship went down, he explained.

"My most serious injury was a skull fracture," he continued. The bone around his eye socket was broken, but he said he didn't know it at the time. He said his whole body was one big pain. "I was covered with oil, grease, burns and lacerations. One injury I didn't understand was a rope burn. I don't know where that came from."

As the ship sank lower in the water, he said, the rescue boats circled closer and closer, until they got close enough to take him and Kennedy aboard. "After that, I don't remember anything until about three days later."

While Kemp was still in the hospital recovering, Kennedy was released and went on a War Bond-selling tour. That, Kemp said, was the last time they saw each other, although they corresponded for a number of years.

The families present included Rachel Esqueda and her son David. She is the sister of crew member Seaman 2nd Class Emilio Cruz Gonzalez. Edward Stillman, son of Chief Pharmacist's Mate Washington Edward Stillman, also attended, as did Joe Burke, brother of Seaman 2nd Class Leo Henry Burke, and Robert G. Breen, son of Fireman 2nd Class Gerald C. Breen.

Stillman, born after his father went to sea on his last voyage, was never with his father.

Breen, however, said he was two years old when his father was killed and he has vague memories of him. "I have pictures of us together, and I remember a little Coast Guard uniform he bought me," he explained.

He added that he was glad for the ceremony because, until recently, his family still thought that the *Serpens* was sunk by a midget submarine. That was the initial and only information his family received, he said, although later it was determined that the explosion probably was not caused by enemy action.

Joe Burke said he was 13 when his brother went to sea, and 15 when he was killed. "What can I say? He was a great guy. We were a close-knit family—he was my big brother, and I looked up to him."

"There is one thing I'm thankful for," he continued. "A lot of families got telegrams when someone in their families got killed. The Coast Guard sent a chaplain to inform us—I'm thankful for that."

Coast Guard Rear Adm. Richard M. Larrabee was the guest speaker at the commemoration ceremony, which was attended by MDW [Military District Washington] Command Sgt. Maj. Edwin Johnson;

Coast Guard Master Chief Petty Officer William C. Phillips, command enlisted advisor for Reserve Forces; and Master Chief Timothy M. Lackey, command enlisted advisor. The chaplain for the service was Navy Cmdr. Timothy J. Demy.

During the ceremony, Larrabee presented commemorative plaques to Kemp and the families, along with copies of a postage stamp commemorating the sinking of the *Serpens*.

In 2005, another memorial commemoration, this one representing the 60th Anniversary of the loss of USS *Serpens* and her crew, was held at Arlington National Cemetery.

The Master of Ceremonies was Commander Chuck Polk, USCGR. His opening remarks are recorded here:

"On behalf of the DC Chapter of the Coast Guard Chief Petty Officers Association and USCG Flags Across America, I want to welcome you to a solemn, but very special, 60th Commemoration of the USS *Serpens* disaster...the largest single Coast Guard disaster in World War II.

"Joining us today are:

"Vice Admiral Thomas J. Barrett, US Coast Guard (Retired), former Vice Commandant of the Coast Guard, and his wife, Sheila;

"Master Chief Petty Officer Frank Tatu, Command Master Chief, U.S. Coast Guard Headquarters, representing the Commandant of the Coast Guard;

"Command Sergeant Major Jeffery L. Greer, U.S. Army, representing Major General Galen B. Jackman, Commanding General, Military District of Washington, and his wife Jenny;

"Captain Louis Farrell, U.S. Coast Guard Reserve, Chief, Office of Reserve Affairs, U.S. Coast Guard Headquarters;

"Captain Frank Buckley, U.S. Coast Guard Reserve, Retired; former Chief, Office of Reserve Affairs, U.S. Coast Guard Headquarters;

"Commander Laura Rabb, U.S. Public Health Service;

"Chaplain Kalas McAlexander, Commander, U.S. Navy Chaplain's Corps, Chaplain of Coast Guard Headquarters;

"Master Chief Petty Officer Jeffrey D. Smith, Reserve Force Master Chief, U.S. Coast Guard Headquarters;

"Paul Deafenbaugh, U.S. Coast Guard Auxiliary;

"And the following special guests:

"*USS Serpens* survivor Kelsie K. Kemp, Seaman First Class, USCG, his wife Elsie, daughter Glenna Young, grandson's Justin and Jamie Horton, and Jamie Horton, and Jamie's wife Anjie;

"Mrs. Jean Lockerby and her husband; Mrs. Lockerby is the sister of USS *Serpens* fallen hero, Private First Class Fred Gilbert, U.S. Army;

"Retired Coast Guard Boatswain's Mate Michael Zumbach, from Lansing, Michigan, grandson of *Serpens* plankowner;

"Those family members located but who could not attend, include:

"Mr. Charles Boyer, brother of lost *Serpens* crewman, Seaman Second Class Clarence W. Day, USCGR;

"Major Les Brody, U.S. Army Medical Corps, nephew of lost *Serpens* crewman, Seaman First Class Ely Gamsu, USCGR.

"The USS *Serpens* Story:

"Commissioned as a military ammunition supply ship in August, 1943, the 14,250-ton *USS Serpens* operated in the Pacific Theater and had a mixed crew of 203 Coast Guardsmen, 56 Army soldier stevedores, and 1 Public Health Service physician, Dr. Harry M. Levin.

"On the evening of January 29, 1945, the *Serpens* was anchored one mile off Lunga Beach at Guadalcanal in the Solomon Islands. Nearing completion of a full day of loading depth charges, the ship suddenly and inexplicably exploded and rapidly sank, taking with her 250 of the 252 crewmen aboard. Of the 193 Coast Guardsmen who perished, 176 of them were Reservists who served side-by-side with their active duty counterparts.

"In addition to the two shipboard survivors, there were eight others who were ashore on administrative business at the time of the explosion: Lieutenant Commander Peery L. Stinson, Commanding Officer, another officer and six crewmen. One of those six was Seaman Bob Smart, whom our Headquarters crew recently located. Bob now lives overseas and has shared his thoughts and memories with us through e-mail. Although he could not be with us today, he asked us to read the following to you, sent this past January 12: 'On 29 January 1945, I missed the 2200 launch to the USS *Serpens*. I was on the dock, reading a message from the Port Director. All of a sudden I heard a big explosion. I saw a big ball of fire and witnessed the *USS Serpens* disaster. The good Lord did not want me on board, so I was not on board. The bow was blown apart. Two were guys picked up from the water.

I remember both of them. I was on board *USS Serpens* from her commissioning in San Diego until she blew up. We were in service together January 43 until 29 January 45. I eventually left the Coast Guard. At first I did not like the service at all. I was in Long Beach, CA. The first thing I did was to put in for transfer overseas. I returned to Guadalcanal about 5 years ago. There are a lot of people diving there, so I went to a Diver's School there to ask about USS *Serpens*. The ship was so blown apart that there was nothing left. The loss of the ship is not the greatest of my memories. However, I really enjoyed sailing. The best part of my service experience was on board that ship.'

"Indeed, the destruction of *Serpens* that awful night was so swift and so complete that only a miracle could explain the survival of two of its seamen. Both were deep in the bow of the ship, worn out from working all day, when their world turned upside down. Seaman First Class Kelsie K. Kemp of Barren Springs, Virginia, and Seaman First Class George S. Kennedy of San Marcos, Texas, somehow made their way upward until they reached a fiery surface in the bay. Their ship rapidly disappeared along with all of their shipmates. Badly injured, both men spent the following months in and out of VA hospitals back in the States, recuperating and then returning to their homes. For their injuries in Theater, Seaman Kemp and Kennedy were awarded the Purple Heart by Rear Admiral L. T. Chalker, the Assistant Commandant of the U.S. Coast Guard. The two remained in touch for many years until one year the Christmas card from Kennedy to the Kemps did not arrive. Their connection has since bene lost. We are ever so fortunate to have found Mr. Kemp, however, and he and his family have honored us with their presence at both the 50th Ceremony in 1995 and again today.

"For the lost officers and crew, the 250 remains were originally buried at the Army, Navy and Marine Corps Cemetery in Guadalcanal with full military honors and religious services. The remains were repatriated under the program for the return of World War II dead in 1949.

"The mass recommittal of the 250 unidentified dead took place on these grounds. The remains were placed in 52 caskets and buried in 26 graves with two gravesites reserved for this memorial inscribed with their names. We are told it still ranks as the second largest mass gravesite in Arlington National Cemetery.

"A witness described the Dedication Ceremony as 'One of the most elaborate military services accorded our fallen heroes... Words would have been inadequate to express the deep gratitude and admiration... in the hearts of [all] who witnessed the service.'

"The USS *Serpens* Monument was dedicated on Thursday, November 16, 1950, at 2:00 p.m. One hundred relatives and 200 others attended the dedication. Participating units included a Color Guard from the U.S. Coast Guard Cutter *Duane*, a Color Guard from the Old Guard at Fort Myer, Catholic, Jewish and Protestant Chaplains, and the United States Army Band (Pershing's Own). Vice Admiral Merlin O'Neill, Commandant, U.S. Coast Guard, gave a brief address. He said, simply, 'We cannot undo the past... but we can insure/// that these men shall be respected and honored forever,'

"AT THIS TIME I WOULD LIKE TO PRESENT TO YOU OUR GUEST SPEAKER, RETIRED COAST GUARD CAPTAIN FRANK BUCKLEY.

Afterwards, the Guest Speaker, retired Coast Guard Captain Frank Buckley, said a few words and the ceremony concluded with these words from Commander Polk:

"I want to especially thank the sponsors of today's commemoration, the DC Chapter of the Coast Guard Chief Petty Officers Association and the 2005 Flags Across America group. Their dedication is unmatched and leads our service.

"Special thanks to the wife of Coast Guard Lieutenant Commander Aboagye for creating and donating the *Serpens* wreaths.

"Special thanks also to the U.S. Coast Guard Honor Guard, who provided the 4-person Color Guard and 7-person Rifle Team.

"And a very special thanks must go to Chief Warrant Officer Edward L. Kruska, editor of the Coast Guard Reservist magazine. Nearly 15 years ago, it was then-Petty Officer Second Class Kruska who, during a private stroll through these grounds, stumbled across this Georgia granite monument with its many Coast Guard names inscribed. Puzzled at why he had never heard of it, he searched the Cemetery's annals and there learned its heartbreaking, yet forgotten, story. Determined to bring it back to the forefront of Coast Guard history, he published an article on it in 1991. More importantly, he vowed then and there to resurface it four years later in a more official and fitting onsite tribute at the 50th Anniversary mark. Photos and details of that event are now in the records forever. Ed's vision and unselfish devotion to these lost comrades has led to this day. Ensuring Vice Admiral O'Neill's admonition would ring true. And it has.

"Mr., Kruska's singular efforts in 1991 have grown now to include an amazing group of folks who have caught his fervor and patriotism. At the top of that list is our friend and cherished comrade, current President of the DC Chapter of the Coast Guard Chief Petty Officers Association, Master Chief Petty Officer Mark Allen. Together, their enthusiasm has attracted so many fellow patriots, it would be impossible to name them all individually at this time. Suffice it to say they are all around us today and we give our heartfelt appreciation. God bless you all and this great Nation we call our own, the United States of America.

"Now, at this time, we invite everyone to gather for a nice, warm reception at the Women in Military Service to America (WIMSA) Memorial (at the foot of the main entrance to the cemetery). Parking has been extended to our party in the area in front of the Memorial.

"This ceremony is concluded."

As a side note, Kelsie Kyle Kemp, born on 5 July 1925, passed away in Wytheville, Virginia, on Thursday, 1 October 2015 at the age of 90. George Solomon Kennedy, who lived in San Marcos, TX, when he entered service, lived in Reno, NV, after being discharged. His whereabouts has not been determined.

Oral history at the USS Serpens Memorial. USCG Flags Across America, Arlington Cemetery, 8 November 2008. Photo courtesy USCG Press.

Photo of events during a Flags Across America event at Arlington National Cemetery Nov. 5, 2011. U.S. Coast Guard photo by Petty Officer 2nd Class Patrick Kelley.

Members of USCG Auxiliary Fort Washington Flotilla 25-07 together with personnel from the US Coast Guard Active Duty, Public Health Service, and the USCG Chief Petty Officers Association participated at the Annual Commemoration and Wreath Laying Ceremony at the Memorial for the USS Serpens at the Arlington National Cemetery on 5 February 2016. Photo courtesy U.S. Coast Guard Auxiliary, Department of Homeland Defense.

On 28 May 2012 Joe Massa, a former Army cargo checker assigned to the 492nd Port Battalion, remembered that fateful night in an article by Ron Simon of the News-Journal (Mansfield, Ohio) entitled "Local man served in Guadalcanal."

> The night the USS *Serpens* blew up off Lunga Beach in Guadalcanal, Joe Massa says he was lifted three feet off his bunk.
>
> Massa, a cargo checker with an Army transportation company, was ashore when the big ship exploded. The 88-year-old retired president of Mansfield's Key Bank was sleeping under canvas close to shore when the *Serpens*, an ammunition ship manned by Coast Guard Reservists, blew up.

"They never did determine just why the ship blew up. Tokyo Rose on radio claimed a Japanese submarine did it, but that was never proven."

"I think they were loading depth charges when it happened," he said.

Massa recalls running down to the beach after the explosion and seeing the *Serpens'* bow still in the water. The rest of the ship was gone.

Of the Army personnel aboard *Serpens* at the time of the explosion, he said most of those men were stevedores, but six to eight of them were cargo checkers, the men with the clip boards who made sure everything was on board and stored properly. His unit was sent out into the Pacific.

"We thought we were headed for New Zealand, but at New Caledonia we were redirected to Guadalcanal.

He would spend close to two years on that humid and muddy patch in the Solomon Islands chain.

"When we arrived there were still Japs hiding in the hills and Marines searching for them," he said. "It was hot. Very hot. Malaria and dengue fever were common. When we went swimming we had to be on the alert for sharks. We went through a couple of typhoons while we were there."

On 27 June 2018 Rod Hadland from the *High Plains Reader* newspaper (Fargo, North Dakota) interviewed SGT Daniel T. Mihuta, USA, then 95 years old and formerly of the 492nd Port Battalion, Company B, Guadalcanal. He was there when *Serpens* exploded.

"Mihuta was drafted into the United States Army after high school, along with his brother, who ended up in Germany. Dan was sent to Guadalcanal as part of the 492nd Port Battalion, Company B. He earned the rank of sergeant, overseeing men to load and unload cargo ships that came into Guadalcanal.

"He recalled one experience: 'We were loading supplies from the Guadalcanal area to send further up the line. The war had already begun now, according to the island, Guadalcanal was declared safe. Prior to this time we had no lights on the island, at sunset. But now we were declared safe and so we were starting to use lights. And it was about a few months after that we were loading a ship with aerial depth charges which go off on contact. And I had worked that ship until about 4 o'clock that afternoon, and closed that ship and came (aboard) shore. And then they found some more bombs, so a second crew of my men went out to finish up the loading and we had 52 from my company plus the people on the ship, which were sailors and Merchant Marine, a total of 250 men. The ship blew up, we never knew whether a bomb went off, or whether the Japanese torpedoed it. Japan claimed they torpedoed it, but we say we never knew.' That ship was the USS *Serpens*."

The co-author, Douglas Campbell, spent time at the National Archives and Records Administration (NARA) in College Park, MD, researching *Serpens* and the 492nd Port Battalion. With the help of NARA employee David Castillo, approximately 250 pages of historical reports from the 492nd Port Battalion, covering the period 25 January 1943 to 10 May 1946, were located in Record Group 407 (WWII Operations Reports in the Records of the Adjutant General's Office, 1905-1981). Within those 250 pages, the monthly historical reports for January through March 1945 were found to be missing, or possibly never written. These reports would have, of course, reflected the events of 29 January 1945 and the work of the Battalion in the aftermath of the explosion. In early 1946, the historian for the Battalion, in attempting to compile the annual (1945) history of the 492nd, wrote: "This report is particularly sketchy due to the fact there has been a complete turnover in personnel and previous monthly reports have not been located." It is known that the 492nd received their orders to depart Guadalcanal – they departed on 4 May 1945 and arrived at Cebu City, Philippines, on 16 May. They then departed from there on 30 August 1945, arriving Yokohama, Japan, on 8 September. Within those 250 pages of history there was no mention of the Battalion's losses or the loss of *Serpens*.

AWARDING THE PURPLE HEART MEDAL

All crewmembers of *Serpens* as well as the Army's 231st Port Company stevedores who were killed aboard *Serpens* were initially awarded the Purple Heart Medal; a few physically received the medal, many did not. The most notable awardees were the two survivors, Kemp and Kennedy. In the 30 May 1945 edition of the Austin American newspaper, page 5, the following article entitled "Only Survivors of Munitions Ship Explosion Given Awards" was published:

> "Seaman First Class George S. Kennedy and one other USS *Serpens* survivor were awarded Purple Hearts recently by R. Adm. L. T. Chalker, assistant commandant of the U.S. Coast Guard.
>
> The presentation of the awards and citations was one of the features of "Coast Guard Night." Kemp and Kennedy are the only survivors of more than 200 officers and men who were aboard when the USS *Serpens*, carrying a cargo of ammunition, was lost against enemy action as it lay anchored approximately a mile from the Guadalcanal shore on Jan. 29."

Another Purple Heart awardee was the ship's Executive Officer, LT John Gayle Aiken, III. In the book "Northwood Boys in World War II," it states: John Gayle Aiken, III, was born in New Orleans, La., on June 3, 1919. In 1941, after receiving his degree from Yale, he became an Ensign in the U.S. Coast Guard. He served five months on the USS *Mohawk* [WPG-78] and then was transferred to the Coast Guard Academy at New London, Conn., where he was an instructor in navigation. Repeated requests brought ultimate assignment to the USS *Serpens*, an ammunition ship.

LT John Gayle Aiken, III
3 June 1919 – 29 January 1945

Gayle, then a Lieutenant and Executive Officer of his ship, lost his life when the *Serpens* was sunk apparently by enemy action off Guadalcanal on January 29, 1945. He was awarded the Purple Heart. The following is quoted from a letter of his commanding officer to Gayle's parents: "…I considered your son one of the finest officers and finest men that I have ever known. A mark of his ability is indicated by the fact that he had been certified as ready for command of the ship by both myself and my predecessor. He was untiring in his efforts and unswerving in his loyalty to the ship and her crew. I have never had so valuable an assistant and so pleasant an associate. You had a fine son, the service had a fine officer..."

Watertender First Class Harry Edward Aro was another *Serpens* crewmember awarded the Purple Heart as stated in his obituary:

> "[Dead is] Watertender First Class Harry Edward Aro, son of Mrs. Mary V. Aro who resided at 1820 Thomas Avenue, Baltimore, Maryland during the war. Harry served as a Watertender 1st Class on the U.S.S. *Serpens* during World War II. Harry was declared "Missing In Action" when the *Serpens* exploded while depth charges were being loaded off the shore of Lunga Beach. He was awarded a Purple Heart. 198 members of *Serpens* crew and 57 members of an Army stevedore unit were on board the ship and killed in the explosion along with one Army soldier on the shore."

It has also been noted in several articles regarding the loss of USS *Serpens* that Dr. Harry M. Levin, the surgeon and only member of the U.S. Public Health Service aboard, was posthumously awarded the Purple Heart Medal. Another found as having been awarded the Purple Heart Medal was GM3c Woodward Solomon Babcock, USCGR. His father was a Vice President of General Motors at the time of his death.

The reason for being awarded the Purple Heart was because the majority of those sitting on the *Court of Inquiry into the Loss of USS Serpens*, after reviewing all the evidence, concluded that *Serpens* was lost to enemy action; specifically, that *Serpens* had been torpedoed by a submarine that was subsequently seen afterwards, pursued by Navy vessels and escaped. After the war the Findings and Conclusion of the Court of Inquiry were overturned and it was determined that *Serpens* was lost due to an "accident intrinsic to the loading process." This, in essence, placed the blame on the Coast Guard crew and Army stevedores. No one considered another possibility – that there was no enemy submarine and that there was nothing wrong with the way the depth bombs were unloaded off the DUKW's and barges and placed in the hold of the ship. Another possibility was the inherent danger of the explosive material inside the depth bombs – a substance called Torpex, short for Torpedo Explosive – a mixture of 42% RDX, 40% TNT and 18% aluminum powder.

The Great Holston Ordnance Works of Kingsport, Tennessee, which is where RDX was mass produced, is one of the great unknown American production stories of World War II. On what had once been rolling pastureland, the U.S. government authorized the construction of Holston Ordnance Works which would produce RDX. Nearly 18,000 workers were employed in the construction of the massive and secret RDX plant, built at a cost $100 million (over a billion dollars in today's terms). By 1944, the United States was producing 50 million pounds of RDX a month. The Bureau of Ordnance publication OP 1664, U.S. Explosive Ordnance, dated 28 May 1947, explains the difference between Torpex 1, 2 and 3.

"The original Torpex (Torpex 1) was a mixture of 45% RDX, 37% TNT, 18% Aluminum powder (1% wax added). Torpex 2, which is now being used, is 42% RDX, 40% TNT, 18% Aluminum powder (1% wax added). It is used in mines, torpedo war heads, and depth bombs." *Serpens* was loading munitions packed with Torpex 2. The "1% wax added" in the original depth charges was beeswax and the melting point of beeswax is 145 to 147 degrees Fahrenheit. Unfortunately, beeswax is made, of course, by bees, and there was not enough beeswax being produced during the war to keep up with demand. So it was decided to switch out beeswax for paraffin wax, which they called Torpex 2. But paraffin, a byproduct from the refining of lubricating oil, begins melting at 99°F.

Maybe not a problem when fighting U-boats in the North Atlantic, but in the hot tropical sun and high humidity of the South Pacific, the wax would melt. Letters mailed home from *Serpens* crewmembers remarked how much hotter it was than usual. Then once in the increasingly hot holds of the ship, with little if any air circulation, and many sitting next to the heated hull, the Torpex would continue to produce pressure within its casing due to Torpex mixing with humidity and creating explosive hydrogen gas. In the presence of an oxidizer -- oxygen being a good one -- hydrogen can catch fire without any outside catalyst such as an electrical spark.

Knowing that a difficulty with Torpex was that it produced hydrogen gas which built up pressure in the casing during stowage, something had to be done to correct that potential problem. It was discovered that 0.5% by weight of calcium chloride added to the mixture would absorb all the moisture and eliminate the production of gas. It was recommended by the Bureau of Ordnance that this percentage be added to the Torpex mixture and that the resulting mixture be designated Torpex 3. However, Torpex 3 began production years after the loss of *Serpens*.

The Bureau of Ordnance also warned: "Precautions must be taken in the manufacture and loading of Torpex to avoid inclusion of moisture." It only took one to explode (the initial explosion heard by eyewitnesses) before igniting all the others that were sitting there in unstable condition. So that is a workable theory - enough to cast doubt on the other findings of enemy torpedo or something wrong with the loading process. Which brings us back to the Purple Heart.

The Purple Heart is awarded in the name of the President of the United States to any member of the Armed Forces of the United States who, while serving under competent authority in any capacity with one of the U.S. Armed Services after 5 April 1917, has been wounded or killed. Specific examples of services which warrant the Purple Heart include any action against an enemy of the United States; any action with an opposing armed force of a foreign country in which the Armed Forces of the United States are or have been engaged; while serving with friendly foreign forces engaged in an armed conflict against an opposing armed force in which the United States is not a belligerent party; as a result of an act of any such enemy of opposing armed forces; or as the result of an act of any hostile foreign force.

The Purple Heart differs from most other decorations in that an individual is not "recommended" for the decoration; rather he or she is entitled to it upon meeting specific criteria. A Purple Heart is awarded for the first wound suffered under conditions indicated earlier.

A "wound" is defined as an injury to any part of the body from an outside force or agent sustained under one or more of the conditions listed earlier. A physical lesion is not required; however, the wound for which the award is made must have required treatment by a medical officer and records of medical treatment for wounds or injuries received in action must have been made a matter of official record.

When contemplating an award of this decoration, the key issue that commanders must take into consideration is the degree to which the enemy caused the injury. The fact that the proposed recipient was participating in direct or indirect combat operations is a necessary prerequisite, but is not sole justification for award. The Purple Heart is not awarded for non-combat injuries.

Enemy-related injuries which justify the award of the Purple Heart include: injury caused by enemy bullet, shrapnel, or other projectile created by enemy action; injury caused by enemy placed land mine, naval mine, or trap; injury caused by enemy released chemical, biological, or nuclear agent; injury caused by vehicle or aircraft accident resulting from enemy fire; and, concussion injuries caused as a result of enemy-generated explosions.

Injuries or wounds which do not qualify for award of the Purple Heart include frostbite or trench foot injuries; heat stroke; food poisoning not caused by enemy agents; chemical, biological, or nuclear agents not released by the enemy; battle fatigue; disease not directly caused by enemy agents; accidents, to include explosive, aircraft, vehicular, and other accidental wounding not related to or caused by enemy action; self-inflicted wounds (e.g., a soldier accidentally or intentionally fires their own gun and the bullet strikes his or her leg), except when in the heat of battle, and not involving gross negligence; post-traumatic stress disorders; and jump injuries not caused by enemy action.

However, it is not intended that such a strict interpretation of the requirement for the wound or injury to be caused by direct result of hostile action be taken that it would preclude the award being made to deserving personnel. Commanders must also take into consideration the circumstances surrounding an injury, even if it appears to meet the criteria. In the case of an individual injured while making a parachute landing from an aircraft that had been brought down by enemy fire; or, an individual injured as a result of a vehicle accident caused by enemy fire, the decision will be made in favor of the individual and the award will be made. As well, individuals wounded or killed as a result of "friendly fire" in the "heat of battle" will be awarded the Purple Heart as long as the "friendly" projectile or agent was released with the full intent of inflicting damage or destroying enemy troops or equipment. Individuals injured as a result of their own negligence, such as by driving or walking through an unauthorized area known to have been mined or placed off limits or searching for or picking up unexploded munitions as war souvenirs, will not be awarded the Purple Heart as they clearly were not injured as a result of enemy action, but rather by their own negligence.

So herein is the crux of the argument as to why those killed or wounded by the explosion of *Serpens* should have their Purple Heart Medals reinstated: 1) they were clearly in a war zone; 2) the preponderance of evidence provided to the Court of Inquiry indicated that an enemy submarine sank the *Serpens* and that was how the Court ruled; and 3) It was never proven that the loss of *Serpens* was actually due to any singular event – be it being torpedoed, an "accident intrinsic to the loading process," sabotage by the enemy, or because, after securing all munitions and completing the loading process by 4 p.m., a depth charge exploded on its own in the hold nearly 8 hours later. The authors believe that, per Army Regulation 600–8–22 on Military Awards, that taking into account the circumstances and various possible scenarios, "the decision will be made in favor of the individual and the award will be made."

Lastly, if the military changed their mind about awarding the Purple Heart Medal, then they should have officially vacated the award to those killed or wounded in the loss of *Serpens*. There is no evidence that they did. In fact, in 1995, just days before the 50th Anniversary Commemoration of the Loss of *Serpens* at Arlington National Cemetery, the survivor Seaman Kelsie K. Kemp, proudly displayed his Purple Heart encased in a frame with his other World War II ribbons and medals. That photograph was published on the front page of his local newspaper. The precedent had already been set and no one said anything to change it; a handful cannot be awarded and allowed to keep their Purple Heart Medals—either everyone affected should be entitled to it or no one should. He stated, in 1995, that the Coast Guard finally gave him the physical Purple Heart Medal in 1956, seven years after the Court's 1945 conclusion was reversed in 1949.

To remember all the men of *Serpens*, including the Army stevedores who died alongside them, one should consider what the award of the Purple Heart will do to help us remember them by and to consider the words of James A. Michener from his book *Tales of the South Pacific*: "They will live a long time, these men of the South Pacific. They had an American quality. They, like their victories, will be remembered as long as our generation lives. After that, like the men of the Confederacy, they will become strangers. Longer and longer shadows will obscure them, until their Guadalcanal sounds distant on the ear like Shiloh and Valley Forge."

This photograph appeared in the 29 May 2005 edition of the Roanoke Times. The caption reads: "Kelsie Kemp honors his World War II service in the Coast Guard with a small display in his living room. His medals include the Purple Heart for his injuries suffered on the Serpens, a photograph of which hangs in the center of the display." Photograph by Gene Dalton, Roanoke Times.

VISITING GUADALCANAL

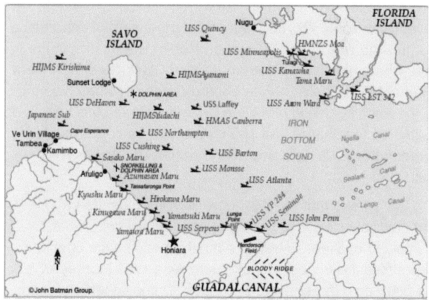

A chart of Iron Bottom Sound, located north of Guadalcanal, showing the numerous ships lying on the seafloor, including the remains of USS Serpens at Lunga Point. Iron Bottom Sound derived its name from the 200 odd ships and 690 aircraft that lie within it. Ships and aircraft from both Imperial Japanese forces and the American Allied Forces are represented. Image courtesy www.Navsource.org.

As the co-authors depleted their source material found through Internet searches and letter writing campaigns, it became increasing important to physically go to Lunga Bay at Guadalcanal, British Solomon Islands. Our interests were varied: 1) to dive and photograph both the *Serpens'* bow sitting in 110 feet of water and the remaining debris field (The wreck is located at: 9°24'37"S 160°0'40"E / 9.41028°S 160.01111°E, or .43 miles directly off Lunga Beach); 2) to visit the Solomon Islands National Museum in Honiara and the Vilu War Museum in Lenggakiki for any possible stored material concerning *Serpens* not available on the Internet; and 3) to interview anyone who still lived in the area on what they remember from the day of the explosion and for the days thereafter as the town and surrounding area cleaned up from the damage. The oral histories were important given that the event was some 75 years ago. One other item of importance for this trip was for the co-author, Robert Breen, to visit the site where his father, Fireman Second Class Gerald Clement Breen, USCGR, lost his life aboard *Serpens* some 75 years ago. Accompanying him were two of his three sons who had gathered together to visit and dive on the gravesite of their grandfather. Also accompanying Robert Breen was a daughter-in-law.

We agreed that the dive team should embark on a methodical process to become better familiar with what remained of *Serpens* before actually spending the time and resources it was going to take to make such a journey. We decided on a three-phase approach: 1) see if there were any Liberty ships still in existence that we could visit, photograph and overall get a sense of the enormity of a 440-foot-long vessel; 2) see if there were any Liberty ships off the coast of the United States that we could dive on in preparation for the 110-foot dive on *Serpens*; and 3) to make the trip to Guadalcanal and dive what remained of the *Serpens*.

Our research for Phase 1 found two Liberty ships that were now floating museums on display within the United

States. One was the SS *Jeremiah O'Brien* located at Pier 45, Fisherman's Wharf, San Francisco, CA.

The SS *Jeremiah O'Brien* located at Pier 45, Fisherman's Wharf, San Francisco, CA, just aft of the World War II submarine USS *Pampanito* (SS-383) which is also open for tours. Photograph by Douglas E. Campbell.

The other was the SS *John W. Brown* located at Inner Harbor, Baltimore, MD. As the *John W. Brown* was only an hour's drive away from Glyn Owen, one of our dive team members, that Liberty ship was selected for an orientation tour. With the assistance of Charles L. "Chuck" Weaver and Dan Donald we received a "behind-the-scenes" tour that included a look below the hatches into the holds and a history lesson on the *Brown* and what Liberty ships meant to the war effort.

Liberty ships were a product of the Emergency Shipbuilding Program that built more than 2,700 such ships during World War II. Designed for quick and relatively easy construction, Liberty ships made possible the massive sealift of troops, arms, and material to all theaters of the war. The *Brown* was built in 56 days by the Bethlehem-Fairfield Shipyard in Baltimore.

The *Brown* made 13 voyages during and immediately after the war. Those voyages took her to the Persian Gulf, the Mediterranean Sea, and Northern Europe. The *Brown* was at the Anzio beachhead and was part of the invasion force at Operation Dragoon, the invasion of Southern France in August 1944. The *Brown* was awarded the Merchant Marine Victory Medal, the Combat Bar, and war zone medals for the Atlantic, the Mediterranean/Middle East, and the Pacific theaters.

After carrying Marshall Plan cargoes to Europe to aid in post-war rebuilding, the ship was used as a vocational high school in New York City from 1946 to 1982. She was then returned to the James River Reserve Fleet until acquired by Project Liberty Ship in 1988. The *Brown* has been fully restored and is an operating museum ship and memorial. She is the only operating Liberty ship on the east coast. The ship conducts 6-hour Living History Cruises about four times a year and travels to other east coast ports.

An accounting of the trip was made by Glyn Owen, who is also a Board member on the Maritime Education and Research Society (MERS), a non-profit 501(c)(3) charity with offices in North Carolina and Florida. Glyn would later make the trip to Pensacola, FL, for the preparatory dives on the Liberty ship *Joseph L. Meek* (testing out the underwater camera gear, etc.) and the trip to Guadalcanal in the British Solomon Islands to dive the remains of the USS *Serpens*. His thoughts are as follows:

"I arrived in Baltimore, MD, at around 6:30 a.m. and walked up to the *Brown*, expecting to be by myself as I wanted to first view the 440-foot-long vessel from the pier on a quiet morning. Instead, what I found were more than 40 volunteers scampering about, preparing, ironically, for a U.S. Coast Guard inspection. The *Brown* was preparing to get underway in a few days on one of their Living History Cruises into the Chesapeake Bay and they first had to pass their inspection. One of the crewmembers, seeing me just standing there looking up at this huge vessel, asked me what I was doing out here so early in the morning as he knew I wasn't a member of the working detail preparing for the Coast Guard's arrival. I explained that a personal tour had been set up and approved in advance, that it had to do with the research and upcoming trip to Guadalcanal to dive the wreck of a related Liberty ship and that I was waiting for the official tour guide to arrive. After a couple of heartbeats, he looked at me and said "Want some coffee?" I said "Sure, would love some" and that's how I got to board the *Brown*. With my first footsteps on her deck, I looked around and thought how something of this size could have just vaporized in an instant. I could not imagine how, in 1945, what it must have been like to the *Serpens* men who perished, but I don't see how they could have expected or felt anything based on the size of the explosion that night on 29 January.

"While topside I was able to see the cover for Hold No. 4. They were wood hatch covers, approximately 8 feet by 4 feet that fit over "I" beams. They are removed by 2 crewmen using hooks. Underneath the wooden cover was another cover to prevent water from going down into the hold. During WWII I was told that the crew may have used canvas to cover over the hold openings as well. As many as four layers of canvas could have been used. The "I" beams can be removed as well. The Liberty ships were so versatile in that it could carry almost the weight of the vessel as cargo. The depth line on the *Brown* showed 30 feet. With the vessel's cargo holds fully loaded, the 30-foot mark would disappear. The vessel's single engine, with little over 2500 HP, allows the 440-foot vessel to wisp along at 9 to 10 knots max. Sitting in the galley with a hot cup of coffee, I was told that if a Liberty ship made one successful trip, it paid for itself. They were ugly, slow, and armed with minimum fire power – in WWII they were simply sitting ducks. These ships got their nickname "Liberty" because the first one built was named SS *Patrick Henry*, famous for his "Give me liberty or give me death" speech. There were 2,710 built and some 2,400 survived WWII – remarkable considering the average time to build one was 42 days. The SS *Robert E. Peary* holds the record – built in 4 days, 15 hours and 29 minutes! Sadly, only two remain seaworthy in the United States. Coffee break over, it was time for the tour!

"Hold No. 4 was different than the other holds in that running across the middle of the hold was the shaft for the single propeller. This took away valuable cargo area for the *Brown* and other Liberty-class boats. There were two ladders you could climb down into the hold to the level of the propeller shaft. From the shaft there were another two ladders (one on each side of the shaft) you could take to climb down to the very bottom of the hold.

The hold was dark. The volunteers aboard *Brown* added lights in the hold but they said that, originally, the area had no lights because when the wood covers were removed, there was enough natural light provided. Hold No. 4, like Hold No. 3, had an emergency egress ladder that had a shroud around it, like climbing up a ladder inside a tunnel. This was for protection. Where light was limited, so was ventilation. Once the "I" beams are replaced and the covers and canvas inserted, she would have been dry. The ladder areas would have been shut as well. As for the heat, the morning I was on board (early April in Baltimore), the outside temperature was mid 40's and down below at the bottom of Hold No. 4 it was downright chilly. My guide said that during the summer, if the temperature hit 80 then the engine room temperature would range over 100 minimum. The Holds would be a bit cooler but very humid and working conditions would have been difficult. So, at the bottom of the Hold, looking up, I can envision the Stevedores above me loading the Hold and the men below guiding the cargo and placing it into position. The heat, the noise, smell of oil, darkness and commotion must have been tedious to be kind.

"When I thought of the explosion, I wondered if someone could have boarded the *Serpens*, made their way to Hatch 4, dropped down into the Hold and purposely set off one of the depth charges being stored there. With no fuse to add to the bomb (they were stored elsewhere under lock and key), it would have been difficult but not impossible. From topside, with 188 crew on board, it could have succeeded if one was very familiar with the precise maneuvering of the boat. They would have to have known where Hold 4 was and that the explosives were in that particular Hold. More importantly, though, the wooden hatch covering Hold No. 4 had already been secured topside, so no, I see this as an improbable feat. Once on board, it's a massive area but with one grenade, would it be 'Boom, it's all over'? Do I believe that a person could board, go through the tween deck unseen, climb below to the engine room area, down the center, open up a door and enter that way? "Tween' is a colloquialism of the word 'between.' In a ship, the tween deck actually means an empty space separating or between (tween) two other decks in the hull of a vessel. Seems less likely by the mere fact I would assume there was 24/7 security on a vessel whose loaded cargo was primarily explosives. But it would also have been pitch black down there – *Serpens* exploded at around 10:30 p.m. local time.

"Above the Tween deck, the sleeping quarters were tight. These Liberty Class ships were known to hold up and more than 500 men – Officers, crew and passengers. It was said that to simply operate a Liberty ship, a crew of under 40 was all that was needed. With that said, there were bunks all over the place. The officer's quarters were small, with a port hole, and with two bunks per room. I did not see the Captain's Quarters.

"Holds Nos. 4 and 5 are the largest and if 4 was loaded with the cargo that *Serpens* had, it would be like having a 4000-square-foot home made completely of explosives go off. In reading the accounts from others who witnessed the explosion, there were two – a small one and then all the explosives going off nearly simultaneously. The blast alone must have been heard for miles around and the fact that the forward area of the *Serpens* survived the blast seems lucky at best. As for the Bosun's locker and anchor/chain area in the forward bow, where the two men survived, they thought they had escaped or were blown out through holes in the hull. My two immediate thoughts were: God was there watching over them and escorted them through those holes or they were already next to escape routes and knew what was going to happen. The locker area is small, dark and with anchor chain all around you, you would have had to think they knew what was going to happen. But in the darkness, the cramped area, moisture, slippery floor, etc., I just don't see it. Certainly, the hand of God guided them to safety.

"Overall, it was a great experience and *Brown* is a great boat. The volunteer crew treats the vessel like a real lady and I would highly recommend everyone who can make the trip to visit this last remaining operational WWII Liberty ship on the east coast. I cannot wait to dive the Liberty ship off Pensacola to test out the underwater cameras. I now know more about the layout and design, and with limited bottom time on scuba tanks, I hope to get a sense of what the bow of *Serpens* will be like when we dive on her in Lunga Bay off Guadalcanal."

The 440-foot-long gray Liberty ship, John W. Brown, is one of only two fully operational Liberty ships, which transported vast numbers of military personnel and countless tons of cargo during World War II — and the only one sailing regularly out of the port city where it was built. Photo courtesy National Park Service.

Hatch No. 4 of the Liberty ship John W. Brown in Baltimore, MD, covered by wood and tarp, much as they would have appeared on the sister ship USS Serpens (AK-97). Photo by Glyn Owen.

Forward anchor chains of the Liberty ship John W. Brown in Baltimore, MD, much as they would have appeared on the sister ship USS Serpens (AK-97). Photo by Glyn Owen.

Bunk area of the Liberty ship John W. Brown in Baltimore, MD, much as they would have appeared on the sister ship USS Serpens (AK-97). Photo by Glyn Owen.

"Brownie," a WWII morale booster unique to the Liberty ship John W. Brown in Baltimore, MD. Photo by Glyn Owen.

The next phase of our research was to find if any Liberty ships were now shipwrecks suitable for scuba diving off the U.S. shoreline. Before expending a large amount of resources to get to the remains of *Serpens*, we thought it best to run some practice dives on a Liberty ship closer to home – making sure we had cameras set correctly, etc. We were surprised to have found so many of these 440-foot behemoth Liberty shipwrecks off the Atlantic and Gulf Coasts! Although we don't think we found every Liberty Ship sunk as an artificial reef, we did find the stripped hulls of 12 Liberty Ships which were intentionally sunk as artificial reefs in the Gulf of Mexico off the Texas coast during the mid-1970s. These type EC-2 Liberty Ships include the: *George Vancouver, William H. Allen, B.F. Shaw, Jim Bridger, George Dewey, Dwight L. Moody, George L. Farley, Edward W. Scripps, Joshua Thomas, Charles A. Dana, Rachel Jackson,* and *Conrad Weiser.*

Off North Carolina we found Liberty ships SS *Dionysus*, SS *Zane Grey*, SS *Theodore Parker* (sunk in 50 feet of water just off Fort Macon near Morehead City) and SS *Alexander Ramsey.*

SS *Wallace* and SS *Allen* are Liberty ships sunk off Alabama's coast. Off Florida's coast we found SS *Thomas Heyward* off Okaloosa County, SS *Joseph E. Brown* off Santa Rosa County, SS *Benjamin H. Grierson* off Bay County, and SS *Joseph L. Meek* off Escambia County.

That was enough research for what we wanted to do. After a few phone calls we opted to dive SS *Joseph L. Meek* off Pensacola, FL.

The *Joseph L. Meek* was built in 1942 by the Oregon War Industries Ship Building Company in Portland, OR. The ship was named after the Oregon trapper, pioneer and first U.S. Marshal of Oregon. She was built for the Maritime Commission, operating under the U.S. war shipping administration. She was just one of the many "Ugly Duckling" ships rapidly constructed in civilian shipyards during World War II. Her keel was laid on 20 October 1942, launched on 16 November and was delivered to the Alaska Steamship Company on 26 November. In 1946, *Joseph L. Meek* was laid up in the James River Reserve fleet. In June of 1976, she was withdrawn from the reserves and had her superstructure removed. She was sunk on November 5, 1976, as an artificial reef by the Department of Commerce. She now rests in 80-95 feet of water seven miles east-southeast of Pensacola Pass at 30 16.390N, 086 09.567W. Her sides rise 20 feet off the flat bottom.

The Liberty ship Joseph L. Meek was built in 1942 by the Oregon War Industries Ship Building Company in Portland. Photo courtesy William Hultgren collection.

MERS member Glyn Owen and co-author Douglas Campbell flew into Pensacola, FL, in late July 2019, to dive the Liberty ship *Joseph L. Meek*. The primary purpose was to test out all the camera gear and to orientate ourselves to what we should expect to see when we dive on the 30 feet remaining of the *Serpens'* bow.

The charter boat Captain taking us to the dive site was Captain Andy Ross of Niuhi Dive Charters. The Hawaiian word *niuhi* simply means big man-eating shark and is often translated as large tiger shark. Supporting Captain Ross was Divemaster Adam Wise. Earlier this year (2019) Captain Ross responded to a "missing diver" emergency by taking his boat and some divers out into the Gulf of Mexico to assist. Observing the current's easterly direction, Captain Ross calculated a speed of one to one and a half miles per hour multiplied by the amount of time the diver had been missing. Other boats and helicopters had been searching for the diver for some 8 hours. Captain Ross and his crew found him – the diver had drifted about nine miles from where he had begun his dive from a private boat.

With additional support from Gulf Coast Dive Pros, probably one of the finest dive shops along the Gulf Coast, we were in good hands. Inclement weather prevented us from achieving our primary goal of diving on the Liberty ship, but the cameras were tested out on secondary shipwrecks – the Ocean Wind and the Russian Freighter.

The 82-foot *Ocean Wind* tugboat was sunk on January 13, 2016 as an artificial reef 10 miles southeast of Pensacola in 82 feet of water. Over the years, *Ocean Wind* was itself commissioned to sink many artificial reefs off Escambia County. Escambia County, with the aid of private donations, purchased the decommissioned tug to fittingly join the others she towed to their final resting place off Pensacola. Funding from the Florida Fish and Wildlife Conservation Commission

(FWC) paid for the preparations of the boat for sinking (removing glass, cutting holes in the hull, etc.), the towing and other expenses related to sinking a ship.

The 82-foot Ocean Wind tugboat was sunk on January 13, 2016 as an artificial reef 10 miles southeast of Pensacola in 82 feet of water.

The second dive was on one of the most popular dive sites in the Pensacola area is the merchant steamer San Pablo, erroneously called the Russian Freighter. This ship is probably the most misunderstood shipwreck in the Pensacola area! It was built by Workman, Clark & Co., Ltd., Belfast, Ireland, in October 1915. The Irish company built the freighter for Unifruitco SS Co Ltd (United Fruit Co), Glasgow. In 1931 it was found to be registered in Panama (Panamanian-flagged) for Balboa Shipping Co. Inc. (United Fruit Co), Balboa. Her length was 315 feet 3 inches (not 400 feet), with a beam of 44 feet 3 inches, a draft of 28 feet 9 inches, and displacing 3,305 tons. This freighter was actually torpedoed by a German submarine, U-161, on July 3, 1942 (not 1944) while it was tied up to a pier in Puerto Limon, Costa Rica – not underway in the Florida Straits. Her position when torpedoed was 9° 59'N, 83° 02'W and she was just completing a voyage which began in New Orleans, LA. She did not "explode off Pensacola's coast" either. It is true that 24 crew were killed in the attack.

The report that "even with the threat of the U-Boat still in the area, Pensacola-based tug boats brought the San Pablo in tow and pulled her closer to shore" is nonsensical. The facts are:

At 4:01 a.m. on 3 July 1942, U-161 fired a spread of two stern torpedoes at the San Pablo, which laid berthed at the fully illuminated pier in Puerto Limón, Costa Rica and was discharging cargo. The ship was hit amidships and near the bridge in #1 and #2 holds and quickly settled to the bottom with only her superstructure above the water because the watertight doors between all holds had been left open. One crew member died on watch below and 23 Costa Rican stevedores working in the holds were killed. All but three crew members of the vessel were ashore at the time of the attack.

On January 9, 1943, San Pablo was raised and after temporary repairs on March 6, taken in tow by the tug Crusader to Tampa via Puerto Castilla and Key West, arriving on March 28. It was first planned to repair the vessel, but she was declared a total loss and purposely sunk 9 miles south-southeast of Pensacola Pass on September 25, 1943. She was not being towed to Mobile. Today she rests in 80 feet of water at 30 11-33 N, 087 13-09 W, about 9 miles off Pensacola Beach.

Diving the San Pablo reveals her stern and three huge boilers to be intact, but the majority of her hull is twisted steel surrounded by a field of metal debris and rubble. Most of the wreckage resulted from dynamite charges used to reduce the wreck's height as she was considered a hazard to navigation. Schools of snapper and other fish hover over the wreck.

One of the most popular dive sites in the Pensacola area is the merchant steamer San Pablo, erroneously called the Russian Freighter. She was purposely sunk on September 25, 1943. Photo courtesy www.floridapanhandledivetrail.com.

Now it was off to the South Pacific! A collective gathering of six made the journey to Guadalcanal, arriving on different flights at different times but all having started from the East or Gulf Coast of the United States and all meeting up in Honiara on Guadalcanal at either the Heritage Park or Sea Coral Hotels. They were:

- Co-authors Douglas E. Campbell and Robert G. Breen.
- Glyn Owen who sits on the Board of Directors of the Maritime Education and Research Society (MERS) which partially paid for this project.
- Robert Breen's son, Jeff, and Jeff's wife, Kim.
- Robert Breen's son, John.

Prior to our arrival we had made contact with the curators of both the small but very interesting Solomon Islands National Museum in Honiara, Guadalcanal (giving us a very good historical look at the Solomon Islands including, of course, the island during World War II) and the Vilu Military Museum in Lenggakiki, Solomon Islands (their display of the remains of American and Japanese WWII aircraft and other relics is an experience not soon forgotten). We were hoping that files or photographs existed in these museums that had never made it to the Internet. Unfortunately resources are very limited on this small island and nothing new was learned about *Serpens*.

We had also made contact with the leading regional newspaper of the Solomon Islands, the *Solomon Star*. We wanted to reach out to the local community through the newspaper to see if anyone had any interest in talking to us about what they remembered or what their relatives had told them about that fateful night when the *Serpens* exploded, the damage inflicted to the surrounding community and the clean-up afterwards. Oral history, especially trying to record an event that occurred some 75 years ago, was particularly important to us as that historical venue is quickly disappearing. But disappeared it had – the average age on Guadalcanal is 63 and possibly no one left on the island was alive in 1945. No one contacted us wanting to talk about what their relatives had said about the big ship exploding off Lunga Beach.

Undeterred, we made contact with Troy Shelley of the Tulagi Dive Shop. Planning for the vagaries associated with working on a small island with limited resources, we felt a one-week trip would include at least one day in which we would be able to dive *Serpens*. On days we could not get out to the remains of *Serpens*, shore dives to other WWII wrecks of interest filled in – including the remains of two Japanese transport ships *Hirokawa Maru* and *Kinugawa Maru* (both grounded and lost to Allied air attack on 15 November 1942), a B-17 Flying Fortress which had limped back to Guadalcanal but fell short trying to reach Henderson Field, and the Japanese submarine I-1.

The I-1 has some interesting history to it. On 29 January 1943 she encountered the New Zealand minesweepers, *Kiwi* and *Moa*. Unable to penetrate I-1's hull with their deck guns, the minesweepers rammed and chased her to shallow water, eventually driving her aground on the reef at Kamimbo Bay, Guadalcanal. Critical material remained on board and the Japanese command tried unsuccessfully to destroy the boat with air and submarine attacks. The U.S. Navy salvaged code books, charts, manuals, the ship's log, and other secret documents, as well as equipment. The code books were written on rice paper meant to quickly dissolve in water, but they were found in the Commanding Officer's waterproof safe and at the time the wreck partially protruded from the water. Of note, I-1's pennant is on display at the National Museum of the Pacific War in Fredericksburg, Texas. In 1968, I-1's main deck gun was recovered and brought to Auckland, New Zealand aboard the HMNZS *Otago* for display at the Torpedo Bay Navy Museum.

From left to right, Jeff Breen, John Breen, Glyn Owen and Tulagi Dive Shop Divemaster Alwin James enter the water heading to the remains of the Japanese submarine I-1. Photograph by Douglas Campbell.

On a side note, co-author Robert Breen is a member of the Coast Guard Combat Veterans Association (CGCVA). The CGCVA's By-laws includes Article 1a which states that one of the purposes of the CGCVA is to "ensure illumination of the Flags displayed at the gravesite of Signalman First Class Douglas A. Munro, USCG (Deceased), recipient of the Medal of Honor, located at Cle Elum, Washington, on a 24-hour daily basis." The gravesite was designated an "Historical Site" by the State of Washington and the CGCVA assumes the responsibility of paying for the electrical power required. By chance, the Tulagi Dive Shop at Guadalcanal is attached to the building housing the Point Cruz Yacht Club. On the Yacht Club's patio is a memorial to S1c Munro placed at the nearest location that could be determined where he was killed by enemy fire. His actions by going into harm's way and saving some 500 fellow military comrades, while he himself was fatally wounded, was what earned him the Medal of Honor posthumously. The citation that went with the Medal tells the story:

> "For extraordinary heroism and conspicuous gallantry in action above and beyond the call of duty as Officer-in-Charge of a group of Higgins boats, engaged in the evacuation of a Battalion of Marines trapped by enemy Japanese forces at Point Cruz, Guadalcanal, on September 27, 1942. After making preliminary plans for the evacuation of nearly 500 beleaguered Marines, Munro, under constant risk of his life, daringly led five of his small craft toward the shore. As he closed the beach, he signaled the others to land, and then in order to draw the enemy's fire and protect the heavily loaded boats, he valiantly placed his craft with its two small guns as a shield between the beachhead and the Japanese. When the perilous task of evacuation was nearly completed, Munro was killed by enemy fire, but his crew, two of whom were wounded, carried on until

the last boat had loaded and cleared the beach. By his outstanding leadership, expert planning, and dauntless devotion to duty, he and his courageous comrades undoubtedly saved the lives of many who otherwise would have perished. He gallantly gave up his life in defense of his country."

Co-authors Robert Breen (l) and Douglas Campbell at the memorial established for Signalman First Class Douglas A. Munro, USCG, at the Point Cruz Yacht Club, Guadalcanal. Solomon Islands. Photograph by Glyn Owen.

On Thursday, 5 September 2019, four divers flipped over the side of their dive boat now anchored over *Serpens* in Lunga Bay for their first of two dives. Two of the divers, John and Jeff Breen, were the grand-sons of F2 Gerald Breen who was killed when *Serpens* exploded. They were here to visit the gravesite of their grandfather, while their father and co-author of this book, Robert Breen, remained aboard the dive boat, soaking in the history and nostalgia from another era, viewing the same shoreline that his father did some 74 years previous. All were here for the first time. Another diver, Glyn Owen, brought the *Serpens* memorial wreath down with him to a depth of 115 feet and with the help of the fourth diver,

Troy Shelley, tied the wreath to the bow of the ship. Along with the wreath, a *Serpens* commemorative coin was placed on one of the entranceways into the interior of *Serpens'* bow.

While preparing for the boat out to the remains of USS Serpens, co-author Robert Breen (center) holds the memorial wreath later attached to the Serpens' bow. His sons, Jeff (l) and John were two of the four divers. Photograph by Douglas Campbell.

Even in the clearest of water, at 115 feet, underwater cameras lose their ability to absorb enough sunlight for crisp images. Here is John Breen, son of co-author Robert Breen and grand-son of F2 Gerald Breen (who died aboard Serpens on 29 January 1945), alongside the remains of Serpens and next to the memorial wreath placed there by the dive team on their first of two dives on the wreckage and debris field. Photograph by Glyn Owen.

After a brief rest period to purge the accumulation of nitrogen out of the divers bodies, called a surface interval, a second dive took place that included the nearby debris field. At that depth, time on the wreckage was only about 15 minutes per dive. All pieces of *Serpens* were left intact – the only thing taken were photographs. The dives were the culmination of hours of planning and coordination and of 30+ hours of travel each way, to and from Guadalcanal. It was the one thing that had to be done that made any sense for this final chapter of the book – to visit the wreckage and to tell those lost on 29 January 1945 that we have not forgotten them.

Earlier, mention was made of a *Serpens* commemorative coin that was placed next to the wreath. A few months before the Guadalcanal trip, Robert Breen initiated the striking of a coin commemorating the upcoming 75th Anniversary of the loss of *Serpens* to coincide with the 75th Anniversary ceremony being held at Arlington National Cemetery in Arlington, VA, on 29 January 2020. The obverse, or "heads" of the coin, is an image of *Serpens* superimposed over the island of Guadalcanal. Around that image are the words "Lunga Beach, Guadalcanal, BSI" and "These men shall be respected and honored forever". On the reverse side, or "tails", is the image of the Monument located at Arlington National Cemetery which is inscribed with the names of those lost aboard *Serpens* and who could not be identified – now buried there around that monument. Surrounding the monument on the coin are the words "75th Anniversary of the Loss of USS *Serpens* (AK97).

POSTSCRIPT

It is with great honor to have been given this opportunity to add my personal voice to the others in this book. I realize its somber responsibility as National President of the Coast Guard Combat Veterans Association (CGCVA). I am very proud to represent our membership in remembering those combat Coastguardsmen, U.S. Army stevedores and others aboard *Serpens* who gave their lives for our country.

For those unfamiliar with the CGCVA, let me introduce our Association's Preamble to our By-Laws: "Being mindful of the traditions, duties and purposes of the United States Coast Guard, our duty to uphold and defend the Constitution of the United States of America and believing that through social association and mutual acquaintance, we may further perpetuate the memory of our fallen comrades, assist their widows and orphans, assist honorably discharged and retired Coast Guard Combat Veterans, and promote and enhance the image and posture of the United States Coast Guard."

Reflecting on why that Preamble has existed since the CGCVA was formed in 1985, I would like to personally thank the co-authors and say that it is about time that someone was able to take such a tragic but significant event in the history of the U.S. Coast Guard – that is, the largest loss of life in a single event in the history of the Coast Guard – and "perpetuate the memory of our fallen comrades" by writing this book. This book should be placed in the Coast Guard Academy Library!

The Preface of this book was written by Admiral James Loy, the 21st Commandant of the USCG and himself a combat veteran. As a Coastguardsman he served in combat as commanding officer of a patrol boat in the Vietnam War. Many of our CGCVA members served in Vietnam, as did I. It comes as no stretch to the imagination to believe one particular scenario - that the loss of *Serpens* could have been brought about through sabotage by the enemy. On several occasions during Vietnam, sampans had been spotted alongside U.S. vessels with saboteurs climbing the anchor chains. One vessel attacked in this manner was SS *Rainbow*, anchored in an explosives anchorage in Da Nang Harbor. Another, the ammunition ship SS *Jefferson City,* was attacked in the Port of Da Nang by sappers, which resulted in a fire and flooding in the hold. The fire was extinguished and the ship was grounded to prevent further flooding. These attacks could have become another *Serpens*.

Sandwiched between Preface and Postscript is finally an in-depth and well-researched story of a historical Coast Guard-manned ship and her crew. It begs to be read by all Coast Guard men and women who formed this long blue line. The loss of nearly 200 Coastguardsmen in one explosive instant should not and cannot ever be forgotten.

Lastly, I take the awarding of the Purple Heart as a serious matter; it is time to correct this injustice. Through dogged research, the co-authors have found newspaper references and photographs of the Purple Heart being awarded to at least 7 of the crew, including two from the Serpens who survived the explosion. If a formal letter from the Government rescinding the award of the Purple Heart was sent to the two Serpens survivors or to the family members of those killed, none ever received it. At the 50th Anniversary Ceremony of the *Serpens'* loss, held at Arlington National Cemetery in 1995, one of the two survivors, Kelsie Kemp, proudly showed his Purple Heart in a frame with a photo of his ship. No one said he didn't deserve it; no one accused him of stolen valor.

No one can prove how it came to be that *Serpens* exploded – enemy torpedo, shipboard accident, sabotage, a mechanical failure inside one of the depth charges... it shouldn't matter at this point. What matters now, and what has always mattered, is that they ALL were placed in harm's way and a handful were aptly rewarded for their sacrifice and nearly 250 others were not. It is time to right this wrong.

As my last words in this Postscript, I turn my attention to the CGCVA. We are a fraternal organization, dedicated to fellowship among its members, and dedicated to making the public aware of the Coast Guard's service and participation in those significant historical events in United States history. The story of USS *Serpens* is very much a part of Coast Guard history and in closing, and on behalf of the CGCVA, I say that co-authors Dr. Douglas Campbell and Robert Breen have done us all proud. *Semper Paratus!*

Stephen K. Petersen

APPENDIX A: DECEASED AND SURVIVORS

Those who died in the explosion:

U.S. COAST GUARD COMMISSIONED OFFICERS

1. LT John Gayle AIKEN, III, USCGR
2. LT William Charles KOTKAS, USCG
3. LTJG George Coleman AUBLE, USCGR
4. LTJG Robert Joseph JOHNSON, USCGR
5. LTJG Warren Clyde PRANCE; USCGR
6. ENS Max Edward DAVIS, USCGR
7. ENS Roy Arthur QUESTAD, USCGR
8. ENS Jacob Harold SHOGREN, USCGR

U.S. COAST GUARD WARRANT OFFICERS

9. MACH Edward Albert BAKER, USCG
10. Chf Pay Clk John Kenneth GORAL, USCGR

U.S. COAST GUARD ENLISTED

11. EM2c Edwin Atwater ABLES, USCGR
12. PhM2c Roy Gordon ANDERSON, USCGR
13. COX Edwin Frank ANTKOWIAK, USCGR
14. WT1c Harry Edward ARO, USCG

15. AS Clifford Daniel ASHBY, USCGR
16. GM3c Woodward Solomon BABCOCK, USCGR
17. S1c Jacob (n) BARER, USCGR
18. S1c Charles Richard BARNHOUSE, USCGR
19. S1c Joseph (n) BIELINSKI, USCGR
20. SK1c Billy LaVere BOYD, USCG
21. S1c Lester Leonard BRANDLEN, USCGR
22. F2c Gerald Clement BREEN, USCGR
23. Std2c Chester BROOKS, USCGR
24. QM3c James Melvin BROSHEAR, USCGR
25. S2c Leo Henry BURKE, USCGR
26. S2c Keith Dale BURNS, USCGR
27. F1c Junior Walter BUTLER, USCGR
28. S1c Raymond Francis CALLAHAN, USCGR
29. S2c Gilbert Joseph CAMARLINGHI, USCGR
30. S2c Michael Louis CAMMARATA, USCGR
31. S2c Anthony (n) CAMBRIA, USCGR
32. S1c Louis Stanley CAREY, USCGR
33. S2c Charles Edwin CARR, USCGR
34. S1c Peter Angelus CASSARIS, USCGR
35. S2c Pete (n) CATGENOVA, USCGR
36. GM3c Philip Reyes CERVANTEZ, USCGR
37. MM2c James Ernest CHADWICK, USCGR
38. S2c Leslie Earl CHAMBERS, USCGR
39. S1c Frank Joseph CIANCO, USCGR
40. S1c Joseph (n) COPE, USCGR
41. S1c James Victor COTE, USCGR

42. S1c William (n) COWHEY, USCGR
43. S1c Charles Edward CRAFT, USCGR
44. S2c Lawrence "F" CREECH, USCGR
45. S1c Lovell Romayne CROOK, USCG
46. S1c Ranard Mason CROWE, USCGR
47. MM1c Arden Orville CUMMINGS, USCG
48. F1c Albert Bradley CURTIS, USCGR
49. S1c John Clifford DALY, USCGR
50. S1c John Albert DANCISAK, USCGR
51. S2c Clarence Willard DAY, USCGR
52. S1c Howard Edward DAY, USCGR
53. RD3c John Clifford DEDMON, Jr., USCGR
54. S2c Henry Karl DEERMER, USCGR
55. S1c Samuel (n) DeGAETANO, USCGR
56. S1c Robert Myles DEGREVE, USCGR
57. S1c Marvin (n) DEROUEN, USCGR
58. StdM1c George Lester DICKERSON, USCGR
59. S1c Lee Henry DIEHL, USCGR
60. F1c Harold George DISTEL, USCGR
61. S2c, Homer Allen DIX, Jr., USCGR
62. S1c William Charles DOHERTY, USCGR
63. CM3c Edward Joseph DONATO, USCGR
64. S1c Donald Robert DONOVAN, USCGR
65. S2c James (n) DRAGO, USCGR
66. S1c William Curt DUNN, USCGR
67. COX Edmund Joseph DURSO, USCGR
68. MoMM3c Robert Allen EASTERDAY, USCGR

69. COX Gustave Fredrick ECKART, USCGR
70. S1c Sylvan Bernard ELSASSER, Jr., USCGR
71. COX Joseph David FAUST, USCGR
72. S1c John (n) FIDURSKI, USCGR
73. S1c Ira Vernon FLETCHER, USCGR
74. S1c Murray Caldwell FLOWERS, USCGR
75. EM3c Fieldon "B" FORKNER, USCGR
76. CM2c Warren Emmett FOX, USCGR
77. S2c Roger William FREGIA, USCGR
78. S1c Jay Fred FRENCH, USCGR
79. S1c Ralph Charles FRITZ, USCGR
80. COX Jime (n) GALLO, USCGR
81. S1c Ely (n) GAMSU, USCGR
82. F1c John Louis GARZON, USCGR
83. S1c Mack Everett GIBSON, USCGR
84. CBM Robert Leland GLAZE, USCG
85. HA2c Sheldon Gordon GOLDSTEIN, USCGR
86. S2c Emelio Cruz GONZALES, USCGR
87. PhM3c Charles Edward GRAEBER, USCGR
88. SC3c Warren Joseph GRANGER, USCGR
89. Y3c Daniel Laban GRANT, Jr., USCGR
90. S1c Jean Pierre Dessaint GRAY, USCGR
91. S1c Freeman (n) GREGORY, USCGR
92. S1c Frank Jerome GRETZ, USCGR
93. S1c Lorren Edward GRISAMORE, USCG
94. S1c Stanley Raymond GRISBAUM, USCGR
95. RT3c Boyce Frank GUTHRIDGE, USCGR

96. WT2c Elmer Pratt HAGEMEIER, Jr., USCGR

97. PhM3c Arthur Charles HAGENDORN, Jr., USCGR

98. RD3c Raymond Charles HAMILTON, USCGR

99. BM2c John William HAMPTON, USCGR

100. F1c William Henry HARLOW, USCGR

101. F2c Kenneth Harold HARMON, USCGR

102. S2c Donald James HART, USCGR

103. F1c James (n) HARTLEIB, USCGR

104. MM3c William Carleton HARTZLER, USCGR

105. S1c Melvin (n) HASKELL, USCGR

106. S2c Perry Paul HEADRICK, USCGR

107. MM2c Leslie (n) HELSEM, USCG

108. F2c Felix Leon HENIGAN, USCGR

109. SC2c George Arthur HENSHAW, USCGR

110. F1c Robert Allen HERRINGTON, USCGR

111. StdM3c Marcus Runnel HICKMAN, USCGR

112. S1c Thomas Leland HIGGINS, USCGR

113. GM3c Henry Cannon HINSON, USCGR

114. S1c, Robert Blake HODGE, USCGR

115. S1c Bernard James HOUCHEN, USCGR

116. S1c Robert Laverne HOYT, USCGR

117. QM3c Raymond Earl HUBACHER, USCGR

118. S1c Otis Dewert HULL, USCGR

119. S1c Colon Joseph HUTCHINSON, USCGR

120. MoMM2c Vernard Connin JACOBS, USCGR

121. S2c Paul Robert JAISSLE, USCGR

122. S2c Norman Anthony JOHNSON, USCGR

123. SK1c Frank (n) KADILAK, USCG

124. S2c Milton Russell KELLAR, Jr., USCGR

125. F1c Arnold Edward KETTUNEN, USCGR

126. S1c Ralph Dana KILEY, USCGR

127. MoMM3c Melvin Marceline KOLAR, USCGR

128. S1c Norbert Edward KRUEGER, USCGR

129. S1c Vincent John KURDILLA, USCGR

130. S1c Stanley John KUSEK, USCGR

131. StdM1c Charlie Golden KYLE, USCGR

132. S1c James Edward LAIRD, USCGR

133. S1c Walter Paul LAMBERT, USCGR

134. S1c Woodrow (n) LANHAM, USCGR

135. S2c Nolan Raymond LEGO, Jr., USCGR

136. MM3c Russell Carl LEVERENTZ, USCG

137. SC3c David Fielding LEWIS, USCGR

138. SK3c Walter John LIMBACHER, Jr., USCGR

139. MoMM3c Charles Thomas MacFARLAND, USCGR

140. COX Joseph James MACKEY, USCGR

141. S2c Samuel Monroe MADDOX, USCGR

142. COX Albert Junior MANKE, USCGR

143. COX Raymond Gregory MAZZANTI, USCG

144. MM3c John Herman McCARTER, USCGR

145. WT3c John Lewis McCAW, USCGR

146. MM3c William Joseph McCULLOUGH, Jr., USCGR

147. RDM3c Malcolm "W" McDANIEL, USCGR

148. SK3c Harold Myers McGUCKIN, Jr., USCGR

149. RM2c Lloyd Arthur McLARTY, USCGR

150. MM3c Alvis Joseph MENARD, USCGR

151. StdM2c Madge Victor MILLER. USCGR

152. S1c James Joseph MIRON, USCGR

153. S1c William Fossett NIVIN, USCGR

154. S1c Douglas Harry OAKLUND, USCGR

155. COX William Richard O'DONNELL, USCGR

156. CMM George Edward ORTON, USCGR

157. F1c Charles Clay PAYNE, USCGR

158. SM3c William Oscar PAZUREK, USCGR

159. WT3c Lincoln Fowler PETERSON, USCGR

160. StdM3c Frederick Edward Adolph QUALMANN, USCGR

161. S1c Orville Frederick REUTER, USCGR

162. MoMM1c Hugo (n) RICCARDI, USCGR

163. RM3c Fred Otto ROYER, USCGR

164. CMM Paul (n) RUDY, USCGR

165. CMM Eugene RUGGIERO, USCGR

166. MM3c Roy Anthony SAMPAY, USCGR

167. S1c Alfonso Celso SANDOVAL, USCGR

168. COX Lewis John SARKISOFF, USCGR

169. F1c John Phillip SCHMOOK, USCGR

170. S1c Charles Eugene SCHRADER, USGCR

171. S1c James Daniel SELAYA, USCGR or E

172. COX William "H" SELEMAN, Jr., USCGR or E.

173. WT3c Robert Joseph SMITH, USCG

174. S1c Robert Charles SNEDDON, USCGR

175. WT3c Robert Harry SORENSON, USCGR

176. RM1c Cyril David STEINMAN, Jr., USCGR
177. CPhM Washington Edward STILLMAN, USCG
178. RM3c Myron Kendall STRICKLAND, USCGR
179. COX Floyd (n) STUCKEY, USCGR
180. Y1c Robert Ernest THOMAS, USCG
181. MM1c James Robert THORNBURGH, USCGR
182. MoMM1c Hubert (n) TURNER, USCGR
183. BM2c Vernon Henry TWAIT, USCGR
184. GM2c William Warner VAUGHAN, USCG
185. CEM Edgar Lloyd VEDDER, USCGR
186. WT3c Samuel Earl VILLEMONT, USCGR
187. WT2c Harold Lacier VINCENT, USCGR
188. COX John Francis WALKO, USCGR
189. StdM1c Eugene Jacob WARD, USCG
190. COX Delos Ray WARDLE, USCGR
191. SM2c Kinchion Dale WEST, USCGR
192. S1c Woodrow Herman WETTS, USCGR
193. S1c Alton (n) WHITE, USCGR
194. SC1c Charles Bernard WOOD, USCGR
195. SM3c Tom ZAFFORE, USCGR

U.S. ARMY OFFICERS

196. 1STLT Arnold J. MCGRATH, USA

U.S. ARMY ENLISTED

197. CPL Lawrence L. ARNDT, USA
198. PFC Walter E. BAGINSKI, USA
199. TEC5 Charles E. BAILLARGEON, USA
200. PFC Robert J. BARRETT, USA

201. PFC Leland C. BARRICK, USA

202. TEC5 Alec (n) BESKOSTY, USA

203. PFC Edwin L. BOOS, USA

204. PFC Derious F. BORTON, Jr., USA

205. TEC5 Alfred W. BRIESCHKE, USA

206. PFC Clarence M. BUCHANAN, USA

207. PVT Clifton C. BURKS, USA

208. TEC5 James G. CARMICHAEL, USA

209. SSGT Fred L. CHILDS, USA

210. PFC Howard R COTTON, USA

211. PVT Fritze O. DAHLBERG, USA

212. TEC4 James E. DAVIS, USA

213. PFC Billy G. ELAM, USA

214. PFC Richard M. FEUTZ, USA

215. PVT Glenn B. FRANK, USA

216. PFC Lewis L. FULDA, USA

217. TEC5 Charles D. FURREY, USA

218. PFC Kayah (n) GALE, USA

219. PFC Edward C. GESFORD, USA

220. PFC Fred E. GILBERT, USA

221. PFC Floyd (n) GRAPENTHIN, Jr., USA

222. TEC5 Phillip (n) GUTIERREZ, USA

223. PFC Alan J. GUYETT, USA

224. PFC Alexander (n) HELEMENT, USA

225. PVT Herman T. HELTON, USA

226. PFC Francis V. HENRY, USA

227. CPL Nile W. HINERMAN, USA

228. TEC5 Robert B. HOPKINS, USA

229. PFC Richard C. JOHNSON, USA

230. PFC William G. KAYLER, Jr., USA

231. PFC Herbert C. KEOUGH, USA

232. PVT William J. KRAMER, USA

233. PFC Paul F. KREPS, USA

234. PVT David A. LaTRAILLE, USA

235. PFC Charles E. McDANIEL, USA

236. SGT Ted (n) McMAHAN, USA

237. TEC5 Guy L. MARK, USA

238. TEC4 Curtiss D. MATNEY, USA

239. PFC Nicholas A. MAY, USA

240. PVT Raymond F. MEDVES, USA

241. TEC5 Leo E. MOORE, USA

242. PFC Huie (n) MORGAN, USA

243. TEC5 Walter L. OKICHICK, USA

244. TEC4 Albert L. OWEN, USA

245. TEC5 John J. PREEDOM, USA

246. SGT George H. REILLY, USA

247. TEC5 Linton J. ROBESON, USA

248. TEC5 Marcus A. RUTH, USA

249. PFC William P. STILES, USA

250. PFC Ivan B. THOMAS, USA

251. PFC Lawton (n) WATTS, USA

U.S. PUBLIC HEALTH SERVICE

252. Surgeon Harry M. LEVIN, USPHS

Unknown Loss

S1c Richard Otto KIRCHNER, USCGR, (605 316) has his name mentioned in the list of those missing after the *Serpens* explosion in an article appearing in Lighthouse Digest Magazine dated June 15, 2015. His date of death was 29 January 1945. However, his ship/unit was never officially identified and he was buried at the National Memorial of the Pacific Cemetery, Honolulu (Punchbowl), Plot A, Row 0, Grave 619. His name does not appear on the Arlington National Cemetery *Serpens* monument.

The other unknown loss was the soldier killed on the beach by a fragment of *Serpens* that hit him. This may be a myth perpetuated by everyone copying it and may have originated by the finding of some shoes that had drifted ashore that belonged to an Army stevedore working aboard *Serpens*.

Lastly, Ginger, the mascot.

Those who survived:

Aboard USS *Serpens*

1. S1c Kelsie K. KEMP, USCG
2. S1c George S. KENNEDY, USCG

USS *Serpens* Officers Ashore

3. LCDR Peery L. STINSON, USCG

4. LT John R. CLARK, USCG

USS *SERPENS* ENLISTED ASHORE

5. S2c Fidel O. CARMONA, USCGR
6. Std3c Richard M. FIGGS, USCGR
7. F1c Morris F. HOUSEKNECHT, USCGR
8. S1c William Edward HUGHES, USCGR
9. CCStd Stanley H. JONES, USCGR
10. S1c Robert J. SMART, USCGR

IN U.S. FLEET HOSPITAL NO. 108 FROM USS *SERPENS*

11. LTJG Julius T. STANGES, USCGR
12. COX George O. ELLARD, Jr., USCGR
13. S2c Fred R. KEESEE, USCGR
14. S2c Raymond C. LEOPARD, USCGR

MILITARY RANKS AND RATINGS MENTIONED

U.S. Army

1STLT	First Lieutenant
2NDLT	Second Lieutenant
MSGT	Master Sergeant
1st Sgt	First Sergeant
TSGT	Technical Sergeant
TEC	Technician
SSGT	Staff Sergeant
SGT	Sergeant
CPL	Corporal
PFC	Private First Class
PVT	Private

U.S. Coast Guard

Commissioned Officers

CAPT (CO)   Captain (Commanding Officer)

LCDR	Lieutenant Commander
LT	Lieutenant
LTJG	Lieutenant Junior Grade
ENS	Ensign

Warrant Officers

Chf Bosn	Chief Boatswain
Chf Carp	Chief Carpenter
Chf Pay Clk	Chief Pay Clerk
Chf Radio Elec	Chief Radio Electrician
Mach	Machinist

Enlisted

AS	Apprentice Seaman
BM	Boatswain's Mate
Bmkr	Boilermaker
CBM	Chief Boatswain's Mate
CCM	Chief Carpenter's Mate
CCStd	Chief Commissary Steward
CEM	Chief Electrician's Mate
CFC	Chief Fire Controlman
CGM	Chief Gunner's Mate
CM	Carpenter's Mate
CMM	Chief Machinist's Mate
CMoMM	Chief Motor Machinist's Mate
CMsmth	Chief Metalsmith
COX	Coxswain
CPhM	Chief Pharmacist's Mate
CQM	Chief Quartermaster
CRM	Chief Radioman
CSF	Chief Shipfitter
CSK	Chief Storekeeper
CSM	Chief Signalman
CWT	Chief Watertender
CY	Chief Yeoman
EM	Electrician's Mate
F	Fireman
FC	Fire Controlman

GM	Gunner's Mate
HA	Hospital Apprentice
MAtt	Mess Attendant
MM	Machinist's Mate
MoMM	Motor Machinist's Mate
Msmth	Metalsmith
OC	Officer's Cook
OS	Officer's Steward
PhM	Pharmacist's Mate
QM	Quartermaster
RM	Radioman
S	Seaman
Std	Steward
SC	Ship's Cook
SF	Shipfitter
SK	Storekeeper
SM	Signalman
WT	Watertender
Y	Yeoman

About the Authors

Douglas E. Campbell, Ph.D., was born on 9 May 1954 in Portsmouth, VA, and grew up as a Navy Brat, traveling all over the world and living on or next to U.S. submarine bases at such places as Holy Loch, Scotland; Rota, Spain; Pearl Harbor, Hawaii; and Charleston, South Carolina. The oldest of six children, he was graduated from Kenitra American High School, Kenitra, Morocco, in 1972 – his 13th school. He received his Bachelor of Science degree in Journalism from the University of Kansas on 24 May 1976; the following day was commissioned at his Naval Reserve Officers' Training Corps (NROTC) Unit as an Ensign in the United States Navy. His father, Navy Senior Chief Guy L. Campbell, was still on active duty at the time and rendered him his first salute, thus getting his silver dollar. LTJG Campbell joined the U.S. Naval Reserve Program as an Intelligence Officer in 1980 and was transferred to the Retired Reserves as a Lieutenant Commander on 1 June 1999.

Dr. Campbell received his Master of Science degree from the University of Southern California in Computer Systems Management in 1986 and his Doctor of Philosophy degree in Security Administration from Southwest University in New Orleans, Louisiana, in 1993. Dr. Campbell is president and CEO of Syneca Research Group, Inc., a veteran-owned small business incorporated in 1995 supporting several Government and commercial clients primarily in aviation and maritime security. He is also Director of the 501(c)(3) non-profit organization Maritime Education and Research Society (MERS, www.MERSFoundation.org), involved in various undersea ventures such as studying the health of the coral reef system off the Yucatan Peninsula. He currently resides with his wife Trish in Southern Pines, North Carolina.

Dr. Campbell recently completed a 6-volume set of books on U.S. Navy, U.S. Marine Corps and U.S. Coast Guard aircraft lost during World War II, Korean War and the Vietnam War. His 600-page book investigating the loss of the U.S. submarine USS DORADO (SS-248) during World War II as a result of "friendly fire" has received critical acclaim (www.ussdorado.com). His book *Save Our Souls*, about the rescue of some 2,400 military and civilian personnel by U.S. submarines during WWII, has been turned into a screenplay for a possible movie. For a complete list and abstracts of his more than 30 books, go to www.syneca.com under Publications.

Robert G. Breen, CFE, was two years old when his father died aboard USS *Serpens* on 29 January 1945. His mother never remarried. Mr. Breen went on to obtain a Bachelor of Arts degree from San Jose State University, CA, followed by 31 years of service within the Central Intelligence Agency (CIA). His assignments within the CIA were with the Office of Finance, the Office of Logistics and the Office of the Inspector General. Mr. Breen served in these offices both domestically and overseas. His career within the CIA spanned assignments dealing with contract audits; international banking; planning, programming and budgeting; contracting; security investigations; financial operations and internal audit functions.

Upon retirement from the CIA, Mr. Breen took his research, auditing and investigative skills and formed RGB Investigations Agency in the State of Florida. He continued to provide his expertise in areas of fraud and background investigations under contract to U. S. Customs and Border Protection, Defense Security Service, and Defense Intelligence Agency. His areas of expertise involved domestic and international loss prevention, asset recovery, asset searches and all areas of due diligence when it came to domestic and international physical security issues.

Mr. Breen currently lives in Venice, Florida. He has been researching and compiling information from various sources on the loss of USS *Serpens* for several years, building a case for reinstating the award of the Purple Heart medal to the *Serpens'* crew after the U.S. Government retroactively changed their mind.

Other Books by Douglas E. Campbell

MILITARY & U.S. HISTORY

Volume I: U.S. Navy, U.S. Marine Corps and U.S. Coast Guard Aircraft Lost During World War II - Listed by Ship Attached

Volume II: U.S. Navy, U.S. Marine Corps and U.S. Coast Guard Aircraft Lost During World War II - Listed by Squadron

Volume III: U.S. Navy, U.S. Marine Corps and U.S. Coast Guard Aircraft Lost During World War II - Listed by Aircraft Type

USS DORADO (SS-248): On Eternal Patrol

BuNos! Disposition of World War II USN, USMC and USCG Aircraft Listed by Bureau Number

Patent Log: Innovative Patents That Advanced the United States Navy (co-author Stephen J. Chant)

U.S. Navy, U.S. Marine Corps and MATS Aircraft Lost During the Korean War

U.S. Navy, U.S. Marine Corps and MATS Aircraft Lost During the Korean War: 2017 Updated Edition

FLIGHT, CAMERA, ACTION! The History of U.S. Naval Aviation Photography and Photo-Reconnaissance

U.S. Navy and U.S. Marine Corps Aircraft Damaged or Destroyed During the Vietnam War. Volume 1: Listed by Ship Attached and by Squadron

U.S. Navy and U.S. Marine Corps Aircraft Damaged or Destroyed During the Vietnam War. Volume 2: Listed by Bureau Number

Save Our Souls: Rescues Made by U.S. Submarines During World War II

Letters from a Soviet Prison: The Personal Journal and Correspondence of CIA U-2 Pilot Francis Gary Powers (co-author Francis Gary Powers, Jr.)

VPNavy! USN, USMC, USCG and NATS Patrol Aircraft Lost or Damaged During World War II - 2018 Edition.

United States Navy Patrol Aircraft Lost or Damaged During World War Two

VPNavy! USN, USMC, USCG and NATS Patrol Aircraft Lost or Damaged During World War II – Listed by Bureau Number - 2018 Edition.

The Submarine Has No Friends: Friendly Fire Incidents Involving U.S. Submarines During World War II (co-author Charles R. Hinman)

CYBER & NATIONAL SECURITY

Compu-terror: Computer Terrorism and Recovery from Disaster

Building a Global Information Assurance Program (co-author Raymond J. Curts, Ph.D.)

Computer Terrorism

Cybersecurity Policies and Strategies for Cyberwarfare Prevention (edited by Jean-Loup Richet, contributing author Douglas E. Campbell)

Continuity of Government: How the U.S. Government Functions After All Hell Breaks Loose

NATURE & TRAVEL

On the Potomac River (co-author Thomas B. Sherman)

A Remote Sensing Survey to Locate the Remains of USS DORADO (SS-248) Off of Bahia de la Ascension, Quintana Roo, Mexico

The Identification of Potentially Hazardous Material Discovered In and Around the Mesoamerican Reef Region of Mexico's Yucatan Peninsula

Shipwrecks and Submerged Cultural Resources In and Around Pensacola, Florida

A Gathering of Extraordinary Individuals: Thomas Mack Wilhoite/Kenitra American High School, Morocco, 1956-1976